YORKSHIRE AIRFIELDS
IN THE SECOND
WORLD WAR

YORKSHIRE
AIRFIELDS
IN THE SECOND
WORLD WAR

Patrick Otter

COUNTRYSIDE BOOKS
NEWBURY, BERKSHIRE

First published 1998
© Patrick Otter 1998

Reprinted 1999, 2002, 2003, 2005, 2007

COUNTRYSIDE BOOKS
3 Catherine Road
Newbury, Berkshire

To view our complete range of books,
please visit us at
www.countrysidebooks.co.uk

ISBN 978 1 85306 542 2

The cover painting by Colin Doggett shows
Mark IV Halifaxes of 78 Squadron returning to Breighton
following a daylight raid in 1944.

Designed by Mon Mohan

Produced through MRM Associates Ltd., Reading
Typeset by Techniset Typesetters, Merseyside
Printed by Cambridge University Press

*All material for the manufacture of this book
was sourced from sustainable forests.*

CONTENTS

YORKSHIRE'S WORLD WAR II AIRFIELDS

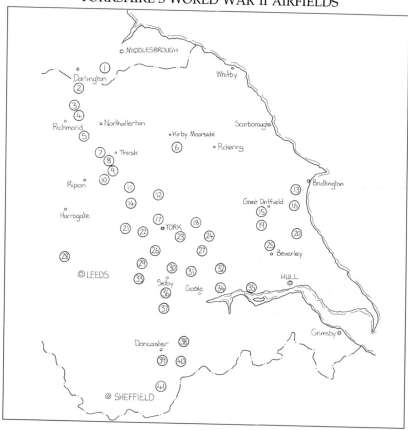

KEY TO MAP

1 Middleton St George
2 Croft
3 Scorton
4 Catterick
5 Leeming
6 Wombleton
7 Skipton-on-Swale
8 Topcliffe
9 Dalton
10 Dishforth

11 Tholthorpe
12 East Moor
13 Carnaby
14 Linton-on-Ouse
15 Driffield
16 Lissett
17 York
18 Full Sutton
19 Hutton Cranswick
20 Catfoss

21 Marston Moor
22 Rufforth
23 Elvington
24 Pocklington
25 Leconfield
26 Acaster Malbis
27 Melbourne
28 Yeadon
29 Church Fenton
30 Riccall
31 Breighton

32 Holme-on-Spalding Moor
33 Sherburn-in-Elmet
34 Bellasize
35 Brough
36 Burn
37 Snaith
38 Lindholme
39 Doncaster
40 Finningley
41 Firbeck

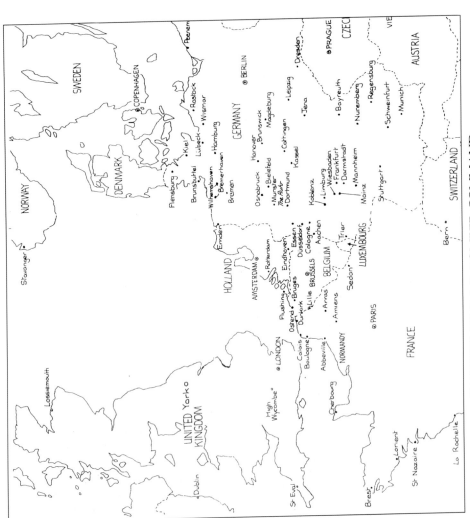

TARGETS OF R.A.F. BOMBER COMMAND

I
SETTING
THE
SCENE

At three minutes past nine on the morning of 3rd February 1940, radar stations along the Yorkshire coast picked up echoes of an unidentified aircraft some 60 miles out to sea. Hurricanes of 43 Squadron, then stationed at Acklington in Northumberland, were scrambled to provide cover for a convoy off Whitby.

Shortly afterwards one of the Hurricanes, flown by Peter Townsend, intercepted a He 111 of KG26 close to the North Yorkshire port, more famous for its abbey and its links with Captain Cook and Dracula than the first air battle in British air space of the Second World War.

Townsend's bullets killed one of the Heinkel's crew and soon afterwards the bomber flew low over Whitby trailing smoke from a damaged engine. It cleared the roofs of a row of houses before crash-landing at a nearby farm. Among the first on the scene was special constable Arthur Barratt and he helped lift the survivors out of the wreckage. A group of local women arrived soon afterwards complete with blankets and flasks of hot tea. A local doctor pulled up in his car to administer first aid. One of the survivors was to die from his injuries and later both men were buried with full military honours at Catterick. Among the wreaths was one from 43 Squadron 'with sympathy'. The air war had arrived in Yorkshire.

During five and a half years of war Yorkshire was to lay claim to many 'firsts'. Its Whitleys were the first RAF bombers to fly over

HRH The Duke of Kent pictured during a visit to the bomb dump at Linton-on-Ouse in January 1942 as S/Ldr Jones, the station armament officer, shows off one of Bomber Command's new 4,000lb bombs. Centre left is the station commander, G/Capt Whitley, and on the extreme right is Air Vice Marshal Roderick Carr, 4 Group AOC. (Eddie McKinna)

Germany in wartime; that Heinkel was the first Luftwaffe aircraft to fall on English soil. Yorkshire was to see the debut of two of the RAF's three heavy bombers, the Halifax and the Stirling; it was the first county to contain two complete bomber groups as well as elements of two others; its bombers were the first to use pathfinder techniques in 1941 and one of its squadron commanders went on to lead Bomber Command's Pathfinder squadrons; it was the home of the only overseas-funded bomber group, No 6, which was paid for by the people of Canada. Yorkshire suffered the only major air raid on a bomber airfield. And, in March 1945, it was in Yorkshire that the very last Luftwaffe aircraft to crash in Britain came down.

More than 18,000 airmen died flying from the county's airfields. Most of those served in Bomber Command, which by the spring of 1945 had 25 squadrons of Halifaxes and Lancasters operating from Yorkshire airfields, second only to neighbouring Lincolnshire where

The complex camouflage scheme used on the hangars at Leeming is clearly shown in this photograph, taken shortly after the airfield opened in 1940. In the foreground a 10 Squadron Whitley and bomb load await the squadron armourers. (RAF Leeming)

there were 32 squadrons, including three Pathfinder units. Fighter Command also had a strong presence in Yorkshire, particularly in the early years of the war when its fighters took part in one of the major engagements in the Battle of Britain. This involved large-scale attacks on northern airfields by Luftwaffe units based in Denmark and Norway. Much to the surprise of the Germans, they were met by a large force of fighters. One of the attacking forces was driven away while the second incurred severe losses before badly damaging the bomber airfield at Driffield.

Bomber Command

Yorkshire's military aviation history had its roots in the First World War. Geography determined then that the scattering of airfields in the county would be used largely for training. Few survived the end of the

11

Debriefing following a raid on Ottignies, 21st April 1944 at Holme-on-Spalding Moor. Pictured are (l to r): F/O Fred Hall, navigator; the squadron Intelligence Officer; Sgt Joe Josey, wireless operator; F/Lt Roy Bolt, pilot; P/O Cal Rathmell, bomb aimer; Sgt Harry Van den Bos, mid-upper gunner; P/O Jack Bates, flight engineer. (Grace Van den Bos)

war and the ones that did closed soon afterwards. By the late 1920s the county began to figure once again in the future plans of the RAF and was one of the major beneficiaries of the expansion programme which got under way in the mid-1930s, with no fewer than eight major airfields planned – Church Fenton, Driffield, Dishforth, Finningley, Leconfield, Leeming, Lindholme and just over the county's northern border, Middleton St George. This latter airfield, together with its near neighbour at Croft, has been included within the scope of this book for both played an integral part in the fortunes of Yorkshire-based squadrons.

Most were planned as bomber airfields and the first of them predated the formation of 4 Group itself, which came into being on 1st April 1937 at Mildenhall, Suffolk under the command of Air Commodore Arthur Harris, the man who was later to lead Bomber Command. Three months later 4 Group's headquarters moved to the newly completed airfield at Linton-on-Ouse, north of York. It was to

A morning briefing at 4 Group HQ at Heslington Hall, AVM Carr is in the centre. On his right are W/Cmdr Guy Lawrence, the Group Training Officer and the Group Royal Navy Liaison Officer, who was consulted on mining operations. On his left are the Group Senior Air Staff Officer, Air Commodore Brooke and S/Ldr Robinson, the Group Navigation Officer. (Sir Guy Lawrence)

move once more, in April 1940, to Heslington Hall on the outskirts of York where it remained until the war ended. Heslington Hall, which is now part of York University, was the family home of Stephen de Yarburgh-Bateson who was a serving RAF officer. Remarkably, he later found himself posted to his own home where he ran the 4 Group operations centre in his old drawing room.

Harris was replaced in 1938 by Air Commodore Blount who was in command until July 1939 when Air Vice Marshal Arthur 'Mary' Coningham took over what he described as the 'world's only specialised night bombing force'. It was a claim which would be put to the test sooner than he thought. 4 Group comprised eight squadrons of Whitleys based at Linton, Driffield, Dishforth and Leconfield (the bomber airfield at Finningley, near Doncaster, was part of the Lincolnshire-based 5 Group and later became the home of a training unit) and the leaflet raids flown that first winter demonstrated the enormous difficulties which lay ahead for RAF bomber crews. Bad weather and rudimentary navigation posed a far greater threat to the 4 Group crews than did the German defences. This was all to change dramatically in the years to come but the lessons learned by those Whitley crews were crucial in the forging of Bomber Command into the fearsomely destructive force it became. AVM Coningham commanded 4 Group until July 1941 when he was replaced by another New Zealander, AVM Roderick Carr, a dynamic leader who was to remain in command of 4 Group until the war ended.

The onset of war sparked a major airfield building programme in Yorkshire. The county is dominated by a series of hills, the Pennines in the west, the Wolds in the east and the Cleveland hills to the north. But there was still room for some 40 airfields, most concentrated in the flat plains around the Ouse. Others were built on the rising land of the Wolds, alongside the Swale and Tees in the north or on the coastal strip south of Bridlington.

Not all of these were initially destined for 4 Group. 1 Group, which was based mainly in North Lincolnshire, was allocated the airfields at Snaith, Breighton and Holme-on-Spalding Moor, all of which were later to be used by 4 Group. Another, at Lindholme, near Doncaster,

Flying control at RAF Full Sutton. (Ron Barrowcliffe)

14

was used initially by 5 Group before being allocated to 1 Group, first as a bomber airfield and later as the base for the group's training.

6 Group formally came into being on 1st January 1943. It was under the command of the Royal Canadian Air Force and, like 4 Group, had its initial headquarters at Linton-on-Ouse when it was formed in 1942, moving to Allerton Park Castle, near Knaresborough, which had been requisitioned from the Mowbray family, in December of that year. It was from there that 6 Group formally began operations under the command of AVM Brookes.

By now Yorkshire was neatly divided in half: 4 Group were south and east of York, 6 Group north of the city. Between them the two groups were to fly 102,399 sorties from Yorkshire, losing some 2,255 aircraft. They operated from 25 airfields, several of them being used for the training of heavy bomber crews.

Four different types of bomber were to see service in the county – the Whitley, Wellington, Lancaster and, of course, the Halifax, the aircraft which is synonymous with Yorkshire's bomber squadrons. The majority of the 6,000-plus built were to fly with either 4 Group (which was all-Halifax) or 6 Group (which used some Lancasters, including the Mark X Canadian-built version). History has not always been kind to the Halifax. Look at any account of the bomber campaign and a picture of a Lancaster, not a Halifax, will adorn the dust jacket. But those who flew the 'Halibag', particularly the Mark III, loved it and will defend its qualities to their last breath. Earlier versions were, in truth, not so highly thought of. They could be difficult to handle and could not reach the same operational height as the Lanc (or the later Halifaxes). And rudder problems could make them unstable and no doubt contributed to the losses of many aircraft. But they were tough machines. They were also, crucially, easier to get out of in an emergency. Proportionally more men survived from Halifaxes than Lancasters and those who did thank their lucky stars for the Handley Page designers.

Many of the outstanding figures in the bomber war were to serve on Yorkshire airfields – Leonard Cheshire, Percy Pickard, Willie Tait, Don Bennett, Gus Walker, Hank Iverson, David Wilkerson, John Searby and many more – and two of the Victoria Crosses awarded within Bomber Command went to men in 4 and 6 Group, both posthumously. P/O Cyril Barton won the first on the Nuremburg raid at the end of March 1944 while flying with 578 Squadron from Burn, while P/O Andrew Mynarski of 419 Squadron at Middleton St George won his during a raid on Cambrai some ten weeks later.

Kassel here we come! 76 Squadron at Holme-on-Spalding Moor, 22nd October 1943.
(Grace Van den Bos)

Fighter Command

It wasn't all bombers, of course. Yorkshire had a number of fighter airfields, built to provide protection for the northern industrial cities and ports and fighter cover for North Sea convoys. Church Fenton, near Leeds, and Catterick, close to the northern home of the British Army, were the two major fighter airfields at the outbreak of war. Others were to open at Catfoss, between Bridlington and Hull, Hutton Cranswick, near Beverley, and Scorton, not far from Darlington. The big pre-war bomber airfield at Leconfield was also pressed into use early in the war to provide fighter cover for the Hull area.

Fighter squadrons operating from Church Fenton, Leconfield and Catterick were to provide a nasty surprise for Goering's Luftwaffe in the early stages of the Battle of Britain when a two-pronged daylight attack by bombers from Norway and Denmark against a supposedly unprotected region of the country was bloodily repulsed, but only after severe damage was caused to the bomber airfield at Driffield. The county's fighter airfields were used by numerous Fighter Command squadrons, which were rotated through northern airfields during the Battle of Britain to give them time to rest and re-equip.

Aircraft Production

Yorkshire was also an important centre of aircraft production throughout the war. Lancasters and Ansons were produced at Yeadon (now Leeds-Bradford International Airport) and Swordfishes and Barracudas for the Fleet Air Arm at Sherburn-in-Elmet and Brough, where American aircraft were also adapted for use by the Royal Navy.

After The War

The rate of expansion of the Royal Air Force in Yorkshire was matched only by its contraction once the war in Europe ended. Today the RAF retains only a major operational base at Leeming together with a scattering of training units. But everywhere there are reminders of the role the county played in the air war of 1939–45. Memorials dotted throughout the county mark the exploits of 29 heavy bomber squadrons which served in Yorkshire. Others mark individual crash sites and many of these have been erected by individuals or civilian organisations whose members will never forget the debt of gratitude they owe to the men and women who served in the RAF. Elsewhere, the remains of the derelict airfields can still be found, a patch of crumbling concrete here, a building there. Surviving hangars now store agricultural equipment, bales of hay now fill huts where once men slept, ate and prepared to go into battle. In York Minster a memorial stands to the 18,000 men lost flying from Yorkshire in the Second World War, around 15,000 of them in Bomber Command.

But perhaps the most fitting memorial of all can be found a few miles from the Minster on the old wartime airfield at Elvington. There a wonderful museum has been created by RAF veterans and enthusiasts. Wartime buildings have been renovated, memorabilia collected and a new hangar erected to house a collection of historic aircraft. Among these is a complete reproduction of *Friday the Thirteenth*, a Mark III Halifax which flew 128 operations from Lissett before being unceremoniously scrapped when the war ended.

Today associations representing squadrons which flew from Yorkshire are as strong as ever although each year that passes inevitably leaves a few empty places at annual reunions. The bond which was forged between the young men and women who served in the British, Canadian, Australian, Polish, Czech, Norwegian and American squadrons which flew from Yorkshire is as strong as ever.

Mona Clowes was a Yorkshire girl who served as a WAAF driver in 6 Group and later married a Canadian airman. Her feelings will be shared by many on both sides of the Atlantic: 'Most of the young men who survived went back to their own country with warm feelings for Yorkshire, feelings which have lasted through all the years. They will never forget their time there.'

2
BREIGHTON

Yorkshire bomber airfields will always be associated with 4 and 6 Groups. But a handful were used in the early years of the war by the largely Lincolnshire-based 1 Group. Among them was RAF Breighton, which officially opened early in January 1942.

It was a typical bomber airfield – three runways (unusually laid in a star shape) and three hangars – built on land close to the villages of Bubwith and Breighton some three miles north of the small town of Howden. Within days of opening the first of two squadrons to use the airfield moved in. 460 Squadron had been formed a few weeks earlier at Molesworth in Huntingdonshire as one of the first RAAF squadrons in Bomber Command and arrived at Breighton with its Wellington VIs. Over the next three and half years it was to establish itself as one of the premier squadrons in Bomber Command, dropping a greater weight of bombs than any other unit and suffering among the highest casualties.

460 flew its first operation from Breighton on the night of 12th-13th March 1942 when five Wellingtons headed for Emden, only one bombing the target area. Initially, many of the aircrew were British but the squadron's first loss from Breighton, a Wellington shot down in a raid on Kiel on the night of 28th-29th April, involved an all-Australian crew. They were among around 100 men from 460 to die over the next few months as the squadron took its Wellingtons to targets across Germany. By the late summer, however, the squadron was put on notice that it was to convert to 'heavies' and early in September, 460 Conversion Flight was formed with Halifaxes, moving soon afterwards to nearby Holme-on-Spalding Moor, then another 1 Group airfield.

The Flight's departure coincided with a change in Bomber Command policy. 1 Group, like its neighbours in 4 Group, had been earmarked for Halifaxes but the success of the new Lancaster then going into service

A Wellington Mk III at Breighton, mid-1942. (Jim Peterson)

in 5 Group decided Command HQ to equip 1 Group with the Lancaster. 460 Conversion Flight quickly returned and exchanged its Halifaxes for four Lancasters and four Manchesters, the Lanc's twin-engined predecessor. They were joined by 103 Conversion Flight, which brought its Halifaxes from Elsham Wold in Lincolnshire and together formed 1656 HCU, later moving to Lindholme.

460 Squadron, in the meantime, was busy converting to Lancasters and flew them operationally for the first time in November, losing its first aircraft in a raid on Stuttgart, three of the all-RAF crew evading capture while the remainder became PoWs. A second aircraft was lost with all seven of its crew in a raid on Essen on the night of 4th–5th January 1943 and a fortnight later the squadron took its Lancasters on the first of many visits it was to make to Berlin. One ran out of fuel and was abandoned by its crew over Flamborough, the wireless operator being killed when his WT leads became entangled with his parachute. Two nights later one of the squadron's flight commanders, S/Ldr Osborn, was killed when his aircraft was brought down by a night fighter over Holland following a raid on Dusseldorf.

It was to be a hard spring for 460 Squadron. Between 26th March and 5th May the squadron lost twelve Lancasters and all 84 men on board. Three of those lost were shot down in a raid on Pilsen, with three more a few days later over Stettin. Remarkably, one of the Lancasters used

Halifax Is at dispersal, RAF Breighton 1943. (Sir Guy Lawrence)

by 460 Squadron, W4783 G-George, was to survive the war. It was delivered to Breighton on 22nd October 1942 and flew 34 operations from the Yorkshire airfield before the squadron moved to Binbrook in Lincolnshire on 14th May 1943. It completed 90 operations before being donated to the people of Australia, where it now resides in the country's war museum in Canberra.

460's move to Binbrook saw most of the ground crew being transported in gliders and heralded new 'ownership' for Breighton, which was transferred a few days later to 4 Group. On 16th June, 78 Squadron arrived from Linton-on-Ouse, the second and last squadron to use RAF Breighton. Though 78 Squadron flew from five Yorkshire airfields during six years of war, today its veterans still look on Breighton as their true wartime 'home'. The squadron memorial was unveiled in the nearby churchyard in Bubwith in 1986 by Sir Guy Lawrence, who commanded 78 Squadron in 1943 and 1944, and the association is among the most active of all those of wartime bomber squadrons.

78 was quickly operational from its new base and on the night of 22nd-23rd June lost the first of almost 120 Halifax casualties it was to suffer when two aircraft were shot down during a raid on Mulheim. A

Post-op char, Breighton 1943. (Sir Guy Lawrence)

third was lost the following night and all on board were killed, including the pilot, Sgt Morrison, who was just 19. That summer the assault on the Ruhr reached a new height and 78 Squadron suffered its share of losses, including three aircraft lost in a single night on Aachen with the loss of 17 lives.

The squadron emerged unscathed over Peenemünde (although one aircraft crashed on take-off, the crew escaping injury) but less than a week later lost five aircraft in the opening raid of the Battle of Berlin, two colliding near Beverley on their return when they were ordered to divert to Leconfield. The aircraft came down near Hull Bridge on the outskirts of the town with just one badly injured survivor from the 15 men on board the two Halifaxes. Two others were shot down by night fighters while the fifth crashed in the North Sea after being damaged by a fighter. Three of the crew died but the rear gunner, Sgt Russell, managed to get the other three injured crew members onto a fuel tank which had floated from the Halifax when it broke up. One died before they were reached by an air-sea rescue launch while the other two died later from their injuries. Sgt Russell received a DFM for his efforts.

Despite the losses there was no respite for 78 Squadron. Three nights later the squadron lost two Halifaxes in an attack on Nuremburg and three more a few nights after that in an attack on Munchengladbach.

Among the 16 men who died in this raid was Sgt Collins, the pilot of one of the aircraft, who sacrificed his own life to make sure his wounded flight engineer escaped.

The losses went on. Two failed to return from Berlin, four more from an attack on Mannheim and two more from an attack on the same target at the end of September. A raid on Hanover cost the squadron another Halifax and four of its crew. The aircraft had been damaged by flak and the rear gunner was trapped. The flight engineer and mid-upper gunner went to his assistance and the pilot, P/O Thompson, opted to remain at the controls while the rescue attempt went on. All four men died when the aircraft crashed. Two further raids on Hanover that autumn cost the squadron six more aircraft and the lives of 35 men while four were lost in a raid in December on Frankfurt, including an American pilot on an exchange from the 8th Air Force.

The squadron had operated Halifax IIs during its time at Breighton but began converting to the much improved Mk IIIs in January 1944, losing the first of its new aircraft in a mining operation early in February. Sowing mines was an important part of Bomber Command's

A weary 78 Squadron crew awaits debriefing after the Berlin raid, 1st September 1943. They are (rear, l to r): Sgt Ferris (mid-upper), Sgt Hardcastle (rear gunner); (front): F/O Kent (bomb aimer), F/Sgt Petrie (flight engineer), F/Lt Dowden (navigator), W/Cmdr Lawrence (pilot and squadron CO) and Sgt French (wireless operator). (Sir Guy Lawrence)

work and Eddie McKinna, one of the armourers 78 Squadron brought with them from Linton-on-Ouse, remembers undergoing two courses on sea mines at HMS *Vernon*, the Navy's mine school, in Portsmouth. He was one of a number of senior NCOs from 4 Group stations chosen for the courses. In return, the Royal Navy petty officers were allocated to stations throughout Yorkshire to supervise the handling of the mines. Breighton's was CPO Alfred Desborough who, before he left in January 1944, told Eddie that 78 Squadron would soon be taking delivery of 200 special mines fitted with a 'sterilising' clock which rendered the mine safe after the set time expired. Eddie McKinna was later ordered to set the clock at 2 am on D-Day – making all the mines safe for the Normandy landings.

The regular bomb load for 78's Halifaxes was 'Plum Duff' – a single 2,000lb bomb and, depending on fuel load, four or six 1,000lb bombs plus six 500-pounders or incendiaries. It was customary for at least one of the 1,000lb bombs to be fitted with a delayed action pistol.

The spring of 1944 saw the bombing campaign reach a new ferocity. Operationally, the squadron suffered its worst night in the last of the big Berlin raids, six Halifaxes failing to return from the attack on the night of 24th-25th March, five being shot down with the loss of 22 lives. A sixth crashed in Norfolk. Three more were lost on the Nuremburg raid and two more in an attack on Karlsruhe.

Despite these losses, morale at Breighton was high. All those who served there remembered it as a happy station. Nowithstanding the rigours of wartime, there was a relaxed regime with none of the 'bull' many had experienced on other airfields. Among the squadron COs during its time at Breighton was W/Cmdr Markland, who took over in April 1944. He was the first wireless operator to command a squadron.

Accommodation at Breighton was no better or worse than on other wartime airfields in Yorkshire. Jack Boswell, who flew in N-Nan, recalls his was one of two crews accommodated in a single Nissen hut about a mile from the messes and a further mile and a half from the Flight buildings. He remembers the service police coming in one morning to collect the belongings of the other crew for forwarding to their next of kin, an experience shared by many others who survived a tour in Bomber Command. He also recalls the role of the WAAFs at Breighton who handled the parachutes, drove the crews to and from their aircraft and worked in the Intelligence or Met sections. It was a particular morale booster to be greeted by a smiling face or hear one of their cheerful voices on the RT when returning from ops.

Jack Boswell also remembers the funny side of life on a 4 Group bomber station, including the time when it was decided that aircrew required fitness training, which left many barely able to climb into their aircraft. And the occasion when a visiting senior officer was driving around the perimeter track when he passed two airmen who were walking to the distant Flight lines. The airmen failed to salute and the senior officer decided to stop his car and give them a piece of his mind. As he opened the door, one of them said: 'Thank you very much for the lift, sir' and promptly climbed into the car with his companion.

The weather and fuel shortages were still amongst the hazards facing crews at Breighton. Returning from Germany one murky night and running short of fuel, Jack Boswell's aircraft was one of a number from Breighton which mistakenly landed at another Yorkshire airfield. At the next briefing the CO urged crews to take particular care and ensure they landed back at Breighton. Everyone did make it back from the raid which followed – except the CO, who landed away, much to his embarrassment.

Tom Austwick, who worked in the radar section (where they learned the value of microwave cooking long before anyone thought to market the idea) remembers the wet and cold winters' nights at Breighton and

F/Lt Long makes a perfect landing in 78 Squadron's P-Popeye at Breighton after a daylight raid on Essen. (Bob Gilroy)

how, during one of them, one of his colleagues opted to cycle into York for a drink. On the way home, with several pints of the local brew on board, suddenly out of the mist came the sound of rattling chains, followed by a horned and bearded head. The hapless airman sprinted the rest of the way back to his Nissen hut where he leapt, fully clothed, into bed, convinced that old Nick himself had come looking for him. It was only the next day he learned that a local farmer kept goats nearby.

78 Squadron was to play its part in the invasion, losing four Halifaxes in an attack on rail yards at Juvisy on the night of 7th-8th June, three being brought down by flak and the fourth crash-landing at West Malling. Two more were lost in each of the attacks on Amiens and Laon bringing 78's losses in June to eight Halifaxes with 38 men killed, nine PoWs and three evaders. But that proved to be the turning point for 78 Squadron. Losses dropped dramatically and only two aircraft were lost in July with a third ditching off the Yorkshire coast after an engine failure, all the crew being rescued. Two more were lost in August, one crashing near Cheltenham after a mining trip off La Pallice and the second being shot down in a raid on Brunswick.

Just two Halifaxes were lost in September (a year earlier 16 had been lost) but the Grim Reaper had a nasty surprise for 78 Squadron in October. On the afternoon of 6th October the squadron was involved in an attack on the synthetic oil plant at Schloven-Buer. Over Holland two Halifaxes from Breighton collided and crashed, killing all 14 men on board. To add to the squadron's misery, a third aircraft was hit by flak and crashed during an operation which cost 78 Squadron the lives of 22 men. The following day another aircraft and its crew were lost in an attack on Kleve.

Only one more aircraft was lost over enemy territory during 1944, a Halifax which was shot down with the loss of six of the crew over Bochum early in November. Three more were destroyed in crashes, only one of which involved fatalities. That occurred on the night of 21st November as F/Lt 'Buck' Buckden and his crew returned from an attack on the refinery at Sterkrade. Buckden, a Canadian, was among the most popular men on the squadron and this was to be the last operation of his crew's tour. Radar technician Tom Austwick recalls that a celebration was planned by the ground crew on the dispersal pan for the crew when they returned. However, as their aircraft approached the airfield it was ordered to go round again because of a change in the wind. Minutes later there was the unmistakable sound of a crash and rescuers later found the Halifax, F-Freddie, had hit a tree and come down in flames at Spaldington, about two miles from the airfield. There were no survivors and the party planned by the ground crew turned into a wake.

That proved to be the last Halifax lost by 78 Squadron for more than ten weeks, until MZ799 failed to return from a mining operation over the Baltic in mid-February 1945. A week later the squadron lost another aircraft which crashed on landing after being diverted to Holme-on-Spalding Moor, the crew escaping without serious injury. The Halifax had returned from Worms with both starboard engines feathered. Another Halifax was written off in a heavy landing the following month and 78's final losses of the war came in April when one was shot down during a daylight attack on Hamburg and another crashed into high ground near Pocklington on its return from another raid on the North German port.

78 Squadron flew its final operation of the war to Wangerooge on 25th April and on 7th May found itself transferred with the rest of 4 Group to Transport Command. It converted to Dakotas later in the summer and in September finally left Breighton for the Middle East.

The airfield itself quickly closed and much of the land was returned to agriculture. However, some wartime buildings were retained and one runway kept clear and now Breighton houses a flying club and a growing collection of historic aircraft.

3
BURN

At 9.16 pm on the night of 30th March 1944, P/O Cyril Barton lifted Halifax LK797 of 578 Squadron off the main runway at RAF Burn, near Selby on what would be his 19th operation. The target was the southern German city of Nuremburg.

At 5.40 am the following morning villagers in the mining community of Ryhope, near Sunderland, heard the sound of a large aircraft nearby. Minutes later the aircraft crashed in the nearby colliery yard. Rescuers found the pilot fatally injured at the controls but three members of the crew scrambled out of the wreckage of the rear of the Halifax.

Barton's aircraft, which had the name *Excalibur* chalked on its fuselage, was the last of 108 heavy bombers to either crash or be shot down following the disastrous raid on Nuremburg. What had happened in the time which had elapsed between the departure of LK797 from Burn and its crash at Ryhope was to earn Cyril Barton a posthumous Victoria Cross, the only one to be awarded within 4 Group of Bomber Command.

After leaving Burn, *Excalibur* had joined the stream of Lancasters and Halifaxes threading their way across Europe to their distant target in bright moonlight. It soon became clear to the Halifax's crew that this was going to be a difficult trip. Fighter activity was intense and on the outward leg they saw the funeral pyres of numerous aircraft shot down by the Luftwaffe. Then it was *Excalibur*'s turn. Two Ju 88s attacked the Halifax head-on, raking the bomber with cannon shells. Two fuel tanks were hit, the starboard inner engine set on fire, the radio destroyed and the rear turret put out of action. Cyril Barton successfully evaded one attack but a second led to further damage, flames and sparks from the damaged engine leaving a trail across the night sky. It was only after the attacks ended that it was discovered that three of the crew, the

Newly commissioned Pilot Officer Cyril Barton, pictured in January 1944. (Via Alan Mitcheson)

navigator, bomb aimer and wireless operator, had jumped (it later transpired they had mistaken one of the evasive action signals for one devised by the crew for baling out).

By this time *Excalibur* was still some distance from the target and in a desperate situation. But Barton opted to press on and, navigating by the stars, he reached the target (his aircraft was one of many which mistakenly attacked Schweinfurt) before turning for home. With little fuel left, the Halifax finally made landfall as the first light of dawn appeared. It was then that the fuel finally ran out and Barton ordered the three remaining members of his crew to take up their crash positions. Suddenly a row of terraced houses appeared in front of the bomber and he managed to lift the aircraft enough to miss all but the last house in the row, before crashing through some gardens and destroying a footbridge over a railway cutting. At this point the Halifax broke in half, the rear section of the fuselage, containing the other crew members, falling into the cutting while the nose section came to rest in the yard of Ryhope colliery.

Alan Mitcheson was then a schoolboy a month short of his 14th birthday. Early that morning he saw Barton's Halifax as it made its way up the coast close to Sunderland and had then just climbed back into bed when the aircraft came in from the direction of the sea. He noticed the aircraft was making a noise 'like a car back-firing' and then flew low over the roof tops before banking and dropping down near the colliery, followed by a 'sound like thunder'. He and his friend, George Goldsborough, went up to the colliery yard on their way to school. They retraced the route of the crashing aircraft and found the end house in West Terrace, which was occupied by the Richardson family, had been completely demolished but rescuers had been astonished to find a kettle boiling merrily in the wreckage when they arrived. Three of the engines were scattered around the area and they learned that a miner, George Heads, had been killed when he was hit by the wreckage as he made his way home.

Among the first on the scene was John Douglas, who was home on leave from the Royal Marines, and he discovered Cyril Barton badly injured in the cockpit of the Halifax. A local GP, Dr Bain Alderton, was called and found the pilot had suffered serious head injuries. He was carefully lifted out and placed in the colliery ambulance. According to the driver, Harry Hicks, he died soon after arriving at the emergency hospital at Cherry Knowle, Ryhope.

The three surviving members of the crew all suffered minor injuries and later returned to Burn where they told the full story of Cyril Barton's final operation. On 26th June 1944 it was announced that P/O Cyril Barton had been awarded a posthumous Victoria Cross in recognition of conspicuous bravery, a medal which was received by his parents at a ceremony at Buckingham Palace on 5th December.

Alan Mitcheson was later to be instrumental in the erection of a memorial to Cyril Barton on Ryhope village green after a lengthy battle with the municipal authorities in Sunderland. The memorial was unveiled by P/O Barton's sisters, Cynthia Maidment and Joyce Voysey, at a ceremony in 1985 attended by three surviving members of his crew, Harry Wood, Len Lambert and Freddie Bryce. One of the many letters Alan Mitcheson received during his campaign was from Freddie Bryce, the Halifax's rear gunner. He stated simply: 'If it was not for Cyril I would not be writing this now. By staying at the controls of the aircraft as he did, he saved our lives. He was a great guy in more ways than one and I am still proud to this day to have been a member of his crew.'

The airfield at Burn had been one of the many built for Bomber Command in 1941. The 600-acre site was bounded by the A19, the Doncaster-Selby LNER line and the Selby canal. It was November 1942 before work on what was a standard bomber airfield was completed, but even before then Burn had been used briefly by 1653 HCU, a Liberator unit which moved from Polebrook in Northants and eventually disbanded at Burn in October. There was a plan at this time to equip some 1 Group squadrons with American-built Liberators. The plan was never to reach fruition but 1653's move may have had something to do with this project.

Shortly after the airfield opened one of the Canadian squadrons destined for 6 Group, 431 (Iroquois), was formed at Burn on Wellington Xs. Many of the original aircrew were British but, after the squadron became operational, there was a gradual 'Canadianisation' before 431 Squadron moved to Tholthorpe on 14th July 1943. It flew its first operation from Burn on the night of 5th-6th March when three aircraft took part in a raid on Essen. It suffered its first loss at the end of the month when Wellington HE503 SE-S crashed in the North Sea following a raid on Duisburg, killing all on board. The squadron lost 16 aircraft in operations from Burn before its move to Tholthorpe, including two in a raid on Dusseldorf on 11th-12th June, while a third was written off after colliding with a Halifax following a landing at Oulton.

One of the squadron's bomb aimers, Sgt Sloan, won a Conspicuous Gallantry Medal during a raid on the Ruhr. He was only 18 and was part of a 'scratch' crew whose Wellington was hit by flak over the target and went into a steep dive during which the skipper ordered the crew to bale out. Sgt Sloan managed to jettison the bombs and then pulled himself into the cockpit only to find the pilot and rear gunner had jumped. The bomb aimer had hoped to train as a pilot when he volunteered for air crew and had done some time on the Link trainer before being retrained. Now he had the opportunity to put that experience to good use.

He called the rest of the crew, the navigator and wireless operator, and told them he planned to fly the Wimpey home and they volunteered to stay with him. During the long flight the starboard engine started running rough and Sloan shut it down, crossing the North Sea on just one engine. He hoped to make it back to Burn but over Lincolnshire the port engine began coughing. Just at that moment he saw a flare path and made a good landing at Cranwell. There, the station intelligence officer heard the incredible story from the crew and immediately called Sloan's CO at Burn to tell him what had happened. The following day the crew were flown back to Burn in three of Cranwell's Dominies, which all dipped their wings in tribute to the remarkable courage of Sgt Sloan as they took off again for Cranwell. Apart from Sloan's CGM, there was a DFC for the navigator and a DFM for the wireless operator.

431's departure marked the start of a period of inactivity at Burn. It was used as a relief landing ground by the Halifaxes from the heavy conversion units at Riccall and Marston Moor, the Austers of 658 and 659 AOP Squadrons, which moved in briefly from Clifton, and by Hurricanes of the Air Fighting Development Unit at Leconfield.

On 14th January 1944 a new bomber squadron, 578, was formed with Halifax IIIs from C Flight of 51 Squadron at Snaith under the command of W/Cmdr David Wilkerson, who had been their CO. Ground staff came mainly from 51 Squadron while air crew were posted in from other 4 Group squadrons, among them P/O Barton and his crew from 78 Squadron at Breighton.

W/Cmdr Wilkerson was a remarkable character, regarded by those who knew him and served with him as one of the finest leaders in Bomber Command and a man destined for great things. He had flown Whitleys with 58 and 35 Squadrons, serving under Leonard Cheshire, a man who he was later to be spoken of in the same breath. He served as

Pilot Harold Brown (third left) and crew at Burn, mid-1944. Others on the picture are (l to r): Paddy Graham (wireless operator), Taffy Jennings (bomb aimer), Jim Inward (flight engineer), Taffy Lloyd (navigator) and Roscoe (mid-upper). The rear gunner was on leave when the photograph was taken. (Jim Inward)

an instructor on 35 Conversion Flight and 1652 HCU before commanding 158 Conversion Flight and a spell at Group HQ and as Base Training Inspector at 41 Base. He returned to operational flying with 51 Squadron in November 1943 and went on to form the new squadron. 578 Squadron was to have one of the lowest loss rates in Bomber Command during 1944 and those who served on the squadron give credit for this to Wilkerson's leadership.

It was Wilkerson who – naturally – led 578 on its first operation, to Berlin, on the night of 20th January and again the following night to Magdeburg, a raid which saw one of the squadron's aircraft ditch 50 miles off Flamborough. The Halifax, J-Jig, had strayed over the Elbe on the return trip and had been damaged by flak, at least one of the fuel tanks being punctured. After sending out a Mayday, the pilot ditched in rough seas and the aircraft quickly broke up. Two of the crew, Sgts Baldry and Lester, were swept away and a third, F/O Williams, was badly injured but was dragged into the dinghy by the other members of the crew only to die some hours later from his injuries. The survivors began firing off flares at regular intervals and these were spotted eight hours after the aircraft ditched by two rescue launches, 520 and 547, which were out on patrol from Immingham for just such an emergency. The survivors were quickly picked up and were later treated in hospital at Grimsby for the effects of exposure.

578 moved to Burn on 6th February and lost its first aircraft from there on the 24th when two Halifaxes failed to return from Schweinfurt, another Halifax making it back to Burn after losing a propeller.

It was 15th March before the squadron was able to operate at full strength, 16 aircraft taking part in a raid on Stuttgart. One was shot down near the target, with just two of the crew surviving. Another crashed near Selby, five of the crew being killed, while a third crashed at Biggin Hill, killing three of those on board.

A week later LK-R failed to return from a raid on Frankfurt. Flying as second pilot was the station commander, G/Capt Marwood-Elton, who survived along with six members of the crew to become a prisoner of war. He was replaced by G/Capt Warburton as CO of Burn. The squadron lost three aircraft in the final attack of the Battle of Berlin on the night of 24th-25th March, just three men surviving from the 22 men on board. Then came the attack on Nuremburg which resulted in the death of Cyril Barton. Two other aircraft from Burn were lost, with no survivors.

An attack on Dusseldorf on 23rd April cost the squadron two aircraft, the only losses in a busy month for 578. These were the last losses until the eve of D-Day when one of the aircraft sent to attack the batteries at Mont Fleury failed to return. By this time the squadron was operating three flights and 24 aircraft left Burn that night for Normandy. Over the target S/Ldr Watson's aircraft was hit by flak and he ordered his crew to bale out. Three managed to get clear and were picked up from the sea by ships in the invasion fleet. S/Ldr Watson himself refused to jump because of the instability of the aircraft and died when the Halifax crashed into the sea.

The end of the month saw the departure of W/Cmdr Wilkerson from Burn. In May he had been awarded a DSO to add to his DFC and was posted to 9 Course at the Empire Central Flying School at Hullavington. His departure was marked by an extravagant 'beat-up' of the airfield by Wilkerson following the last of his 47 operations and a ceremonial send-off by the whole squadron, such was his popularity.

A Halifax III of 578 Squadron, 1944. (Yorkshire Air Museum via Peter Green)

Ten weeks after leaving Burn, David Wilkerson was dead, killed when the Martin Baltimore aircraft in which he was flying as a passenger crashed on take-off. He was later buried at his family's request in Selby after a funeral service at RAF Burn. Civilians who lived in the area around the airfield lined the route of the cortège as a tribute to a man they had all come to admire during the brief time the squadron had been at the airfield.

In his excellent history of 578 Squadron, Hugh Cawdron, a boyhood friend of David Wilkerson, records numerous tributes to a man held in the highest regard by everyone who knew him. Cpl Ted Bland wrote: 'We would have followed him through Hell – but God had need of him.' F/O John Bluring: 'I remember W/Cmdr Wilkerson as the best boss I've ever had, in or out of the RAF.' F/Lt Geoffrey Sanders: 'A prince among men, a brilliant pilot, a wonderful squadron commander who led by example.'

Burn's worst night of the war came, ironically, soon after Wilkerson's departure, six aircraft being lost in a raid on Bottrop. One was shot down over the Dutch coast and there were two survivors from a crew on their 32nd operation and a second was shot down near the target. Two others collided over what is now Hull's Bransholme estate as they

The 578 Squadron Memorial at Burn. (D. Wheeler)

headed back to Burn, killing all 14 men on board. A fifth fell to a night fighter while the sixth disappeared without trace on a night which cost the squadron the lives of 36 men.

The pace that summer was furious in 4 Group. On 3rd August 21 Burn aircraft took part in a daylight attack on V1 sites in northern France, all the aircraft returning safely despite one being damaged by a bomb from a Lancaster which tore a huge hole in its starboard wing. That evening the squadron was back over France again, attacking another flying bomb site. One of its aircraft crashed after the crew baled out over Suffolk. Two Halifaxes and their crews were lost eight nights later in a raid on the Opel works at Russelheim, a third just making it back to the emergency strip at Woodbridge with flak damage.

The threat of damage from the bombs of higher-flying Lancasters was always one which Halifax crews had to endure and another 578 aircraft had a fortunate escape when a bomb went right through the fuselage during a daylight raid on Venlo early in September. The aircraft later landed at an American airfield where, ironically, the Lancaster which dropped the bomb also landed. No guesses for who bought the drinks that night.

Casualties were light during 578's only winter at Burn. Just one aircraft was lost in December, during a raid on Bingen, while a second was written off in spectacular fashion at Wormingford. The pilot raised the undercarriage after the aircraft swung on take-off, the Halifax crashing through a row of trees and demolishing some airfield buildings before finally coming to a halt.

An attack on Hanover early in January 1945 resulted in a lucky escape for one crew, all of whom baled out after their aircraft was involved in a mid-air collision over Belgium. Two more were written off in crashes when the squadron was diverted to Waterbeach in Cambridgeshire following an attack on Wesel on 17th February, one Halifax overshooting and the second running into the wreckage. A third 578 aircraft was then involved in a collision on the ground with a USAAF DC3.

Four nights later an attack on a refinery near Dusseldorf resulted in two aircraft being shot down by night fighters and a third was damaged in a heavy landing. The following night 14 aircraft from Burn took part in what turned out to be the only raid of the war on the town of Worms. Again, two 578 Squadron Halifaxes were shot down by night fighters and just one man, F/O Danny McLean, survived.

The attack on Kamen on the night of 3rd-4th March – best

remembered on other 4 Group stations because of the attacks by intruders on the returning Halifaxes – saw two 578 Squadron Halifaxes each complete their 100th operation. Only four Halifaxes were to achieve the 'ton' (compared with 34 Lancasters) and two of them were from 578 Squadron, while a third completed its 100th operation with 51 Squadron at Snaith after spending its early days at Burn. The 578 Squadron aircraft, LW587 LK-V/A and MZ527 LK-W/D, went on to complete 104 and 105 operations respectively and both were scrapped after the war.

Both aircraft flew as part of the 15 from 578 Squadron among the 760 heavy bombers which raided Chemnitz on the night of 5th-6th March. Several later landed at Bovington, where one swung on landing and collided with a second Burn Halifax, the resulting fire destroying both bombers. Two nights later the squadron suffered its final losses of the war when two aircraft failed to return from a raid on the Deutsche Erdoel refinery at Hemingstedt, one being shot down near the target and the second disappearing over the North Sea after sending out a Mayday message.

The squadron flew its last operation of the war in a daylight attack on Wuppertal on 13th March, one of the 14 aircraft despatched returning early. A month later 578 Squadron was disbanded and RAF Burn closed to flying. It was placed on a care and maintenance basis and in 1946 was used for one of the huge War Department disposal sales, its runways lined with all manner of military equipment surplus to requirements.

Much of the airfield has long since been returned to agriculture although there are a few scattered reminders of its wartime role. More importantly, the spirit of 578 Squadron is kept alive by an active squadron association, which unveiled its own memorial in Burn village in 1991 and a second some time later in Wiltshire in memory of David Wilkerson.

4
CARNABY

As early as 1941 senior figures in the Royal Air Force had been looking into the feasibility of special emergency runways to handle aircraft suffering from battle damage or mechanical problems. Crash-landings on operational airfields were becoming something of a serious problem, often curtailing flying for some time while damaged aircraft were removed and runways made good.

The initial idea was to extend the main runway at Wittering, on the Lincolnshire-Cambridgeshire border but, as the air war gathered pace, this was clearly insufficient and so, in August 1942, three sites were selected for development as special emergency airfields, Manston in Kent, Woodbridge in Suffolk and Carnaby in Yorkshire.

The Yorkshire site selected was no stranger to aerial activity. Nearby Lowthorpe had operated as a sub-station to Howden during the First World War and was the temporary home of a flight of DH6s used on anti-submarine patrols. Between the wars, a large grassed area at Speeton was used for private flying. Carnaby itself was absolutely ideal for its new role, only a mile or so from the sea with no obstacles to hamper aircraft. Communications were also ideal as it stood alongside the railway line from Bridlington to Hull, and it was on this line that most of the building supplies arrived.

The contract to build Carnaby went to Monks, the company responsible for many of the airfields in Yorkshire and Lincolnshire. Carnaby was something different for them – an immense runway with only limited ground facilities.

The runway was 3,000 yards long and 250 yards across, some five times the normal width. At each end there were 500 yard grass undershoots and overshoots. The runway surface was a mix of sea sand and bitumen, which was a little more forgiving and easier to repair than the standard surface. The runway itself was divided into three 'lanes', the left designated for emergencies only, aircraft being permitted to land there without seeking permission from flying control. Normal landing procedures existed for the remaining two lanes, across which it was possible for aircraft to land side by side.

Like Woodbridge and Manston, Carnaby (which was under the control of 4 Group HQ) was to get the new FIDO fog dispersal equipment and this was installed at the time of runway construction. A special siding was also constructed at Carnaby station for the deliveries of fuel for the FIDO burners.

The airfield opened for business in April 1944 but the fog dispersal equipment was not ready to be tested until 19th July when the burners were lit for the first time. No warning of the test had been given to the local population – or the National Fire Service – and the great glow in the sky to the south-west suggested to the people of Bridlington there had been some major catastrophe at the new airfield.

FIDO was first used in earnest to land two groups of Halifaxes in poor visibility following a raid on the Pas de Calais on 1st August, the highlight of which was a near miss by two 158 Squadron aircraft from Lissett which landed on the same runway but in opposite directions at the same time. Fortunately, F/Sgt Billy Bishop (who had landed the 'wrong' way) opened the throttles of his aircraft just in time to 'bounce' over the aircraft of F/O Leonard.

During its operational life, Carnaby was to recover more than 1,500 aircraft, around half of which were suffering from mechanical failures while many others had sustained battle damage.

A typical incident came on 17th September 1944 when Lancaster ND356 belonging to 100 Squadron at Waltham in North Lincolnshire reported the loss of an engine, no hydraulics, no flaps, fuselage damage and a badly wounded bomb aimer as it made its way back across the North Sea.

The aircraft, HW-O, was immediately diverted to Carnaby where all the emergency services, fire, rescue and ambulance crews, were turned out to await the arrival of the Lancaster. It came in low and immediately settled on the runway. It was while the Lancaster was rolling along the almost two miles of concrete that the emergency vehicles spotted a 500lb bomb fall from the half-open bomb bay of the Lancaster. It rolled unceremoniously to the side of the runway, to be dealt with later by a disposal team.

The Lancaster, in the meantime, finally came to a halt and six of the crew were able to clamber out while the seventh, bomb-aimer P/O J. Sanderson was helped out by ambulance crews. The aircraft had taken what appeared to be a direct hit in the nose from a flak gun and the crew later counted 117 holes in the aircraft, which had been on 100 Squadron's books for most of that very busy summer.

The Lancaster was later towed off the runway to a civilian repair depot at Carnaby where repairs got under way within a matter of days. ND356 was almost as good as new by the time they had finished with it and later in the year another crew arrived to fly HW-O back to Waltham where it saw out the war before being scrapped.

Two of her crew, the pilot, F/Lt (later S/Ldr) H. F. Scott, and the bomb aimer, P/O Sanderson, who had pressed on with his bomb run despite being wounded, received immediate DFCs and two others, the navigator, F/Lt J. H. Harwood, and the flight engineer, P/O J. B. McQuaid, were later awarded the same decoration.

Sheffielder Jack Morley was the wireless operator in Z-Zebra, a non-ABC Lancaster of 101 Squadron at Ludford Magna in Lincolnshire and

S/Ldr Scott and crew with their new aircraft after 100 Squadron had moved from Carnaby in April 1945. They are (left to right): P/O McQuaid (flight engineer), S/Ldr Scott, F/Sgt Nelson (rear gunner who had just replaced the tour-expired 'Buck' O'Riordan), P/O Jones (wireless operator), F/S Johnson (mid-upper), P/O Sanderson (bomb aimer), F/Lt Hardwood (navigator).

he and his crew were pleased to see the runway lights at Carnaby on the night of 23rd October 1944, a night they hoped would have seen the completion of their tour.

He was part of the crew of F/Lt G. H. Harris and they had taken off from Ludford late in the afternoon on what was to be a raid by over a thousand Halifaxes and Lancasters on Essen. They had with them S/Ldr Gundry-White, who went along as 'second dickey' on his first experience of operational flying over Germany.

An hour out from the Lincolnshire coast, Z-Zebra's port engine began to overheat and F/Lt Harris had to shut it down. The Lancaster gradually fell behind the stream but the crew members were unanimous when the pilot asked them what they wanted to do – press on. As Essen approached, however, Z-Zebra ran into more problems when the starboard outer was damaged, probably by flak, and caught fire. The flames were quickly extinguished but the Lancaster was left with only its emergency battery supply to provide power. This meant that the load of one 4,000lb high capacity bomb plus 2,070 incendiaries could only be dropped manually. But again the crew opted to continue with the attack.

Over Essen, however, they found the bombs would not release so they decided to go round and do it all again, despite their target being the heaviest defended city on earth. Again the bombs refused to budge so, reluctantly, they turned for home.

Their problems were compounded by the fact that the bombs were now fused and posed a very serious threat to the Lancaster should they come loose on the return flight. Over the North Sea they tried repeatedly to release their deadly load but the bombs just wouldn't budge. The one bright moment came when the pilot managed to restart the port outer engine. When they managed to raise Ludford on the R/T they were immediately ordered to divert to Carnaby where the emergency services would be waiting for them.

They were ordered by the tower at Carnaby to fly out to sea while preparations were made for their arrival. They inadvertently heard what these were when someone left their transmitter switch on – all non-essential personnel were to move as far away as possible as the Lancaster was expected to explode when it touched down!

But F/Lt Harris got everything right and Z-Zebra made the smoothest landing of her life on the long, wide runway at Carnaby. The bad news was yet to come. When they arrived back at Ludford they were told as they had not dropped their bombs on Essen the operation did not count towards the completion of their tour! Happily, they and Z-Zebra returned safely from a raid on Cologne on 28th October.

Poor weather and the pressing need to halt the German counter-attack in the Ardennes meant a busy Christmas for the staff at Carnaby. On Boxing Day some 20 Halifaxes got down using the airfield's FIDO system and one airman counted over 100 Halifaxes, Lancasters and Stirlings parked nose to tail on the airfield.

One of Carnaby's busiest days came at the end of January 1945 when 65 USAAF bombers, mainly B24 Liberators, were diverted there after an aborted raid on Brunswick. Once they saw the glow of the FIDO burners through the gloom there was no holding the American pilots. Despite being urged to obey orders and remain in a stacking system, they 'came down in droves' according to one eye witness. Several of the American pilots, however, balked at landing in the fiery glow below them and attempted to find a hole in the fog somewhere else. Tragically one or two of the aircraft were to crash with considerable loss of life on the North Yorkshire Moors.

Carnaby was used by 617 Squadron in its initial trials with the 22,000lb Grand Slam bombs, the squadron honing their take-off techniques before flying from their own airfield at Woodhall Spa in Lincolnshire with the monster bombs. On one occasion at the end of March two 617 Squadron Lancasters landed at Carnaby with their Grand Slams after an aborted mission rather than waste them in the sea.

The airfield also witnessed one of the miracle escapes of the air war. Early in April 1945 Halifax E-Easy of 58 Squadron Coastal Command was on an anti-shipping patrol from its base in the Shetlands when a photo-flash accidentally ignited in the bomb bay, blowing a large hole in the aircraft. Much of the fuselage and tail unit was damaged and the crew could find no trace of the hapless mid-upper gunner, whose turret had been blown off in the explosion. The aircraft was low on fuel and poor visibility led it to be diverted to Carnaby, where it landed between the FIDO burners. It was only when the aircraft was on the ground that the mid-upper gunner was found, caught up by his parachute harness underneath the fuselage. He was unconscious and suffering from exposure and shock but otherwise unharmed by his three and a half hour ordeal in the aircraft's slipstream. It was later noticed that the oxygen mask and goggles he was wearing had scraped along Carnaby's runway when the aircraft landed.

Carnaby closed in March 1946 only to reopen briefly seven years later as a relief landing ground for Meteors from 203 Advanced Flying School at Driffield. It later became the base for a Thor intercontinental ballistic missile battery, before these weapons were removed in 1963 and it closed again. The airfield was bought jointly by Bridlington Urban and Rural Councils in 1972 and redeveloped as a major industrial estate and was used for many years as the British distribution centre for Lada cars imported through Hull from the Soviet Union.

5
CATFOSS AND HUTTON CRANSWICK

It was in the mid-1930s that the RAF first began using a windswept spot near the East Yorkshire coast as a gunnery training airfield. It was close to the village of Brandesburton, just off the Hull-Bridlington road, but the airfield took its name from the nearby Catfoss Grange. Those who served there remember RAF Catfoss as one of the bleakest postings in their military career.

Catfoss owed its existence to the bombing and gunnery range established by the RAF during its Thirties expansion programme off the Yorkshire coast between Hornsea and Skipsea. The site chosen for the airfield was less than five miles from the coast and its location ensured that units using its facilities – a word which has to be used with some caution – wasted little time in flying to and from the range. Records show that the airfield was one of only a handful in Yorkshire to have hardened runways laid before the war.

One of the only operational units to be based there was 97 Squadron, which was formed from B Flight of 10 Squadron in 1935 and flew its Heyfords from Catfoss briefly before moving south. The airfield itself was destined to become the home of No 1 Armament School and filled this role until the outbreak of war when the school was moved to the safety of the west coast. In October 1939 a detachment of Spitfires from 616 Squadron, then based at Leconfield, moved in and used Catfoss for North Sea patrols before the squadron left in May 1940.

Catfoss closed for expansion work, which was still going on when the airfield officially reopened in August. It was to be another two months before No 2 (Coastal) Operational Training Unit set up home at Catfoss. It was equipped initially with Blenheims and a handful of Ansons and went on to fill an important role in training the strike crews who would turn Coastal's Beaufighter squadrons into such a potent force. Later it was to be equipped with its own Beaufighters, the Blenheims being relegated to providing initial training.

Facilities at Catfoss were stretched almost to breaking point for much of the time it was used by 2 OTU. At one time the station strength numbered almost 2,500, yet the dining hut could only accommodate 250. Some airmen who served there remember that meal breaks had to be extended to 90 minutes to give the men time to queue for their food.

The officers' mess was in nearby Brandesburton Hall and accommodation huts were scattered over a wide area. LAC Ralph Dargue, who spent some considerable time at Catfoss, remembered that the camp was so widespread he never did get to see all of it.

Outside Bransburton itself, one enterprising member of the local

Beaufighter VIs of 2 OTU operating from Catfoss in 1943. (Andrew Thomas)

community provided bathing facilities for airmen while two equally enterprising London prostitutes set up in business in the village.

The airfield itself still had a single Bellman hangar and there were no huts provided on the flight lines. The men who worked on those lines had to do what 'erks' throughout the RAF did – improvise. Shelters were knocked together from packing cases and bits of corrugated iron and engine covers were used to provide shelter from the elements for tool boxes.

Esther Wilford (née Spavin) served at Catfoss with the Waaf contingent as an R/T operator from January 1944 until February 1945 when she transferred to Melbourne, and has fond memories of the airfields, not the least because that was where she met her future husband. During her time there the Waafs were accommodated in the married quarters and it was only when she learned to ride a cycle that she began to discover the delights of this part of the East Riding, visiting places like Hornsea, Skipsea and Ulrome. Discipline was relaxed, particularly after an RAF Regiment contingent left, and the Waafs were able to stay out late without being noticed, using the opportunity to visit the cinema at the Brandesburton end of the camp and making occasional visits to Hull, although most of the cinemas in the badly-bombed city were still closed. Farms surrounded the airfield and occasionally they provided fresh eggs for breakfast at Catfoss' Naafi canteen. Then there was always the local fish and chip shop and Smokey Joe's Café on the main road. Life was good at Catfoss during her time, she remembers, so much so that they were hardly touched by the war. Reminders came, however, over the radio as bombers, badly damaged in raids over Germany, called for assistance and were diverted to the nearby emergency strip at Carnaby.

Catfoss's runways provided a haven in the early days of the war for bombers from Yorkshire airfields struggling to make it home or those suffering from mechanical defects. Typical of these was a 76 Squadron Halifax, MP-O, which had taken off from Pocklington on the afternoon of 31st August 1942. Soon after take-off the port engine cut and smoke began pouring from it. The aircraft would not climb above 300 feet and, 15 minutes after take-off, the pilot, Sgt Moir, attempted to land at Catfoss, the undercarriage collapsing and the bomber colliding with a parked Blenheim. Moir and his crew climbed out uninjured and were later collected and taken back to Pocklington. He later completed his tour with 78 Squadron, was commissioned and awarded a DFC but was killed while instructing at Marston Moor on 25th May, 1944. At Catfoss itself flying went on almost non-stop and Ralph Dargue recalled numerous accidents, 13 aircraft being lost in one 11-day period, many coming down in the sea with fatal consequences for those on board.

On 15th February 1944, 2 OTU was finally disbanded at Catfoss and was replaced by the Central Gunnery School, which moved from Sutton Bridge in Lincolnshire, bringing with it an assortment of aircraft including Wellingtons, Spitfires, Beaufighters and Martinets. Its work was regarded as of supreme importance within the RAF, covering all aspects of aerial gunnery. The school ran a Gunnery Leaders' course and also provided refresher training for fighter pilots and attracted some of the best instructors. Its last wartime commanding officer was the Battle of Britain ace, G/Capt 'Sailor' Malan.

The Central Gunnery School moved to Leconfield in November 1945 and plans were drawn up for Catfoss to become a civilian airport, serving the city of Hull. These plans, like so many others around the country, came to nothing and the airfield closed, reopening briefly in 1959 when Catfoss became a satellite of Driffield and Thor missiles were deployed there. These were removed in 1963 and what remains of RAF Catfoss today is used for storage or agricultural purposes.

In contrast with Catfoss, facilities at Hutton Cranswick were much better when it opened as a fighter airfield within 12 Group in January 1942. Day-time fighter cover for much of East Yorkshire and the Hull area had been provided from Leconfield for the previous two years but this pre-war airfield was about to return to Bomber Command control.

The airfield at Hutton Cranswick lay across the Beverley-Driffield road from the village which gave it its name and was close enough to the bomber airfield at Driffield for the circuits to overlap, a common occurrence in Yorkshire in those days.

The airfield had been built with three concrete runways – something of a luxury in Fighter Command – together with a pair of T2 hangars. It was, like most of the airfields of the day, a dispersed site with many of the accommodation huts being situated around the neighbouring village of Watton. Its first of many Fighter Command occupants was 610 Squadron, which arrived with its Spitfire Vbs from Leconfield soon after the airfield opened. Their's was, like all the squadrons to follow them, to be only a brief stop. Fighter Command rotated its squadrons with almost frightening speed through operational and training areas, Hutton Cranswick falling very much into the latter category. With the worst of the blitz now over, many of Fighter Command's activities were focused on fighter sweeps across France and the Low Countries and these had to be conducted from airfields in the south, south-west and East Anglia. After periods in the front line, squadrons moved north to airfields like Hutton Cranswick for rest, re-equipping and additional training. They were also expected to fly patrols along the East Coast and deal with any intruders.

610 Squadron was replaced by another Spitfire squadron, 19, which stayed for less than a month before being replaced by 308 (City of Krakow) Squadron, the first of several Polish units to spend some time at Hutton Cranswick. It had been flying fighter sweeps from Exeter and remained in Yorkshire, apart from a six-day detachment to Redhill, until the end of July. Its replacement was another Polish squadron, 316 (City of Warsaw), which had been formed the previous year at Pembury and had most recently been operating from Heston. It was to remain at Hutton Cranswick for almost eight months, the longest of any wartime squadron, before it eventually moved to Northolt.

The Poles of 316 were joined in November 1942 by 195 Squadron, which had recently re-equipped with Typhoons. 195 left for Woodvale in February followed shortly by 316, their replacements being two more Polish squadrons, 306 (City of Torun) and 302 (City of Poznan). The latter had, in fact, been formed at Leconfield in the summer of 1940

HRH the Marharatta of Baroda in a visit to 124 Squadron at Hutton Cranswick in 1945. With him are W/Cmdr Saunders and G/Capt H. W. Harrison, OC 124 Squadron. (Andrew Thomas)

from the remnants of No 3 Poznan Air Regiment and Polish units which had flown with the French Air Force.

306 remained at Hutton Cranswick for less than a month before leaving for Catterick while 302 Squadron left a couple of weeks later. Their replacements were more Polish units, 315 (City of Deblin), which flew in from Northolt, and 308 which made a return visit to Hutton Cranswick from Church Fenton. Both had gone again on the Fighter Command merry-go-round by September, when they were replaced by three British squadrons, 234, which brought its Spitfires from Rochford, and 168 and 170 with Mustangs. The Mustang squadrons were in Yorkshire for only a week for trials to be carried out at Huggate Wold, near Driffield, a site which had been considered at one time as a suitable location for a bomber airfield. Now it was one of a number of sites around the country being used to try out experimental steel mesh runways. These had been devised in the United States and could be laid easily and cheaply as temporary airstrips by engineers. The trials at Huggate Wold and elsewhere were to prove the value of the strips and the RAF was to make great use of them on its forward air strips in Normandy following the D-Day landings. The trials at Huggate Wold lasted for about a week before the Mustangs left, 170 going to Leconfield and 168 to Thruxton.

Hutton Cranswick's role was now changing and in December, 291 Squadron was formed there from 613, 629 and 634 Anti-Aircraft Co-operation Flights. Its job was to provide target towing facilities for anti-aircraft gunners along the coast and it used an assortment of well-used Hurricanes and Martinets for the job, and was to remain at Hutton Cranswick until the war ended.

The airfield was still being used by fighter squadrons, which paid fleeting visits during the spring as part of the build-up for the invasion. Among them were several Canadian squadrons, including 401, 403, 412, 441, 442 and 443, all flying Spitfires, and Typhoon-equipped 439 Squadron. 310 (Czech) Squadron also spent part of July and August at Hutton Cranswick before moving south once again. The final unit to arrive was 124 Squadron, which flew in with its Spitfire IXs ten days before the war in Europe ended, the squadron finally leaving in mid-July. A month earlier 291 Squadron had disbanded. Hutton Cranswick was used by No 16 Armament Practice Camp until mid-1946 when the airfield was finally closed.

6
CATTERICK AND SCORTON

It is perhaps fitting that Yorkshire's oldest military airfield should be at Catterick, which has been a cornerstone of Britain's defences since Roman times. It was in 1914 that a site between the River Swale and the Great North Road was laid out as a training centre for the fledgling Royal Flying Corps and it grew to become one of the major centres for aviation in the north of England.

Between the wars what was by then RAF Catterick was retained and the 1935 Expansion Scheme saw the airfield virtually rebuilt. Two large C-type hangars were added and are still in use today. Catterick's role was to be within Fighter Command and in the late summer of 1939 it was home to 41 Squadron equipped with Spitfires and 64 Squadron, which operated Blenheims in the fighter role under the command of S/Ldr Rogers. 26 Squadron was also at Catterick with its Lysanders, later leaving to join the BEF in France in the Army Co-operation role. A few days before the war began a fourth unit, 609 (West Riding) Squadron, moved in from Yeadon with its Spitfires. It was a pre-war Auxiliary squadron and its twelve pilots found conditions very cramped when they arrived at Catterick. The airfield was also being used as the call-up point for reservists, several of whom had served there during its RFC days. 609's pilots found themselves quartered in the Great War officers' mess, part of which had been closed for almost 20 years.

The Dornier 217 was used extensively by the Lutftwaffe on bombing raids from 1941 (MAP).

Over the next six years Catterick, like all northern fighter airfields, was to see a steady stream of units coming and going. It was to provide aerial defence for the nearby Army garrison and the industrial areas on the Tees and air cover for coastal convoys in the North Sea. It was also to fill its Great War role, that of training both day and night fighter pilots and Catterick was also used to rest and re-equip squadrons during the Battle of Britain and the fighter activity over Northern France in the months and years to come.

In those early days the airfield was used to provide valuable experience for the squadrons which passed through it. 609, which spent just five weeks there, was brought up to operational readiness at Catterick. Those who flew with the squadron remember the novelty of having to wait for a gap in the traffic on the adjoining Great North Road before being given permission to take off (later traffic was halted to allow aircraft to use the runway which ended alongside the road). They were also heartened to see how easy it was to achieve a 'wheels-up' landing in a Spitfire during their time there. It was 'demonstrated' for them by F/O Paul Edge, who received a severe ticking off because of the shortage of Spitfires (his was later repaired), but gave a great deal of confidence to his fellow pilots, already by then great admirers of the qualities of their aircraft.

By late September Catterick had become a sector station within

Spitfire Is of 41 Squadron at Catterick in March 1940. (Andrew Thomas)

Fighter Command's 13 Group and the following month one of its squadrons, 41, celebrated its first 'kill'. F/Lt Blatchford, F/Sgt Skipton and Sgt Harris shot down a He 111, which was on an armed reconnaissance from its base at Munster, some 20 miles off Whitby. Two of the Heinkel's crew survived for 43 hours in their dinghy before being washed ashore at Sandsend, near Whitby and becoming the Luftwaffe's first PoWs in England.

Shortly after this 41 Squadron moved to Wick for a brief stay before returning. During their absence 219 Squadron was reformed on Blenheims and quickly moved to Catterick's new satellite airfield a few miles further north at Scorton.

The late spring of 1940 saw the arrival of 54 Squadron and its Spitfires from Hornchurch, swapping places with 41 Squadron while 64 Squadron moved to Church Fenton. However, 41 was to make a number of return visits to Catterick during the summer and it was there for the major attack by the Luftwaffe on Yorkshire on 11th August. That evening the squadron successfully shot down a Ju 88 at Ugthorpe, near Whitby and a few minutes later a second was brought down at Mulgrave Moor.

The airfield was used occasionally by diverted aircraft from Yorkshire's bomber airfields. One of these was a Whitley of 77 Squadron which was returning from a raid on Cologne. As it approached the airfield, the bomber struck a telegraph pole and crashed close to Catterick village, killing one of the crew.

During the Battle of Britain Catterick was used by several fighter squadrons following spells in the front line over southern England, including 64, 600 and 504 Squadrons. Spitfires of 41 Squadron were scrambled on 15th August as a large force of He 111s escorted by some 20 Me 110s approached the North East coast from their base at Stavanger in Norway. The attack, part of the same operation as that intercepted by fighters from Leconfield further south, was quickly broken up by a large force of RAF fighters (which the Luftwaffe assumed were now all based in southern England) and seven of the twin-engined escorts and several bombers quickly shot down. The remainder dumped their bombs and turned for home.

As winter approached, Catterick's role embraced the RAF's growing night fighter arm and 256 Squadron was reformed there on Defiants in November. It worked up under S/Ldr Gatheral and finally left for Middle Wallop in January 1941. It was replaced by 68 Squadron which reformed on Beaufighters, later leaving for Ercall. 600 Squadron also converted to Beaufighters before leaving for Drem in Scotland.

In May that year Catterick saw the formation of the first of many overseas squadrons to use the airfield, 313 (Czech) working up on its Spitfires before moving to Leconfield under the command of S/Ldr Findlay. They shared the airfield for a time with 122 Squadron and were replaced at Catterick by 131 Squadron, which included many Belgians amongst its pilots.

At the end of July, 145 Squadron arrived without its Spitfire Vs, which it had left at Tangmere. The air and ground crews flew to Catterick in Harrow transports and took over 41's Spitfire IIs, the Harrows then flying 41 Squadron to its new home at Merston. 145 Squadron then began flying convoy patrols, a far cry from the low-level fighter sweeps over northern France they had been flying at Tangmere.

Later in the summer 313 moved to Castletown and 131 to Tern Hill, followed by 122 Squadron. Newcomers included 17 Squadron, which spent two months at Catterick with its Hurricanes, and 134 Squadron, which had just completed a spell in Russia. Early in 1942 a second Norwegian fighter squadron, 332, was formed at Catterick and flew its Spitfires from North Yorkshire for some six months before moving to North Weald. Its replacement was a Canadian squadron, 403, which arrived from Martlesham Heath with Spitfire Vbs, a detachment immediately being sent to West Hartlepool for convoy work. 403 was, in turn, replaced by a second Canadian squadron, 401, before it left for Kenley. In the meantime, 145 Squadron had moved to the Middle East.

The pace at Catterick was beginning to slacken as fewer fighter squadrons were rotated through the airfield. Fighter Command's operations were now focused largely on the South and East Anglia. During the summer of 1942, 1472 Flight was formed at Catterick to work in conjunction with the Army's Battle School at nearby Barnard Castle. It operated a number of mainly obsolete ground attack aircraft, including Battles and Tomahawks, and was to fly from Catterick until it was disbanded in the late autumn of 1943.

It shared the airfield with a number of fighter squadrons during its time at Catterick. Amongst them was 306 (City of Torun) Squadron, a Polish unit which had already spent some time in Yorkshire. It operated from Catterick from May 1943 until the summer of 1944 during which time the squadron's affection for the friendly folk of Yorkshire, first encountered at Church Fenton, grew noticeably.

Several of the new fighter bomber squadrons being formed for the coming invasion were to spend some time at Catterick. Among them was 183 which was formed at the North Yorkshire airfield in November 1942 under the command of S/Ldr Gowers and worked up on Typhoons before moving to Cranfield in March 1943. Other visitors included two more Spitfire squadrons, 527 and 130, and 219

A Blenheim If, FK-F, of 219 Squadron at Catterick, March 1940. (Andrew Thomas)

Squadron, a night fighter unit which flew its Beaufighters briefly from Catterick.

In February 1944, 222 Squadron arrived with Spitfire IXs from Woodvale for a five-week stint at Catterick before leaving for Acklington. It was to be the last operational squadron to operate from RAF Catterick. The airfield's geographic restrictions meant it was unsuitable for larger aircraft and for the remainder of the war it was used only occasionally by Army Co-operation and communications aircraft. When the war ended Catterick was used to process the thousands of surplus aircrew awaiting demob and in 1946 it became the home of the RAF Regiment, whose depot was moved from Lincolnshire.

Catterick's satellite at Scorton had, unusually, been built in peacetime, opening within 13 Group in October 1939. Its facilities were very basic but it was kept busy as the overflow airfield for Catterick which, during the first 18 months of war, was one of the busiest airfields in the north.

Scorton's first resident unit was 219 Squadron, which moved in with its Blenheims soon after the airfield formally opened. These were the days when the Blenheim was perceived as a high-speed twin-engined fighter, an illusion which was quickly to disappear when it was first used in combat with the Luftwaffe. 219 remained at Scorton until October 1940 when it moved to Redhill.

Its departure was the signal for an expansion programme at Scorton, which included the laying of three Tarmac runways and the erection of twelve Blister hangars. By October 1941 Scorton was back in business and 122 Squadron moved in from Catterick, exchanged its Spitfire IIs for Vs and began flying convoy patrols along the North East coast. It was largely unexciting work livened only by the frequency with which naval gunners fired on RAF aircraft. 122 moved out in the spring of 1942 to Hornchurch as the airfield's role switched mainly from day to night fighters. Large-scale attacks by the Luftwaffe were now a thing of the past but raids by single aircraft were causing problems and four Beaufighters of 406 Squadron, which was based at Ayr, moved in to provide night fighter cover. Eventually, the whole squadron moved to Scorton to fly patrols over the North East and remained until September when it moved to Predannack in Cornwall.

It was replaced by another Canadian unit, 406, which moved from Ayr and was to be involved in several brushes with the Luftwaffe during its time in North Yorkshire. 406 was replaced in turn by 219

Squadron which later moved to Catterick with its Beaufighters. During this period 167 Squadron was reformed at Scorton on Spitfires before moving to Castletown.

The spring of 1943 saw 604 Squadron arrive from Ford in Hampshire and, re-equipped with Beaufighters, take over night fighter cover for the area during the winter. During the autumn 130 Squadron moved in from Catterick with its Spitfires and, after a spell at Ayr, flew convoy patrols before becoming non-operational and being disbanded in January 1944. The squadron was later reformed at Lympne.

In February 1944, 56 Squadron brought its Typhoons from Martlesham Heath. It had spells at Acklington and Ayr before returning to Scorton where it converted to Spitfire IXs and moved to Newchurch. 604 Squadron, in the meantime, exchanged its Beaufighters for Mosquitos and, under the command of W/Cmdr Constable Maxwell, moved to Church Fenton.

The late spring of 1944 saw unusual visitors to Scorton – two squadrons of P-61 Black Widows, big twin-boomed night fighters then being introduced into the US 9th Air Force. Both squadrons, 422 and 425, moved from Charmy Down for a period of training in night fighter tactics. Several experienced RAF night fighter pilots were seconded to the American units as they flew a series of exercises with Halifax and Lancaster bombers from the Yorkshire-based 4 and 6 Groups. Towards the end of June both squadrons moved briefly to Hurn, near Bournemouth, to provide night fighter cover over Normandy. They returned to Scorton but left again for Charmy Down at the end of July.

Scorton itself was now surplus to requirements and it ended the war as a storage depot. The airfield was closed in 1946 and the land reverted to agriculture.

7
CHURCH FENTON

Among the first phase of Expansion Programme airfields in Yorkshire was one close to the village of Church Fenton, between Selby and Tadcaster. It was designed from the outset as a fighter airfield and opened on 1st April 1937, although construction work was to continue at a gentle pace for the next two years on further additions.

Like other airfields of its generation, Church Fenton was built with large brick C-type hangars. It was planned to erect three but by the time the war began only two had been completed and the space earmarked for the third was later to be occupied by a T2. Its first occupants were 72 and 213 Squadrons, which flew Gladiators and Gauntlets. 213 moved the following year and was replaced by 64 Squadron, which immediately converted from Hawker Demons to Blenheims. 72's Gladiators were replaced by Spitfire Mk Is a few weeks before the war began, by which time the airfield had been allocated to 13 Group, Fighter Command.

Six weeks after the war began, and still with not a shot fired in anger, 72 Squadron left for Leconfield where it was to be used for North Sea patrols. Its replacements were 245 and 242 Squadrons, which were both reformed there in December 1939 on Hurricanes. A month later Church Fenton was home to four squadrons of fighters with the return of 72 Squadron from Leconfield. This was a pattern which was to be repeated through the next three years, with squadrons rotated through Church Fenton at regular intervals.

Much to the delight of its pilots, 64 Squadron replaced its Blenheims with Spitfires in April 1940 and a month later they left for the south coast, quickly followed by 242 Squadron which went to Biggin Hill. On 16th May 249 Squadron was formed at Church Fenton. One of its flight commanders was James Brindley Nicolson, who was no stranger to the place. After completing his training, he had joined 72 Squadron at the

A 72 Squadron Spitfire I in need of a new propeller at Church Fenton, winter 1939. (Andrew Thomas)

Yorkshire airfield in 1937, and quickly earned a reputation as an outstanding pilot. He had later flown his first operational sortie with the squadron from Leconfield before returning to Church Fenton. Five days later 249 went to Leconfield to be equipped with Hurricanes and brought them back to Church Fenton where they worked up to operational readiness.

249 Squadron was to get its share of action during its time at Church Fenton. On 8th July, three aircraft from the squadron's B Flight intercepted a Ju 88 off the Yorkshire coast. The pilots, P/Os Parnell and Beazley and Sgt Main, each claimed a third share of the Ju 88 as it crashed. Three of the Junkers' crew baled out and landed at Aldbrough, where they were captured by Mrs Nora Candwell, armed only with her husband's unloaded shotgun. She was later awarded an OBE.

On 14th August the squadron moved south to Boscombe Down – its ground crews and baggage being carried in Imperial Airways' Hannibals – and it was while flying from there three days later that Nicolson became Fighter Command's only Victoria Cross winner of the Second World War, attacking a Me 110 in his blazing Hurricane before baling out with severe burns.

Back at Church Fenton, 87 and 234 Squadrons flew briefly on coastal patrols before moving out. 87's replacement was 73 Squadron, which was to have some considerable success when Sgt McNay and P/O Carter each shot down a Ju 88 in the major air raid on Yorkshire's bomber airfields on 15th August, the attack which caused extensive damage at Driffield.

That month also saw the formation of the first all-Polish squadron in Fighter Command, 306 (City of Torun). It was to remain at Church Fenton until November and during that time the Poles learned at first hand about the kindness of Yorkshire people. It was a particularly cold and damp autumn. Villagers in Church Fenton noticed how badly equipped the young Poles were to deal with the conditions and so a group of women collected wool and knitted enough scarves for the entire squadron.

The Fighter Command round-about saw 73 Squadron swap places with 85 Squadron at Castle Camps early in September. The squadron had been in the thick of the fighting over the South East and had lost four pilots on 1st September, including one of its flight commanders. So depleted was the squadron that it was left to one of its sergeant pilots to lead the remnants of 85 into Church Fenton. Among the pilots 85 left behind was S/Ldr Peter Townsend, the man who had helped shoot down the first German aircraft over England earlier in the year. He had been wounded in the leg on 31st August when his Hurricane was shot down over Croydon. Townsend was determined not to be absent for long, however, and arrived at Church Fenton on 22nd September. He was able to walk with the aid of a stick and immediately went to see the MO and reported himself fit for flying. To prove his case, he took off in one of the squadron's Hurricanes and did a series of aerobatics over the airfield. On 21st October 85 Squadron was selected for training as a night fighter unit and left for Kirton-in-Lindsey two days later.

Soon after 85's arrival in September the first American 'Eagle' Squadron in Fighter Command, 71, was formed at Church Fenton under S/Ldr Walter Churchill, who had previously been with 605 Squadron. Three of its pilots were Americans who had flown with the French Air Force, while others had crossed the border into Canada and volunteered to fly with the RAF.

There was a desperate shortage of aircraft within Fighter Command at the time and the only fighters available for 71 Squadron were four American-built Brewster Buffaloes, which were hopelessly obsolete and regarded as downright dangerous by most who flew them. All four aircraft were quickly written off in 'accidents' and within a fortnight new Hurricanes began arriving for the Eagle Squadron pilots, the aircraft being delivered by Peter Townsend and his fellow 85 Squadron pilots.

November saw the departure of the Poles of 306 Squadron to Tern Hill and the Americans of 71 Squadron to Kirton. Church Fenton itself was destined for a new role in Fighter Command and early in December No 4 Operational Training Unit was formed for the purpose of training night fighter pilots. It was later renumbered 54 OTU and initially had on its strength over 80 aircraft, including 31 Blenheims and 24 Defiants. Its task was to provide the night fighter pilots which Britain badly needed in that second winter of war. Its CO was W/Cmdr 'Batchy' Atcherley DFC and, in February 1941, among its instructors was F/Lt Nicolson VC, who had still not fully recovered from the burns he suffered in his blazing Hurricane. He did not fly during his second spell at Church Fenton but by September 1941 was deemed to be operational again and was posted to Hibaldstow in Lincolnshire.

Among the early pupils during Nicolson's time was A Flight of 85 Squadron, which arrived at Church Fenton to convert to Blenheims in readiness for flying Havocs. Among their instructors was George Stainforth, a former Schneider Cup pilot.

Church Fenton was one of a number of airfields attacked by the Luftwaffe during the night of 26th-27th April. 54 OTU had a number of Blenheims and Defiants in the air as a Ju 88 flown by Lt Heinz Volker arrived in the Church Fenton circuit. His first victim was Blenheim L7232, the pilot managing to bale out before the burning aircraft crashed. Minutes later Volker found a second Blenheim, this one flown by Sgt Spungin, and badly damaged it before it made good its escape. Volker then flew low across the airfield, dropping a stick of bombs and wrecking a third Blenheim which had been waiting clearance for take-off.

Flying resumed from Church Fenton after the all-clear sounded but it appears flying control were unaware of the presence of a second intruder. This Ju 88, flown by Lt Rudolf Pfeiffer, intercepted a Defiant flown by Sgt Crozier soon after it had taken off. The gunner, F/Sgt Bell, returned fire as the pilot dived to avoid the night fighter. The Defiant hit a row of trees near Thorp Arch church and crashed, badly injuring both members of its crew.

It wasn't just the Luftwaffe which could prove lethal to the pilots of 54 OTU. The crew of a Blenheim which crashed at Poppleton, near

York on the night of 28th February were killed. Shortly afterwards a second Blenheim crashed near Cawood. Again, there were no survivors. Two aircraft were also lost on the night of 18th July, one crash-landing on the North Yorkshire Moors, the pilot escaping with minor injuries. The pilot of a second Blenheim which crashed in the same area later that night was not so fortunate.

On the night of 15th November that year P/O Cleaver and his air gunner, Sgt Cohen, were returning to the airfield in their Blenheim when it was attacked by a Spitfire of 121 Squadron, one of the American Eagle squadrons in the RAF. The Spitfire pilot mistakenly identified the Blenheim as a Ju 88 and promptly shot it down. The pilot baled out but the gunner was unable to escape and was killed when the Blenheim broke up and crashed onto Wetherby race course. Brian Lunn and Lee Arbon record this incident in their book on wartime crash sites in the Wetherby area. They note that a race meeting was held the following day at Wetherby and the horses ran on the steeplechase course with the wreck of the Blenheim still in the middle of the track.

54 OTU moved to Charterhall in May 1942 and was replaced by two night fighter squadrons, 25, which was flying Mosquitos, and 488 Squadron, which was reformed on Beaufighters. The latter unit was commanded by W/Cmdr Transdale, a night fighter 'ace' with eight kills to his credit, five of them at night. The squadron worked up at Church Fenton before moving to Ayr in September 1942, being replaced by 600 Squadron.

25 Squadron, which arrived at Church Fenton under the command of S/Ldr Watkins, was initially equipped with Beaufighters but re-equipped with Mosquito Mk IIs in February 1943 and by that summer had 26 aircraft on its strength. In August, the squadron's C Flight re-equipped with Mosquito FBVIs and began flying extended sorties across Europe before the whole squadron moved to Acklington in December.

During the summer 25 had been joined at Church Fenton by 26 Squadron, which operated Mustangs, and a second Mosquito squadron, 96. The latter moved to Drem while 26 Squadron went to Hutton Cranswick in East Yorkshire and was replaced briefly by 234 Squadron.

Resident squadrons in 1944 included 124, 604, 288 and 307, a Polish squadron which moved in with its Spitfires from Coleby Grange in Lincolnshire.

On the last day of the year 456 (RAAF) Squadron re-equipped with

Mosquito NF XXX NT245/G of 125 Squadron operating out of Church Fenton, 1945. (Andrew Thomas)

the high altitude fighter variant of the Mosquito in readiness for flying bomber escort duties. Once the new aircraft arrived, the Australian squadron, which was commanded by W/Cmdr Howard, began working up on them and by the end of February were deemed ready for operations. Two days later the ground crews began moving out for Bradwell Bay with the aircraft and aircrew due to follow the next day. That night the Luftwaffe staged Operation Gisella, a mass attack by long-range fighters on bomber airfields in eastern England, with those in Yorkshire particularly badly hit. Despite lacking most of its equipment and ground crews, 456 Squadron managed to get five Mosquitos airborne, although by that time it was very much a case of closing the stable door. The following day ground crew and equipment were hurriedly flown back to Church Fenton by Transport Command in case the Germans mounted a second attack. This duly came and once again five 456 Squadron aircraft were scrambled, one Ju 88 being intercepted and claimed as damaged over East Anglia. It turned out to be the final fling of the Luftwaffe and the last occasion aircraft from Church Fenton were in action. 456 Squadron finally left for Bradwell Bay later in March and were replaced by 68 Squadron, which was to disband there just days before the war ended.

   Church Fenton was retained by the RAF after the war and, following

Church Fenton's first post-war open day, September 1945. On display are Mosquito NF30s of 125 Squadron. (Yorkshire Air Museum via Peter Green).

the laying of concrete runways, became the first station in the country to house a fighter squadron equipped with jet aircraft, 263's Meteors. In the late 1950s it was transferred to Flying Training Command and over the next three decades played a major role in training aircrew for the RAF. Today the airfield is still used to house a university air squadron and as a relief landing ground for the Tucanos of 1FTS.

8
CROFT

In the early evening of 28th January 1944 some 28 Halifax Mk Vs of 431 (Iroquois) and 434 (Bluenose) Squadrons RCAF began taking off from RAF Croft for Berlin. When the ground crews gathered to count their aircraft home early the following morning, eight were missing and a ninth written off in a heavy landing, almost a third of the station's strength.

Five from 434 Squadron failed to return, three being shot down in the Berlin area while a fourth was lost without trace. A fifth Halifax was hit by flak and lost an engine over the target, the aircraft finally being abandoned by its crew over Filey, all but the rear gunner surviving. Flak accounted for three Halifaxes from 431, two crashing near Berlin with the loss of ten men. The third made it back to the Lincolnshire coast where the crew baled out. Three of them drowned but the survivors were picked up by Grimsby minesweepers. A fourth 431 Squadron Halifax was written off in a crash-landing at Dishforth.

The raid had cost Croft the lives of 35 men with another eleven later being reported as prisoners of war. The aircraft were to be among almost 150 Whitleys, Halifaxes and Lancasters lost in the three and a half years Croft served as a front-line bomber squadron.

It was the second most northerly of all Bomber Command's airfields, pipped for this honour by its neighbour and parent station, Middleton St George, and had opened as a satellite of Middleton in October 1941. The airfield was built in a little over a year by a series of contractors and lay just inside Yorkshire close to the main Northallerton-Darlington road. It was bounded on one side by the LNER main line and this may have been behind the thinking behind installing arrester gear on two of the runways. Whether this was ever used is uncertain, but elsewhere trials with both Lancasters and Halifaxes had shown their unsuitability for this equipment.

When it opened, Croft was part of 4 Group and its first occupants

A low level pass by a visiting Blenheim IV of 13 Squadron, Croft, October 1941. (13 Squadron via Peter Green)

were 78 Squadron, which arrived with its Whitleys on 20 October 1941 from Middleton St George. The squadron was in action almost straight away, losing its first aircraft from Croft in a raid on Kiel on 2nd November.

Bad weather was as much the enemy of the Whitley crews as the German defenders and that winter several of the dozen Whitleys 78 Squadron lost went down in the North Sea, short of fuel or covered in ice. Typical of their experiences was that endured by Sgt Lloyd-Jones who landed his Whitley at Coltishall with just two gallons of fuel left in the tanks after a raid on Berlin. The aircraft had experienced 70mph head winds on the return flight and the crew had thrown out everything possible to keep their aircraft in the air.

In the spring of 1942, 78 Squadron's Conversion Flight was formed as the squadron began its switch to four-engined Halifaxes. Little time was lost in putting the squadron's new aircraft to use. 78 Squadron was to leave Croft early in June and by that time had already flown numerous sorties with its new Halifaxes, losing half a dozen to enemy action and seven more in crashes. One of these came after the first 1,000 bomber raid at the end of May when 78 Squadron put up 20 of its Halifaxes. On the way home F/O Foers emerged from cloud at 2,000 feet over Huntingdon and collided with a Hampden from 14 OTU, which was also returning from Cologne. The Hampden pilot survived the crash, as did F/O Foers and three of his crew.

Croft had by now been earmarked as a base for the growing Royal Canadian Air Force contingent within Bomber Command and in mid-September the advance elements of 419 (Moose) Squadron began arriving from Topcliffe. The squadron, which was flying Wellington IIs, arrived on 1st October and immediately began converting to Halifax IIs, moving to Middleton at the end of the month.

They made way for the formation of a new Canadian unit, 427 (Lion) Squadron, which was adopted by the MGM film studios in California and took its name from the film company's lion symbol. There was little to roar about, however, on the squadron's first operations, two of the three Wellingtons sent on a mining trip to the Frisians on 14th December 1942 aborting because of technical problems.

It was during this period that 6 Group (RCAF) was being formed and both Croft and 427 Squadron were to play a major part in the group's fortunes over the coming years.

Croft itself was transferred to 6 Group on 1st January 1943 and officially became a Royal Canadian Air Force station, though still 'belonging' to the RAF. 427's first operational sortie as a 6 Group squadron came on the night of 15th-16th January when six Wellingtons took part in a heavy raid on the French port of Lorient, one failing to return.

Croft was destined to become 64 Base Sub-station under the control of Middleton St George when the Canadians adopted Bomber Command's base structure in March. The move coincided with the conversion of 427 Squadron to Wellington Xs, which were to be used only sparingly before conversion to Halifaxes in May. They were in action on the night of 12th-13th March when an attack on Essen was led by the CO, W/Cmdr Dudley Burnside. His Wellington was hit by flak on its way to the Ruhr, an 88mm shell killing the navigator and wounding the wireless operator. Despite losing his oxygen supply and not being able to climb above 10,000 feet, Burnside pressed on and bombed the target, the wounded wireless operator plotting a course for home which brought the damaged Wellington back to Stradishall. The trip earned him a CGM and there were DFMs for three other members of the crew.

Operational losses went on during this time but lives were also lost nearer to home. On 6th April a 427 Squadron Wellington swung on landing and eventually came to rest in an orchard on the adjoining East

Charles Lott, Stuart Cliff, Alec Stuart and two other members of their 427 Squadron crew at Croft, June 1943. (Charles Lott)

Vince Moor Farm. The pilot, Sgt Ash, was killed along with his bomb aimer while the other members of the crew were badly burned when the aircraft exploded just after they had got out. Soon afterwards another Canadian pilot, F/Sgt Ash, died when he made a force-landing on Stressholme golf course on the outskirts of Darlington after suffering engine failure.

427's conversion to Halifaxes was completed by the end of April and the squadron moved to Leeming, its place at Croft being taken by the 1664 Heavy Conversion Unit, which formed at the airfield on 10th May. The unit remained at Croft until 7th December when it moved to Dishforth, and lost nine aircraft in crashes during that time. The worst of these came on 23rd September when Halifax EB181 flown by P/O Highshead flew into high ground near Helmsley, killing five of those on board, and on 22nd November when EB150 dived into the ground from 500 feet soon after take-off, crashing into the grounds of Blue Anchor Farm, near Scotch Corner. Six men were killed and one, F/Sgt Milloy, the student pilot, injured. Five days before 1664 HCU left Croft, DG282 collided with a haystack on a low pass near the airfield killing six of those on board, including the pilot, F/Sgt Peter Gray.

434 Squadron's Pistol Packin' Bomba *and her crew at Croft in the winter of 1943-44. (Yorkshire Air Museum via Peter Green)*

Croft became an operational bomber airfield again on 7th December when 1664 HCU was replaced by 431 and 434 Squadrons, which both moved from Tholthorpe.

They arrived in the midst of the Battle of Berlin and took their Halifaxes to the German capital for the first time at the end of the month, two 431 Squadron aircraft being shot down near Berlin itself with the loss of 13 of the 14 men on board. 434 Squadron was to lose three aircraft on another Berlin raid on 20th-21st January, six of the 21 crew escaping with their lives. Five Halifaxes, three of them from 434 Squadron, were lost in an attack on Leipzig on 19th-20th February with the loss of 27 lives.

One of the great escapes of the war came on 25th February 1944 for ten men who had climbed on board Halifax LK907 for a fighter affiliation exercise. The aircraft was about 1,000 feet up after take-off when it collided with some seagulls. One of the birds crashed through the windscreen, virtually blinding the pilot. The bomb aimer, F/O Roy, took the controls and, guided by advice from the injured pilot and by controllers at Croft, managed to land the damaged Halifax, which eventually ran off the runway into a pile of rubble.

There was no such good fortune for the two gunners on board a 431

Squadron aircraft which landed back at Croft after a raid on Le Mans on 15th March. As the aircraft was taxiing off the main runway, a 'hung-up' bomb fell through the partially opened bomb bay doors and exploded, killing both the mid-upper and rear gunners instantly. The Croft squadrons also suffered badly in a raid on Montzen on the night of 27th-28th April, losing six aircraft, four of them from 431 Squadron.

Among the replacement crews to arrive at Croft in the late spring of 1944 was that of F/O Jack Harris, a Canadian who headed a multi-national crew which included two Americans, navigator F/O Eddie Gill and rear gunner P/O Red Mills; two other Canadians, bomb-aimer Sgt Mervyn Brown and mid-upper P/O Harry Grant; and two Englishmen, wireless operator Sgt Eddie Eastwood, whose home was in Bedford, and the flight engineer, Londoner Sgt Bob Haill.

One of their early operations led to them coming close to being posted missing. On the way home they were ordered to divert because of bad weather at Croft and the only airfield Sgt Eastwood could raise was East Moor. 'The squadron was at the point of posting us missing when the control tower at East Moor realised there were two aircraft with the 'B' squadron letters on the airfield, one from the 434 and ours from 431,' recalled Mr Eastwood.

Another raid on an oil storage depot near St Nazaire resulted in Flying Officer Harris's crew landing at Woodbridge in Suffolk following problems on the return flight. The crew were whisked to the station medical station for a check-up, despite their protestations that they were uninjured. They were given a tot of rum and then taken to the mess where a table was quickly cleared for a meal to remember. It was, the crew agreed, typical of American hospitality.

They were quickly in action, flying in operations which spanned the D-Day period before, in mid-July, they were given a week's leave. Back at Croft, they were briefed for a daylight attack on a wooded area in Belgium where a German Panzer unit was believed to be refitting. This operation was cancelled, but the 421 Squadron crews were put on stand-by for an attack that night on Hamburg. It was to be a mainly 6 and 8 Group show with some support from ABC-equipped Lancasters from 1 Group's 101 Squadron in the first major attack on Hamburg for almost a year. It was also to be one of the worst nights of the war for Croft – and the most memorable in the short life of Eddie Eastwood.

Seventeen of 431's Halifaxes were all away by 2200 hours, and crossed the North Sea in the stream at 1,000 feet before beginning a steep climb to their bombing height of 20,000 feet.

The flak was moderately heavy on the bomb run and Jack Harris managed to keep 431's B-Baker steady when, in Eddie Eastwood's words, 'all hell broke loose'. The Halifax was hit, and hit hard, by what turned out to be a night fighter. 'Before you could say corkscrew both our starboard engines were on fire and both gun turrets out of action. The skipper asked the navigator for a course to Sweden for it was clear we were not going to make it home. We had just dropped our bombs when we were hit again by flak, this time in the bomb bay.

'The skipper shouted to abandon the aircraft as he couldn't hold it much longer. When my turn to go arrived I put my feet through the hatch and as I did so the slipstream whipped off my flying boots. As I tried to grab them my 'chute caught on the hatch and the next thing I remember was hurtling through space. I pulled the cord and seemed to swing a few times before I hit the ground in a field beside a ditch. All I could hear was what I took for gunfire and loudspeakers saying "Achtung". After a while I realised the "gunfire" was ammo exploding from a burning aircraft.'

B-Baker was not alone among the Croft Halifaxes to fall to a combination of night fighters and flak that night. Only twelve of the 17 Halifaxes which took off were to return the following morning.

A fine shot of a 434 Squadron Halifax and crew, Croft, 1944. (Yorkshire Air Museum via Peter Green)

Back in Germany, Sgt Eastwood was wondering how he was going to escape without even so much as a pair of shoes. He buried his parachute and began walking along a dirt track until he eventually came to a minor road. He stood trying to decide which direction to take when he heard the sound of a small motorcycle coming towards him. He dived through a hedge and fell almost into the arms of two civilians, both of whom were carrying rifles.

He managed to convince them he wasn't carrying any weapons – this was the time when aircrew were being issued with pistols – and by this time the motorcycle rider had arrived, complete with Prussian-type helmet and breastplate. It turned out he was an official in the Todt Organisation and told the two civilians to take their captured airman to the nearest small town where he was locked in what appeared to be a café awaiting the arrival of the military.

Sgt Eastwood, still without boots, was taken to what he took to be a German Army depot and from there to the Wehrmacht equivalent of a glasshouse where he was given two slices of black bread and a mug of something unidentifiable to drink. It was very cold and each time he

Home are the raiders. 434 Squadron's T, Y and W fly in formation following an attack on the oil refinery at Sterkrade, September 1944. (Yorkshire Air Museum via Peter Green)

tried to make his guard understand he wanted a blanket he found he was escorted to the toilet!

The following morning he was taken to the local railway station and there he met up with bomb aimer Mervyn Brown and Bob Haill, B-Baker's flight engineer. German efficiency, it seemed, didn't extend to reading train timetables. The 9pm to Obereusel in fact left at 9am the following morning and the three had to spend their second night of captivity in a Gestapo cell where they were kept under very careful observation.

It was a long and tedious journey, broken only by a stop in Frankfurt where the three airmen were given some food. At the interrogation centre in Obereusel Sgt Eastwood was put into a cell where there was a small bunk covered in straw. After only a few minutes he realised he wasn't the only occupant of the bunk and spent most of the remainder of his time there trying to rid himself of lice.

When it was his turn to be interrogated, he was surprised to find that his captors knew he was from 431 Squadron. They told him no trace had been found of his aircraft or his pilot. They did tell him that Red Mills had baled out but had died on his way to hospital and that Harry Grant, the mid-upper gunner, had been wounded in the head but was recovering in hospital. The remainder of the crew were PoWs. His interrogator also surprised him by reeling off the names of other crews at Croft, some of whom Eddie had never heard of, and asked about the new H2S ground-mapping radar, yet to be fitted to the Croft Halifaxes.

Sgt Eastwood then accompanied some 70 other captured aircrew on the journey, by train, tram and on foot, to Stalag Luft 7 at Bankau. It was an uncomfortable place. He and five other men shared a hut little bigger than a garden shed, sleeping in what amounted to a paper sack covered by a blanket.

The 431 Squadron survivors were among the occupants of Stalag Luft 7 who took part in one of the notorious forced marches early in 1945 as the Russian advances led to the evacuation of prison camps in eastern Germany. They were forced to march over 150 miles in appalling weather conditions with little food before being crammed into cattle wagons for the final stage of their journey.

The pace of operations at Croft was unrelenting and so, it seemed were the losses, including eight in one night – four from each squadron – in an attack on the refinery at Sterkrade. One of the many crashes around the Croft area still remembered locally occurred on 30th August 1944 when a Halifax on a navigational exercise crashed in a wheat field near Croft Spa railway station. The crew had completed only one operation and had just taken off in Halifax MZ626 WL-T when the pilot, P/O Todhunter, appeared to lose control and the bomber plunged into the field and caught fire. All seven men aboard were killed instantly. Six of them, including the pilot, were Canadians while the flight engineer Sgt James McMahon, was a 22-year-old Irishman. During the same month two aircraft from 431 Squadron were flying in formation near Selby when the starboard inner propeller on one came off and struck the second aircraft. The aircraft then collided and fell together into open fields near RAF Burn, killing all those on board. Among them was a corporal who was being given a lift back to Croft. His bicycle was later found in the wreckage. More fortunate were the crew of eight and the 17 unauthorised passengers crammed into a 431 Squadron Halifax which swung and crashed during a transit from Membury. All survived.

In October 1944 Halifaxes at Croft began to be replaced by new Canadian-built Lancaster Mk Xs, 431 Squadron converting that month and 434 during December. The two squadrons were to lose some 20 Lancs between them, the first SE-S (KB813) crashing during a cross-country exercise during 431's conversion on 25th October. The last were two Lancasters, again from 431 Squadron, which collided over the North Sea on the last operational sortie flown from Croft when 15 aircraft from each squadron took part in the attack on gun batteries on the island of Wangerooge.

Both squadrons were later involved in airlifting PoWs to Britain, before finally taking their Lancasters back with them to Canada in June in preparation for becoming part of Bomber Command's Tiger Force, which was to operate in the Pacific. However, events overtook them and the squadrons were disbanded in Nova Scotia in September 1945.

Croft itself was used briefly by 13 OTU before the station closed in 1946. After the war Croft was developed into one of the leading motor racing circuits in the North East and there are now plans to develop it still further. Some of the wartime buildings are still visible to visitors as a reminder of the airfield's proud wartime history.

9
DALTON AND WOMBLETON

Just off the busy A168, which links the town of Thirsk with the A1, can be found the remains of a wartime airfield which took its name from the nearby village of Dalton. The site was one of many identified in the first great sweep of the Air Ministry surveyors early in the war and RAF Dalton opened in November 1941.

Its first occupants were 102 Squadron, one of the original Yorkshire bomber units. They moved in from nearby Topcliffe with their Whitleys and were quickly in action from the new airfield, providing seven aircraft for an attack on Emden on the night of 30th November. Six made it back, the seventh being abandoned by its crew low on fuel after a difficult trip back from Germany in an ice-covered aircraft. The squadron lost a second aircraft on the night of 16th December when 14 Whitleys went to Dunkirk, the 102 Squadron Whitley disappearing without trace.

The Whitley's days were numbered and the squadron was to lose just two more from Dalton before it began converting to Halifaxes. One of these turned back from an attack on Brest with engine failure. Over Sheffield the second caught fire and the pilot, Sgt Hollingsworth, ordered his crew to bale out. Three managed to do so before the pilot tried to crash-land, the aircraft hitting buildings in Cresswell Street at Pogmoor, near Barnsley, killing the pilot and the rear gunner. An attack on Emden at the end of the month saw the squadron lose its last Whitley, Sgt White and his crew disappearing without trace. Among them was Sgt Hazeldine, a survivor of the crash at Barnsley.

During January 102's Halifax Conversion Flight began retraining

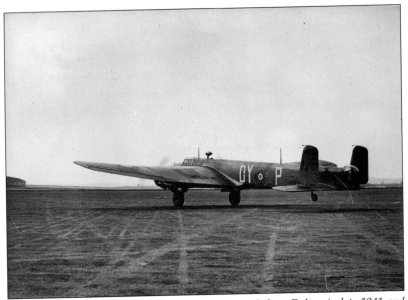

A Whitley of 102 Squadron, which flew these aircraft from Dalton in late 1941 and early 1942. (Peter Green)

crews on the new four-engined bomber then going into service with 4 Group. Early Halifaxes were notoriously difficult to handle and this may have been responsible for the first loss the squadron suffered on 14th April when an aircraft crashed near Ripon during an air test, with the loss of the pilot, F/Lt Williams and seven men on board. The aircraft was seen doing right and left turns before suddenly stalling and spinning into the ground.

By the end of the month 102's Halifaxes were operational and the squadron was to lose two in one night, one shot down by a night fighter while taking part in an attack on Cologne and the second falling victim to flak in a raid on Dunkirk. Six men died in the two crashes, four became prisoners and, remarkably, four managed to evade capture and later returned to the squadron.

The squadron was to leave Dalton early in June, taking its Halifaxes back to Topcliffe. Before it went it lost three more aircraft, one on 1st-2nd June over Essen and two the following night in a second raid on the city. One went down in the sea off Harwich with the loss of the entire crew, and the second, which had suffered severe flak damage, crashed on its approach to the airfield, all those on board surviving.

These were to be the last losses from Dalton for over nine months.

102's departure was followed by the arrival of 76 and 78 Squadron Conversion Flights which together joined 1652 HCU and moved to Marston Moor in August when Dalton closed for redevelopment.

When Dalton reopened in November 1942 it was earmarked for the Royal Canadian Air Force and 428 (Ghost) Squadron was formed there on Wellington IIIs that month. By the time 428 Squadron was ready for business, it and Dalton had been transferred to 6 Group, which came into being on 1st January 1943.

The squadron flew its first operation on the night of 26th-27th January when six aircraft returned safely from an attack on submarine pens at Lorient. The squadron enjoyed a period of good fortune in its early days at Dalton and it wasn't until the end of March that it suffered its first losses, two Wellingtons failing to return from an attack on Bochum. There was just one survivor from the ten men on board the two aircraft.

The RCAF Wellingtons suffered severe losses in the spring of 1943 during what became known as the Battle of the Ruhr. 428 Squadron lost another 13 aircraft – four on them in mining operations – before it left Dalton at the beginning of June, with the loss of 59 men. Four of those who survived were picked up by a rescue launch off Grimsby early on 28th May when their flak-damaged aircraft ditched. The unfortunate rear gunner drowned when the tail of the aircraft broke off during the ditching and sank.

During this period Dalton was used on a number of occasions by the RCAF Wellington squadrons at nearby Dishforth, 425 Squadron losing a Wellington over Duisburg on 8th-9th April and 426 Squadron two aircraft over the same target on 12th-13th May.

When 428 left Dalton for Middleton St George its departure marked the end of the airfield's operational role. Two weeks earlier 1666 HCU had been formed at Dalton and it was to work up there before moving to Wombleton in October.

1691 (Bomber) Gunnery Flight had been formed at Dalton early in July and it remained there until the end of the war – it became 1695 Bomber Defence Training Flight in February 1944 – providing support training for 6 Group. During August 1944 the 6 Group Aircrew School was also formed at Dalton, a holding unit providing training for crews from 22, 23 and 25 OTUs before they went on to the 6 Group HCUs. Both these units were disbanded at Dalton in August 1945 and the airfield closed soon afterwards.

The airfield at Wombleton opened in October 1943 and was used exclusively for training within 6 Group. Its resident unit until the end of the war was 1666 Heavy Conversion Unit, which operated both Halifaxes and Lancasters to meet the needs of 6 Group's squadrons. The airfield was also used briefly by 1679 Heavy Conversion Unit, which moved in from East Moor before being disbanded and its aircraft and staff incorporated into 1666 HCU.

Wombleton was an unlikely spot for a heavy bomber airfield. It was built close to the village from which it takes its name in the fertile valley between the Hambleton Hills and the North Yorkshire Moors. Both must have caused problems for crews relatively new to flying largely clapped out aircraft, many of which were squadron discards.

Wombleton was typical of wartime airfields, its Nissen huts and T2 hangars constantly, it seemed, awash in a sea of mud. It was unusual in that several of the country lanes the airfield bisected were never closed, probably unofficially, to the local populace. It was with a sense of amazement that newcomers watched farm workers criss-crossing the airfield as though it and its heavy bombers were not there. One country road linking the villages of Wombleton and Nunnington was incorporated into one of the runways and, so the story goes, was shared at times by aircraft and local traffic.

The airfield was built close to the pre-war airfield at Welburn Hall at a height of 120 feet above sea level, which added to the problems of the HCU crews. It was a credit to them, and the hard-working ground crews who worked round the clock to keep the aircraft serviceable, that there were not more crashes.

But crashes there were, many of them killing some or all of the crews of the aircraft involved. Typical of these were a series of crashes, all involving Halifaxes in October 1944. One aircraft suffered an engine fire at 15,000 feet on a cross-country run. Three of the crew managed to bale out before the aircraft went into a spin and crashed on the outskirts of Manchester, killing the remaining four on board. Ten days later another cross-country exercise saw a 1666 Halifax collide with another aircraft from 1664 HCU at Dishforth at 18,000 feet over Devon. Two nights after that another aircraft hit the ground near Dishforth after the bomb doors came open in flight. Two men were killed three nights later when Halifax LW235 crashed at Nunnington. The official report later decided the aircraft was flying too low in poor visibility. The final crash of the month came a week later when Halifax HR723 – a veteran which had seen service with 35, 77 and 405 Squadrons – was

Halifax II LW235 pictured here as EY-B of 78 Squadron during the autumn of 1943. Shortly afterwards it was transferred to 1666 HCU at Wombleton. It was destroyed in a crash on 20th October 1944 at Nunnington. (Sir Guy Lawrence)

abandoned due to heavy icing, the aircraft eventually crashing near Llandudno. One civilian died in addition to one of the crew whose parachute harness was not correctly fastened.

The unit also wrote off a number of its Lancasters. Some like ND656 were real veterans. This particular aircraft had seen service in 1 Group with 460 and 103 Squadrons before being damaged. It was later repaired at 38 MU and issued to 1666 HCU where it was written off in a crash in March 1945. Towards the end of the war, however, some of the Lancasters delivered to Wombleton were brand new. One of them, HK756, disappeared during a diversionary operation by 126 aircraft over the North Sea during the night of 14th-15th January just a week after being delivered from the Vickers Armstrong factory at Castle Bromwich. No trace was ever found of the aircraft.

1666 HCU was disbanded in August 1943 and Wombleton was returned to RAF 'ownership'. It was used for some years by the RAF Regiment as the home of its Battle School before the airfield finally closed in the early 1950s.

10
DISHFORTH

Five major airfields in Yorkshire were commissioned by the RAF in a nine-month period between the summer of 1937 and the spring of 1938. Among these was Dishforth, which was built alongside what was then known as the Great North Road, a few miles from Ripon. By 1941 it had actually expanded across what is now the A1, with dispersals for 78 Squadron's Whitleys on the west side. Barriers had to be dragged across the road to enable aircraft to be moved to and from the dispersals.

Dishforth was the second of the airfields to be handed over to the RAF – Driffield had opened a few weeks earlier and Finningley was to open a few days later – and it was to play a major role in the coming conflict in Europe. It started the war as one of 4 Group's principal airfields, later became a Canadian bomber station and ended the war as the headquarters station for training within 6 Group.

Like its contemporaries, Dishforth was a big, comfortable station, contrasting strongly with some of its wartime-built neighbours. Its five hangars were big, brick-built C-types, in the familiar arc pattern. Its messes, accommodation blocks and technical sites were the envy of all those who had to endure winters at places like Tholthorpe, Dalton or Wombleton.

Dishforth's pre-war squadrons, 10 and 78, were both equipped with Whitleys in September 1939. 78 had been designated 4 Group's reserve squadron, providing training for new crews in days long before conversion units. It was, therefore, 10 Squadron which first went to war from Dishforth, scattering leaflets hopefully across north-west Germany. These first operations quickly brought home to crews the difficulties of navigating over Europe at night, one Whitley crash-landing in Lancashire at the end of September. The following night the squadron suffered 4 Group's first casualties when F/Lt Allsop and crew were killed when their aircraft crashed into the North Sea.

A Whitley IV of 10 Squadron which crash-landed on the outskirts of Grimsby following a leaflet raid on 7th April 1940. (Peter Green)

King George VI made the first of two wartime visits to Dishforth in November 1939 accompanied by the Chief of the Air Staff, ACM Sir Cyril Newall, and was shown around one of 10 Squadron's Whitleys. Two weeks later 78 Squadron swapped places with 51 Squadron at Linton-on-Ouse and both squadrons operated together in the first bombing raid against a German target. It came on the night of 19th-20th March 1940 on the seaplane base at Sylt on the island of Hörnum and was retaliation against an attack on the Scapa Flow naval base during which misplaced bombs fell on a nearby village.

The attack was led by Whitleys of 102 Squadron at Driffield, but at Dishforth invited national newspaper reporters were awaiting the return of 10 and 51 Squadrons. When they heard that 10's CO, W/Cmdr Bill Staton had arrived early and flown several times over the target before bombing, he was selected as the hero of the hour and the following day all the credit was given to 'Crack 'Em Staton'. There was barely a mention of the Driffield squadrons, 102 and 77. Needless to say, this was to lead to some degree of friendly rivalry between the airfields. 51 Squadron, in the meantime, had suffered the only loss of the night, F/Lt Baskerville's Whitley being shot down.

A 10 Squadron crew following an air test in their Whitley, summer 1940. (RAF Leeming)

Both 10 and 51 were involved in the Norwegian campaign, two of 51's Whitleys failing to return from operations on 23rd April while a third crashed out of fuel at Slaidburn a week later, killing two of the crew. 51 Squadron lost another aircraft in an attack on the refinery at Wanne-Eickel in May and, during the same raid, W/Cmdr Staton's aircraft was badly damaged while he carried out one of the earliest examples of target marking.

An attack on targets in the Ruhr at the end of May demonstrated the difficulty of navigation and target location. P/O Warren and his crew in 10 Squadron's P4952 ran into a magnetic storm over the North Sea and were too late to bomb the primary target. Warren opted for the secondary target – the airfield at Flushing – and dropped his bombs after identifying what he thought to be the Rhine. It was only when he tried to land at Dishforth and found himself close to the Lancashire coast that he realised his compass had been thrown out by the effects of the storm. Back on the ground he discovered to his dismay that the 'Rhine' was actually the Thames and the target he bombed was the Fighter Command airfield at Bassingbourn in Cambridgeshire.

Fortunately, there were no casualties or serious damage but the unfortunate bomber pilot earned the nick-name 'Von' Warren.

Soon after this 10 Squadron moved to Leeming and was replaced by 78, which returned as an operational squadron from Linton, flying its first operation to the Ruhr on 19th July. It suffered its first loss two nights later when Sgt Monkhouse and his crew failed to return from Soest.

Early in 1941 the Dishforth squadrons were selected to carry out an operation dear to the heart of Winston Churchill – an assault by paratroopers on the Tragino aqueduct in southern Italy. The attack was to be carried out by X Troop 11 SAS Battalion and, as the RAF had no specialist aircraft for the purpose, Whitleys were selected because of their range and original design, which included the provision of a ventral turret. The frame of this was still present in the RAF bombers and it was easy to adapt to provide an exit point for paratroopers.

Four crews from each squadron were selected for Operation Collosus and, after training at RAF Ringway (now Manchester Airport), they flew to Mildenhall on 3rd February. There they picked up 39 soldiers before flying on to Malta, where they all successfully landed on a bomb-damaged airfield. Six aircraft were selected for the drop, carrying 36 soldiers and their equipment in addition to several 250lb bombs. The remaining two aircraft were to bomb railway yards at Foggia.

The Dishforth aircraft, led by W/Cmdr Willie Tait, who was later to command 617 Squadron, dropped the SAS unit from less than 300 feet and, despite some of the explosives being lost, the aqueduct was severely damaged. One of the Foggia aircraft developed engine trouble and had to be abandoned, the crew becoming PoWs. Their capture led to the planned pick-up of the SAS soldiers by a Royal Navy submarine being cancelled and all the attackers were later captured and spent the rest of the war as prisoners.

A year later Whitleys of 51 Squadron were involved in a similar operation, this time the dropping of paratroops on the Luftwaffe's Wurzburg radar installation at Bruneval, near Le Havre. The Dishforth aircraft, led by W/Cmdr Percy Pickard, dropped the paras close to the radar station and vital equipment was captured and brought back to England. The success of the raid prompted a second visit by the King, this time accompanied by the Queen, to Dishforth, where he congratulated W/Cmdr Pickard on the squadron's exploits. Pickard was later to command the low-level attack on the Amiens prison in 1944, where he was killed when his Mosquito was shot down.

LUFTPOST

Von der Royal Air Force abgeworfen

Nr. 3

9. Juni 1941

Verboten überall, wo die Wahrheit verboten ist

EIN BILD, DAS BÄNDE SPRICHT

Deutschland erhält einen Vorgeschmack

Treffsicherheit!
Das hat mit einer Bombe die R.A.F. getan

DIESES Luftbild — eine Autobahnbrücke über den Rhein in der Nähe von Mannheim — wurde von der R.A.F. aufgenommen, nachdem die Brücke von Bomben entzweigeschnitten worden war. Ein paar interessante Folgerungen können aus diesem Bild gezogen werden.

Erstens: die R.A.F. zielt gar nicht schlecht.

Zweitens: die R.A.F. stattet ihre Besuche in Deutschland nicht nur bei Nacht, sondern auch bei Tage ab, sei es, um Bomben abzuwerfen, oder um Bilder aufzunehmen.

Drittens: die R.A.F. weiss, dass das Transportsystem einer der wunden Punkte Deutschlands ist — dank der von der britischen Seeblockade verursachten Anspannung. Indem die R.A.F. derartige Objekte mit Bomben belegt, steigert sie diese Anspannung langsam aber sicher bis ins Unerträgliche.

Viertens: um eine Brücke wie diese zu zerstören, bedarf es keiner besonders grossen Bombe; die neue britische Bombe jedoch, die oft "Bezirksbombe" genannt wird — weil eine einzige genügt, um ein riesiges Gebiet zu verheeren — hat eine fünfmal grössere Sprengkraft als jede bisher bekannte.

Fünftens: bis jetzt hat die R.A.F. vorwiegend Bombenflugzeuge benützt, die verhältnismässig klein sind — nicht grösser als die durchschnittlichen deutschen Maschinen. Die neuen gigantischen Flugzeuge wie der britische "Short Stirling" und der amerikanische "Liberator" werden erst jetzt in Massen hergestellt. Ihre Bombenladung und ihre Flugweite übertreffen die von England früher verwandten Maschinen um ein Mehrfaches. Sie sind imstande, den Krieg gegen Deutschland immer weiter nach dem Osten zu tragen.

Zusammenfassend: was Deutschland bisher erlebt hat, war nur ein Vorgeschmack. Und nach dem musste Feldmarschall Milch schon jetzt feststellen: "Dieser Krieg unterscheidet sich von allen vorhergehenden dadurch, dass auch das Heimatgebiet aufs Stärkste mitberührt wird." Deutschland, das seit mehr als 125 Jahren nicht zu spüren bekommen hat, was Krieg auf eigenem Boden bedeutet, muss und wird noch lernen — genau wie Warschau, Rotterdam und Belgrad es erfahren haben — wie der von Hitler 20 Jahre lang gepredigte totale Krieg wirklich aussieht.

ROOSEVELT:

Die historische Proklamation,

am 27. Mai dem amerikanischen Volke verkündigt.

SINTEMALEN der Ablauf der Ereignisse offenbar macht, dass sich die Achsenmächte in einem Kriege wie diesem nicht auf die Ziele beschränken, zu denen sie sich ursprünglich bekannt haben, dass vielmehr diese Ziele nicht nur den Umsturz der demokratischen Ordnung auf der ganzen Erde, sondern auch eine die Völker und ihre Wirtschaft umfassende Weltherrschaft einschliesst, die jeden Widerstand zu Lande, zur See und in der Luft zerstören will, und

SINTEMALEN Gleichgültigkeit von Seiten der Vereinigten Staaten dieser wachsenden Drohung gegenüber gefährlich wäre und die gesunde Voraussicht verlangt, dass wir im Interesse der Sicherung dieser Nation und dieser Erdhälfte vom Friedensstand militärischer Stärke übergehen zu einer Basis, welche uns in Stand setzt, sofort und entscheidend fertigzuwerden mit jedem Versuch, diese Hemisphäre einzukreisen oder einen Stützpunkt für Angriffe gegen sie zu schaffen, ebenso wie jede von ausländischen Agenten erfolgende Drohung eines räuberischen Einfalls in unser Gebiet und unsere Gesellschaft zurückzuweisen,

erkläre ich, Franklin D. Roosevelt, Präsident der Vereinigten Staaten von Amerika,

nationalen Notstand befindet, der es erheischt, alle seine militärischen, See-, Luft- und zivilen Verteidigungsmassnahmen auf Bereitschaftsstand zu bringen, um alle Angriffshandlungen oder -drohungen gegen irgendeinen Teil der westlichen Erdhälfte abzuwehren.

ICH RUFE alle führenden Männer und Beamten in Staat und Gemeinden auf, zusammenzuarbeiten zur Gewährleistung unserer inneren Sicherheit gegen jeden vom Ausland inspirierten Umsturz, und jedes Gemeinwesen in den Stand des Maximums produktiver Leistung und des Minimums an Verschwendung und nutzloser Reibung zu setzen.

ICH RUFE alle loyalen Staatsbürger auf, die Erfordernisse der Nation zuerst ins Auge zu fassen und in die Tat umzusetzen, dahingehend, dass wir alle physischen Kräfte, alle sittliche Gewalt und alle materiellen Hilfsquellen dieser Nation mobil und bereit machen zu sofortiger Abwehr.

"Die Vollmachten des Präsidenten" — siehe S. 4.

VOR EINEM JAHR

Der italienische Journalist Ansaldo im "Völkischen Beobachter" vom 3. Juni 1940: "Italien muss seine Gerechtigkeit und Freiheit im Mittelmeer erlangen. Das muss Italien mit...

8.000 englische Flieger jährlich aus U.S.A.

DER Luftausbildungsplan des britischen Weltreichs sieht vor, dass jährlich 30.000 Flieger aus allen Teilen des Empires in Canada und viele tausende mehr in Australien, Neuseeland und Südafrika ausgebildet werden. Diese Methode hat sich bereits so ausgezeichnet bewährt, dass ein ähnlicher Plan jetzt in den Vereinigten Staaten aufgestellt worden ist.

Achttausend britische Flieger werden nun alljährlich in dreizehn amerikanischen Schulungszentren ausgebildet werden. Ungefähr die Hälfte von ihnen wird speziell im Gebrauch der neuen schweren amerikanischen Bombenflugzeuge geschult. Der erste grosse

One of the leaflets scattered by crews from Dishforth in the summer of 1941. (Sir Guy Lawrence)

In the meantime 78 Squadron moved to Middleton St George in April 1941 leaving 51 Squadron as the sole occupants of Dishforth. It was to be an eventful stay. Among the aircraft lost that spring was Whitley T4270 whose crew had the misfortune to be shot down by a Hurricane over Dorset on their way back from Brest. A second aircraft on the raid was forced to ditch off the French port. Two aircraft were lost from a raid on Cologne, one of them crash-landing on a sandbank off the German coast. Three of the Whitley's crew were later picked up by a German float plane which then crashed at its base at Börkum, killing all on board. An attack on Frankfurt on 6th-7th August saw the squadron lose three aircraft, two being shot down close to the target while the third was abandoned by its crew near Swanton Morley due to severe icing.

Twelve nights later three more were lost in an attack on Cologne, one crashing near Ipswich following a fire on the return journey. The pilot of one of the other aircraft, Sgt James, won a DFM after giving his parachute to the wireless operator and then managing to crash-land the aircraft. Sgt James was later repatriated but died from tuberculosis. Three more were lost when Berlin was the target on the night of 7th-8th September, one over the target, another crash-landing in Sweden and a third stalling and diving into the ground near the airfield.

The winter of 1941-42 saw 51's Whitleys fighting both the Germans and the elements, with varying degrees of success. They lost a number of aircraft and their crews, including two of the eight sent on the night of 7th-8th November 1941 to Berlin, the aircraft flown by S/Ldr Dickenson and Sgt MacMurray both being listed as 'failed to return'. A series of attacks on the port of Emden early in 1942 cost the squadron a further five aircraft.

The squadron was also used to support the Royal Navy's attack on the dry dock facilities at St Nazaire in March 1942, losing three of its aircraft in the process. One crashed near Ilkley and the second on Great Whernside, all those on board being injured. The third ditched in the Channel and the crew were later picked up by a minesweeper after spending ten hours in a dinghy.

51 Squadron flew its last Whitley operation from Dishforth on the night of 27th-28th April to Dunkirk before the squadron left Yorkshire for Chivenor which as one of the 4 Group squadrons went on detachment to Coastal Command to combat the growing U-boat menace.

Plans were already being drawn up for a new bomber group, funded almost entirely by the Canadian government. It was to be based in North Yorkshire and Dishforth was one of the airfields designated to form part of it. On 25th June 1942, 425 (Alouette) Squadron RCAF was formed at Dishforth under W/Cmdr J. M. St Pierre, the fifth Canadian squadron to be formed in England and the first French-Canadian squadron.

It was equipped with Wellington IIIs and was to lose one of its Wellingtons in a tragic accident during its working up period. The aircraft, which was carrying a crew of five, was taking part in a fighter affiliation exercise with Spitfires from 403 Squadron, then based at Catterick. One of the Spitfires, flown by Sgt Norman, an American with the RCAF, collided with the front turret of the Wellington over Pickering and both aircraft fell in flames. The squadron flew operationally for the first time on the night of 5th-6th October, when eight aircraft were sent to Aachen. It was an undistinguished debut, only two aircraft reaching the target area. Five turned back with various problems while the last crashed in Essex, killing all six on board.

A second Canadian squadron, 426 (Thunderbird), was formed on 15th October, taking its title from the Red Indian name for aircraft. It flew operationally for the first time on 14th-15th January 1943, losing one of the Wellingtons sent to Lorient and a second in a daylight operation to Essen two weeks later.

Over the next five months 426 Squadron was to suffer particularly badly, losing a further 19 Wellingtons. Among them was X3420, which was flown by the squadron CO, W/Cmdr Blanchard. He was shot down over Holland by a night fighter in an attack on Cologne on 14th-15th February. All six on board were killed and within days W/Cmdr Crooks had taken over the Thunderbirds.

Two members of the crew of a 426 Squadron Wellington, the bomb aimer P/O Lasky, and wireless operator Sgt Anderson, were picked up by a Royal Naval destroyer off Cromer after the aircraft ditched following a raid on Kiel. Lasky later received the DFC and there was a DFM for Anderson.

425 lost its last aircraft from Dishforth in a raid on Mannheim on 16th-17th April, the squadron flying out two days later to the Middle East. Contractors were now moving in to Dishforth for runway construction and further expansion, but the Thunderbirds were to continue to fly from the airfield until mid-June, their final operation

*RAF Dishforth pictured by a Luftwaffe reconnaissance aircraft, October 1940.
(Peter Green)*

being a raid on Dusseldorf from which one of their aircraft failed to
return with the loss of the entire crew. Two days later the squadron
moved to Linton-on-Ouse. Dishforth's third occupants, 1512 BAT
Flight, which had been formed as 12 BAT Flight in September 1941,
also moved out, taking its Oxfords to Banff.

426's departure marked the end of Dishforth's war as an operational
bomber station. It had been selected as the Base station for 6 Group's
training arm and reopened in November as the home of 1664 Heavy
Conversion Unit, which moved in from Croft. 1664 HCU shared
Dishforth briefly with 'old boys' 425 Squadron, which returned from
the Middle East and re-equipped with Halifaxes before moving to
Tholthorpe. As 61 (Caribou) Base, Dishforth had Dalton and
Wombleton as its satellites and between them they had the task of
supplying crews for the remainder of 6 Group's Halifax squadrons.

The new Halifax Mk III was just beginning to go into squadron
service but 1664 had to make do with a mixed selection of Mk IIs and
Vs, most of which had been well used before they arrived.

One of the first aircraft to be lost from 1664 at Dishforth was a Mk V,
DG282, which crashed half a mile south of the airfield's No 3 runway

on the night of 2nd December when part of the airfield was shrouded in smoke from a train passing on the nearby line. Five of the crew were killed in that crash. On the same day another crew died when their aircraft hit cottages on the outskirts of Northallerton and caught fire. Later in the month a third Halifax broke up in the air over Harrogate. Four of the crew managed to bale out but the remaining three died when the wreckage of the aircraft fell onto the outskirts of the city, hitting a house in Kent Road and the nearby golf course.

There were numerous accidents that spring and summer resulting in Halifaxes being damaged or written off. The fortunate crews were those who walked away.

In October that year 1664 lost six aircraft and with them the lives of 22 men – a higher loss rate than many front-line squadrons. The first suffered an engine fire on 2nd October during a night exercise. Four of the crew baled out but there were still three men on board when the Halifax hit the ground at high speed near Ripon. Eight nights later another Halifax and its crew disappeared on a training exercise. It was thought their aircraft crashed in the sea. On 17th October the pilot of JP197, F/O Hutcheon, opened the bomb doors instead of raising the flaps after take-off and the Halifax crashed near Dishforth village, killing five of the crew. Later that night a second Halifax crashed after taking off on an exercise. This time there were no survivors. Two Halifaxes were then written off after accidents at the end of the month, one after a heavy landing and the second following an engine fire. Both crews escaped.

The final loss of the war sustained by 1664 HCU came on the night of 15th March 1945 when Halifax MZ481 disappeared on a cross-country flight. A little over two weeks later the unit was disbanded and 1695 Bomber Defence Training Flight, which had been formed at Dishforth at the end of January, moved out.

Dishforth was to be used for many years after the war by the RAF, first as a training centre for Transport Command and later by 241 Operation Conversion Unit. When the RAF finally moved out its runways were used by jets from nearby Leeming while many of its buildings were taken over as a regional training centre by the North Yorkshire Police Force.

11
DRIFFIELD

Shortly after 1pm on the afternoon of 15th August 1940 radar operators at Staxton Wold, near Scarborough picked up a series of echoes over the North Sea. They were quickly identified as German aircraft. Twelve Spitfires of 616 Squadron were scrambled from Leconfield and six Hurricanes of 73 Squadron at Church Fenton, which were already airborne, were ordered to the Bridlington area. It was the second element of a two-pronged attack on the North East coast on the Luftwaffe's Adlertag – Eagle Day – when they hoped to eliminate the RAF before the planned invasion.

Some minutes later the fighters caught sight of a force of around 50 Ju 88s approaching the coast just south of Bridlington and immediately dived to attack them. The Junkers were from KG30 based at Aalborg in Denmark. Some were equipped for bombing and others were fitted with 20mm cannon and machine guns. In the air battle which followed nine of the raiders were reported to have been shot down and three more were to crash on their return to Denmark. But it quickly became clear what their target was – the airfield at Driffield, some ten miles inland from Bridlington and then the home of two Whitley squadrons.

Reports of how many of the raiders made it to Driffield are confused, ranging from 12 to 40. What was certain was their efficiency. Within a few short minutes they devastated the airfield. Four of the five big brick-built hangars were badly damaged, many ancillary buildings were left on fire, twelve Whitleys were destroyed and 13 people were killed and numerous others wounded. Of those who died, seven were RAF personnel, including a WAAF attached to the station headquarters staff. Five were members of the East Yorkshire Regiment and one, Frank Ibbotson, was a civilian employee on the station.

The aircraft carefully dive-bombed and strafed the airfield, the only opposition by now being a single Vickers .303 machine gun mounted on the station water tower. It proved to be the heaviest raid of the

Whitley Vs of 102 Squadron in one of Driffield's wrecked hangars following the air raid of August 1940. (Yorkshire Air Museum via Peter Green)

entire war on an RAF bomber station in England and was to put Driffield out of action for several months.

One of the men on the receiving end of the bombing was flight mechanic Vernon Whitehair. 'We were just coming out of the mess after having our lunch when they came. It seemed as though there were 40 Ju 88s overhead all at once. They were so low you could almost reach out and touch them,' he recalls. He and the other men with him ran for cover in a nearby Anderson shelter which, within minutes, was rocked by the explosion of a German bomb. When they finally emerged from the badly-damaged shelter there were fires burning everywhere.

Mr Whitehair, who now lives in Cornwall, recalled it was only after the bombers had begun their attack that the air raid sirens sounded. 'That afternoon Lord Haw Haw came on the radio to say that the Luftwaffe had been to Driffield and knocked out four of the hangars and that they would be back to finish the job the following day,' he went on.

LAC Whitehair was among many men who suffered severe shock as a result of the bombing and was sent to a converted hotel in Buxton to recuperate. It was there that he was later discharged on medical grounds from the RAF.

P/O Richard Pinkham recalled: 'We had been totally unprepared for the attack and after the initial shock we wandered around in a daze and rendered what help we could.'

Eric Martin, who now lives in Driffield, was an NCO air gunner with 77 Squadron and remembers this as a 'terrible time' at the airfield. He recalled that ten days after the attack the squadron moved to Linton-on-Ouse where they were equipped with new aircraft.

Mabel Ulliott then lived at Hutton Vicarage, two miles across the fields from RAF Driffield, and remembers there was no warning of the attack. Seconds before the bombers arrived she saw the family dog taking cover and then came the unfamiliar sound of German aero engines and the awful noise of the bombs as they struck the airfield. She recalls that many of the farm labourers in the area were out in the fields and hid among the stooks of corn as the Luftwaffe gunners opened fire on them.

Driffield was an ideal target for the German bombers, the furthest east of all the big pre-war bomber airfields in Yorkshire and Lincolnshire. It had first been used by the RFC in the First World War but later all the temporary buildings which had been erected on the site at Eastburn close to the market town of Driffield were dismantled and flying ended. However, the site was resurveyed in 1932 and chosen as one of the 14 sites in the North East for airfield construction. Work began three years later and RAF Driffield officially opened on 30th July 1936, complete with five brick-built C-type hangars and standard RAF accommodation and technical blocks. It was the first of the big Expansion Programme airfields to open in Yorkshire.

Initially, it was a 3 Group bomber airfield, housing 58 and 215 Squadrons, with both 51 and 78 Squadrons forming there in 1937. The following year the airfield came under the control of 4 Group and 58 Squadron was replaced by 102 and 215 Squadron by 77, two squadrons which were to spend most of the coming war flying from Yorkshire airfields.

They re-equipped with Whitleys and were put on alert on 3rd September 1939 as Britain declared war on Germany. It was two nights later when three Whitleys from 102 Squadron flew over the Ruhr scattering leaflets, with 77 Squadron repeating the operation with two Whitleys the following night. On their way back, one of the aircraft was forced to land by a Belgian Air Force Fairey Fox for flying over a neutral country, with the second making a forced landing. These were the first of a number of 'nickel' operations carried out by the Driffield

Whitley III K8952/K of 77 Squadron burnt out at Driffield following a forced landing in February 1939. (Yorkshire Air Museum via Peter Green)

squadrons. Their value was questioned by the crews, but the experience gained on night operations over Europe was to stand those who survived the coming months in good stead. The operations themselves resulted in a number of aircraft and their crews being lost. Among them was a 77 Squadron Whitley shot down by light flak on 15th-16th October over Germany. The pilot, F/Lt Roland Williams, was killed while the remainder of the crew baled out to become some of the very first RAF prisoners of war.

Two days later there was another tragedy for the Driffield squadrons when a 102 Squadron Whitley stalled after take-off at Catterick and crashed into a field. It was ferrying stores and ground crew of 41 Squadron to Drem in Scotland. Seven men died in the crash and two others were seriously injured. 102 Squadron lost another Whitley during a leaflet raid on Frankfurt while a 77 Squadron aircraft and its crew disappeared during a reconnaissance over northern Germany.

That winter the Driffield Whitleys ranged far and wide over Europe, scattering their leaflets from Wilhelmshaven to Vienna. The most ambitious of these came on the night of 7th-8th March 1940 when two aircraft from 77 Squadron flew to Warsaw to drop more than six million leaflets across the Polish capital. The squadron was ordered to repeat the operation a week later and one of the crews selected was captained by F/Lt Tomlin, who had flown on the first operation. It was a night which was to go down in RAF legend.

He was flying L-Love, the reserve aircraft for the night and one noted for its lack of power. On the return flight they encountered severe icing and this, combined with the Whitley's thirst for fuel, led to the crew deciding to land as soon as they were over the French border. They were flying on dead reckoning and as soon as the captain and co-pilot believed they were over friendly territory they looked for somewhere to put down.

As they lost height they were fired on by light flak but the pilot thought it was French gunners below him and switched on his navigation lights and lowered his undercarriage. The anti-aircraft fire immediately stopped.

The Whitley landed on a large if somewhat uneven field and the pilot noticed a young man running towards the aircraft. He and the co-pilot switched off the engines and got out to talk to him. It was only when they spoke to him they realised they were some 20 miles on the German side of the French border. Both airmen quickly climbed back into L-Love, the engines fired up immediately and they swung the bomber round and took off in the direction indicated by the young man, landing a few minutes later at Villeneuve airfield, this time on the right side of the border!

Not all the casualties suffered by personnel at Driffield involved aircrew. On 14th April a member of a Whitley's ground crew was killed when he fell under the wheel of the bomber as it was being towed across the airfield.

The Driffield squadrons were heavily involved in the Norwegian and French campaigns and on 11th-12th June took part in Bomber Command's first raid on Italy. Thirty-six Whitleys from Driffield, Dishforth and Linton refuelled at St Peter's airfield on Jersey – shortly to become the home of Lutfwaffe Me 110s – and headed for Turin. Twenty-three aircraft were forced to turn back because icing prevented them flying over the Alps while the remainder attacked Turin and Genoa. On the return a 77 Squadron Whitley crashed in flames near Le Mans, killing Sgt Songest and his crew, Bomber Command's first casualties on operations to Italy.

Driffield was the temporary home of 88 Squadron and its surviving Battles during June before the squadron moved to Northern Ireland. It was during its brief spell at Driffield that, the story goes, an LAC airframe fitter with 88 Squadron took off in one of the unit's Battles and later landed at Colerne in Wiltshire, where he was arrested.

The raid on 15th August left Driffield in a terrible state, as we have seen, and the airfield was to remain closed until January 1941. The RAF, however, was determined to let the Germans believe it was business as usual and a number of dummy Whitleys were left scattered around the airfield while repairs were carried out to the hangars and many damaged buildings.

When it did finally reopen it was as a fighter airfield under the control of 13 Group, Fighter Command. 213 Squadron arrived from Leconfield but moved to Castletown in Scotland in mid-February, exchanging places with 1 (Fighter) Squadron Royal Canadian Air Force. The Canadians spent a fortnight at Driffield before moving to Digby in Lincolnshire, an RCAF station, where it was renumbered 401 Squadron. Its place was taken by 485 (RNZAF) Squadron, which spent seven weeks at Driffield before taking its Spitfires to Leconfield. During this period the airfield was transferred back to 4 Group Bomber Command.

On 1st April 1941 104 Squadron was reformed on Wellingtons at Driffield. It had been a training unit earlier in the war and was to remain at Driffield until early in 1942 when it was transferred to the Middle East. It was joined within three weeks by the first Canadian bomber squadron to be formed overseas, 405 (Vancouver), which was equipped with Wellington IIs.

104 Squadron made its bombing début on the night of 8th-9th May in a 4 Group attack on Bremen, four of its six aircraft bombing successfully. The fifth aircraft attacked Wilhelmshaven while the sixth suffered a bomb door failure. A second successful operation followed the next night when S/Ldr Beare led six aircraft to Ludwigshafen.

405 Squadron made its bow a month later when it supplied four of the aircraft which attacked marshalling yards at Schwerte in the Ruhr. It lost its first aircraft on 16th-17th June when a Wellington crashed in the sea off the Dutch coast with the loss of the entire crew following an attack on Cologne. Three days later 405 moved to Pocklington.

Driffield was still operating with grass runways and it was clear these could not sustain two Wellington squadrons. However, 104 still shared the airfield with 2 BAT Flight (later to become 1502 Flight) which had seven Whitleys on its strength. In October the 4 Group Target Towing Flight was formed at Driffield and was given the number 1481 TTF, flying Whitleys, Battles, Lysanders and Martinets.

104 Squadron was to fly some 373 Wellington sorties from Driffield before it finally moved, losing 13 aircraft in the process. Amongst these was a Wellington which ditched in the North Sea in August 1941 after a raid on Berlin. A week later the Wellington's dinghy was washed ashore on the Dutch coast. All on board were dead. The last of their losses came on the night of 15th-16th January 1942 when two Wellingtons failed to return from a raid on Emden with the loss of ten men. One disappeared without trace while the second crashed on Arden Great Moor.

As 104 Squadron moved out, it left behind its home echelon which formed a new bomber squadron, 158, which was to remain in Yorkshire for the remainder of the war. The new occupants at Driffield made their operational début on the night of 14th-15th February when seven aircraft flew from the concrete runways at Pocklington to Mannheim. It was to be some time before Driffield became an 'all-weather' airfield.

The squadron suffered its first loss from Driffield on 9th-10th March when Wellington NP-W crashed on the airfield after an attack on Essen. Five of the crew were killed in the burning aircraft but the rear gunner was saved by a member of the ground crew, Cpl Hughes, who risked his own life to pull him to safety. It earned him a Mention in Despatches. A second aircraft and its crew were lost over Hamburg while a leaflet raid, a traditional way of easing in new crews, cost the lives of Sgt Amos and his crew when their aircraft crashed in the sea off Ostend.

The spring and summer of 1942 saw Bomber Command involved in an all-out assault on the Ruhr and a raid on Essen in mid-April cost the squadron two Wellingtons. Others went down in attacks on Dortmund, Hamburg, Kiel and Ostend while four aircraft failed to return from a raid on Warnemunde on 8th-9th May, 19 men being killed and just two surviving.

158's spell at Driffield ended with the Cologne raid on 30th-31st May when two aircraft failed to return, one of them flown by the squadron CO, New Zealander S/Ldr Harkness. Also taking part in the raid were five of the Whitleys of 1502 BAT Flight and one of them, flown by its CO, S/Ldr John Russell, was shot down by a night fighter over Belgium. Russell and the wireless operator, Dennis Foster, were the only survivors.

158 Squadron had been earmarked for conversion to the new four-

F/Sgt Nev Page and crew, 466 Squadron, RAF Driffield. (Stan Parker)

engined Halifaxes then coming into service within 4 Group. Driffield, with its grass strips, was clearly unsuitable for the Halifax and soon after the Cologne raid the squadron left the Yorkshire Wolds for the new airfield at East Moor, north of York.

For the remainder of the summer Driffield was left to its beam approach and target towing flights, resuming its role as a bomber airfield with the formation of 466 (RAAF) Squadron, which was equipped with Wellington IIIs. 466 was to remain in 4 Group and East Yorkshire until the end of the war with two spells at Driffield and one at Leconfield.

A second squadron, 196, was formed at Driffield but was transferred almost immediately along with 466 to Leconfield while work got under way on laying the concrete runways the airfield badly needed. 1502 BAT Flight and 1481 TTF continued to use the airfield until the early summer when they, too, moved to Leconfield.

Around this time Driffield, despite its non-operational status, became 43 Base HQ with Lissett and Leconfield as its sub-stations. It was also the home of the 4 Group Battle School which gave aircrew a taste of army life. Soldiers from the King's Own Yorkshire Light Infantry were the instructors, a role they assumed with some

Halifax III LL598/E of 462 Squadron operating from Driffield in 1944. It was written off following a fire in January 1945 after the squadron moved to Foulsham in 100 Group. (Yorkshire Air Museum via Peter Green)

enjoyment, and the aircrew spent several weeks wading through mud, climbing walls, sleeping rough and learning to use rifles and machine guns.

Driffield's runways were eventually completed but it was to be June 1944 before a resident squadron arrived, 466 moving back from Leconfield with its Halifax IIIs. W/Cmdr Forsyth assumed command of Driffield with W/Cmdr Connolly leading the squadron. It suffered its first loss from its new home on the day following the Normandy invasion, F/Sgt Pearce and his crew failing to return from their first operation. Later in the month the squadron CO led a 4 Group attack on Siracourt, S/Ldr McMullan's Halifax being shot down by radar-predicted flak, only two of the crew surviving. The squadron was joined in August by 462 (RAAF) which reformed at Driffield under W/Cmdr David Shannon after serving in the Middle East. It remained at Driffield until the end of the year when it moved to Foulsham as part of 100 Group.

462 Squadron lost its first Halifax in an attack on a V1 site in the Pas de Calais late in August and was to lose a handful of other aircraft

Sgt 'Bunny' Burrows and crew of 466 Squadron at Driffield, who were shot down in an attack on a flying bomb site in August 1944 on their 25th operation. Several members of the crew survived. (Stan Parker)

before its departure for Norfolk in December, one of them in a mid-air collision with a Lancaster from 625 Squadron at Kelstern in Lincolnshire as they returned from Essen. The only survivor was the bomb aimer, F/Sgt Grace, who was blown clear. The squadron also lost two aircraft on the night of 2nd-3rd November in a raid on Dusseldorf. Two men survived, P/O Jubb and W/O Scott, and both evaded capture and were eventually picked up by American soldiers.

Two nights later F/Lt Joe Herman of 466 Squadron had the most remarkable escape of any bomber pilot in the Second World War. His Halifax was badly damaged by flak in a raid on Bochum and caught fire. He ordered the crew to bale out but then learned that the mid-upper gunner, F/Sgt 'Irish' Vivash, was trapped. He tried to bring the blaze under control while those members of the crew who hadn't jumped tried to free the gunner. By this time the flames were getting worse and Herman, who was on his 31st operation, was reaching down to locate his parachute when the Halifax exploded. Seconds later he found himself tumbling through the night sky, his parachute some distance away in the burning wreckage. He was falling with his arms outstretched when suddenly he crashed into something and instinctively grabbed it. 'It' was the left leg of F/Sgt Vivash, who had also

466 Squadron Halifaxes on a daylight raid early in 1945. (Yorkshire Air Museum via Peter Green)

been blown clear but was wearing his parachute at the time. Joe Herman clung on for dear life with Vivash telling him not to touch the right leg because he feared it was broken. Together, the two men and their single parachute crashed into the branches of a fallen tree on the ground which cushioned their rapid descent. Both men were injured but survived to become PoWs. There was only one other survivor from their aircraft.

466 Squadron was involved in most of the major raids in the later stages of the war and lost a further 15 Halifaxes on operations in addition to several more in accidents. Two of its Halifaxes were destroyed in the Luftwaffe's Operation Gisella on 3rd March 1945 when a large force of Ju 88s and He 219s followed the bombers back from an attack on a synthetic oil refinery at Kamen. Both were attacked in the Driffield circuit and badly damaged. The crew of N-Nuts baled out and the aircraft eventually crashed near Skegness while the second Halifax, C-Charlie, crashed near the airfield, only three of the crew escaping. The final losses of the war for the squadron came on the night of 8th-9th April when two aircraft were lost. One, on its 97th operation, crashed near the airfield, killing all on board. The second was brought

down near the target and five of the crew survived and became, very briefly, prisoners of war.

Flying continued at Driffield after the war until, in 1958, it was converted to accommodate Thor ballistic missiles. These remained until 1963 when the missiles were returned to the United States. Driffield was later used briefly as a test centre by Buccaneer aircraft built at Brough and, in 1977, was acquired by the Army which established its school of mechanical transport there.

12
EAST MOOR

Take the B1363 out of York and a few miles north of the city you will come across the pleasant village of Sutton in the Forest, in the centre of which is a simple memorial to the men of three RCAF squadrons which served on the nearby East Moor airfield between the autumn of 1942 and the spring of 1945. The memorial, which is in the form of a sun dial, records the exploits of 429 (Bison), 432 (Leaside) and 415 (Swordfish) Squadrons and was unveiled in 1990, yet another reminder of the huge contribution of the Royal Canadian Air Force to the bomber campaign.

East Moor began life as the home of a 4 Group squadron, 158, in the summer of 1942. The airfield site had been selected in 1940 as an alternative to one identified earlier at nearby Strensall, which was found to be unsuitable because of the number of streams in the area.

It was opened in June 1942 as a standard wartime bomber airfield with three concrete runways and three hangars, one of which collapsed soon after being erected. By the time it was finished the airfield was already earmarked for the Canadians but for the first four months of its life it was used by 158 Squadron, which arrived from Driffield while in the process of converting to the new Halifax II.

158 Squadron had already flown eleven of their Halifaxes operationally on the 1,000 Bomber Raid on Cologne before they moved to East Moor but once at their new home all their efforts were put into conversion work. By the end of June the squadron was operational again and lost its first Halifax early on the 26th. DG225 ditched less than a mile off Scarborough when it ran short of fuel on its way back from Bremen, P/O Bradbury and his crew being picked up within minutes. They were not, however, to survive for long. Three weeks later they were killed when their new Halifax was shot down in the

suburbs of Gelsenkirchen during a raid on Duisburg, the first 158 Squadron Halifax to be lost over Germany. The squadron lost a second aircraft that night when NP-Q crashed in the sea 15 miles off the Norfolk coast. Fifteen men died in the two Halifaxes. Five nights later two more Halifaxes failed to return to East Moor, both falling to night fighters in an attack on the U-boat yards at Vegesack, near Bremen. There were no survivors from either aircraft.

A week later another Halifax was lost over Holland on its way home from Duisburg, five of the crew surviving. Another failed to return from an attack on the same target the following night and a third was lost after hitting the balloon barrage over Hamburg and crashing in the sea. The final loss in July came when NP-T was hit by flak and ditched in the Scheldt estuary during an attack on Dusseldorf. All the crew were picked up by a Luftwaffe flying boat. Six operations in two weeks had cost 158 Squadron eight Halifaxes and the lives of 37 men, with a further 21 prisoners.

Just two aircraft were lost in August, the first of them in an attack on Bochum. The aircraft was attacked by a night fighter and the rear gunner, P/O Marshall, badly injured. The pilot, Australian P/O Phillips, ordered the remainder of the crew to bale out and then tried to crash-land the Halifax to save the life of the gunner but the aircraft broke up and both men died. It was another of those acts of supreme courage with which the wartime history of Bomber Command is studded.

Raids on Duisburg, Bremen and Essen claimed further aircraft from East Moor while another failed to return from Saarbrucken when it suffered structural failure close to the target and broke up in mid-air. The only survivors were the pilot and rear gunner who were thrown clear. The squadron was to lose another four aircraft before it left East Moor at the end of October, one of them crashing at the rear of the Black Horse public house at Wiggington, near York during an air test. The final loss was on the night of 23rd-24th October when NP-D came down in the Channel on its way home from Genoa with the loss of all eight men on board.

At the end of the month 158 left with its Halifaxes for Rufforth. It was replaced on 7th November when 429 (Bison) Squadron was formed at East Moor on well-used Mk III Wellingtons. The squadron was adopted by the people of Lethbridge in Alberta and by the city of Bradford in England and the men quickly took to life in their new surroundings. Flying began almost immediately and the records show

A Wellington IIIa of 429 Squadron after a wheels-up landing at East Moor early in 1943. (Yorkshire Air Museum via Peter Green)

that 429 lost its first aircraft when the pitch control failed and Sgt Black and his five-man crew baled out over Stokesley, near Middlesbrough.

The new year saw East Moor come under the control of the newly-formed 6 Group and 429 became operational on the night of 21st-22nd January when four aircraft were involved in a mining operation, one failing to return after being shot down by flak and crashing in the Zuider Zee. F/O Johnson, P/O Stirton and Sgts Risingham, Dymick and Stuart were among the first men to be killed in a 6 Group operation. Four of them were British and the pilot was a New Zealander. Some 20 years later, as land reclamation work was going on, the remains of their Wellington were found by Dutch engineers.

429's first bombing operation followed four nights later when ten Wellingtons left for Lorient, three turning back with mechanical problems. One failed to return and among the five-man crew was 17 year old Sgt Lewis, the aircraft's wireless operator, one of the youngest RCAF men to die in Bomber Command.

Six weeks passed before there was another empty dispersal at East Moor. On 2nd-3rd March five aircraft from 429 Squadron took part in a major mining operation. One of East Moor's aircraft, AL-K, ditched in the North Sea 87 miles off the Norfolk coast in bad weather. It was nearly two and a half days later that a rescue launch found the aircraft's dinghy. On board was the navigator, Sgt Rothena, and the body of the pilot, Sgt Black, who had died a few hours earlier.

429 Squadron was to play a full part in the coming bombing assault on the Ruhr, losing some 20 aircraft in attacks on German targets before it finally left East Moor early in August for Leeming. Eighty-four men died in those aircraft, 16 became PoWs and just two managed to evade escape. The squadron's worst night came over Krefeld on 21st-22nd June when four aircraft failed to return and 17 of the 20 men on board were killed.

The Battle of the Ruhr cost 429 Squadron two commanding officers. W/Cmdr Savard DFC, who at 22 was the youngest commanding officer in Bomber Command, was killed with his crew over Mulheim on 22nd-23rd June. His replacement was W/Cmdr John Piddington who was ordered by 6 Group to restrict the number of operations he flew. He had already completed one tour and was on his third operation with 429 Squadron when he lost his life. It was the second of the great Hamburg raids. Piddington had a particularly fast Wellington and arrived over the target early. Rather than hang around, he opted to go in virtually alone and his Wellington was intercepted by a Me 109 flying in the 'Wild Boar' role. The fighter attacked from astern and quickly set fire to the bomber, only two of the crew surviving.

This was the last Wellington to be lost by 429 Squadron during its stay at East Moor. It moved out less than a fortnight later for Leeming and was replaced by 432 (Leaside) which moved in from Skipton-on-Swale on 19th September.

By this time East Moor was already being used by 1679 HCU, which had been formed there in May to provide conversion training for 6 Group's Lancaster squadrons, 408, 426 and, by November, 432.

In the meantime 432 had to soldier on with its Wellingtons, losing four in raids from East Moor, all against Hanover. It was there, on the night of 8th-9th October, that LN451, QO-W of 432 Squadron, became the very last Wellington to be lost on Main Force operations, which was of scant consolation to the five men who died on board the aircraft.

By this time 432 was already in the process of converting to Lancasters, losing its first one on a training flight on 16th November, three men being killed when the aircraft crashed near Scampton. Ten days later ten Lancasters were sent to Berlin, all returning safely. However, one was lost over the German capital on the night of 2nd-3rd December with eight men on board, a second crashing back at East Moor. Two more were lost on 16th-17th December, one coming down in Berlin and the second ditching off Whitby out of fuel, the crew being picked up.

1679 HCU moved to Wombleton in mid-December by which time plans had already been drawn up for East Moor to become a two-squadron, all-Halifax airfield. In the meantime, Lancaster operations went on and there was an immediate DFC for P/O McIntosh who brought his damaged Lanc back to the emergency strip at Woodbridge after the aircraft was damaged over Berlin on the night of 2nd-3rd January. Further aircraft were lost in attacks on Brunswick, Leipzig and further raids on Berlin during January before 432 began to convert to the new Halifax III, then coming into service with Yorkshire-based squadrons. Its final Lancaster was lost in a training accident on 2nd February, the aircraft crashing into trees near Ripon killing all seven on board. It was during this period that the squadron was joined at East Moor by 415 (Swordfish) Squadron, which arrived from Bircham Newton after a spell with Coastal Command.

432 lost its first Halifax on the last of the big Berlin raids late in March. The pilot, P/O McIntosh, who had won a DFC earlier in the year, was one of four survivors. Three aircraft were lost from East Moor on the Nuremburg raid, including one, LW429, from 415 Squadron, its first since arriving in North Yorkshire.

There were fortunate escapes for some in those days. Ray Scott was a 19-year-old from Scarborough when he went to East Moor as part of F/Lt Don Speller's crew in 432 Squadron in January 1944. He had joined the Canadian crew as its British flight engineer in 1943 at 1664 HCU at Dishforth and had completed half a dozen trips before one night, during a pre-op briefing, he suddenly realised his hearing was going.

'I had a heavy cold so I was sent to see the MO and he immediately sent me to the hospital. My pilot took a spare engineer with him. The next morning the padre came in and asked me whose crew I was with.

A Halifax Mk V of 432 Squadron touches down at East Moor after an air test.
(C. Jones)

When I told him he said they were missing. They had got the chop and it wasn't until after the war that I learned they were all killed,' said Mr Scott who later completed his tour with 425 Squadron at Tholthorpe.

An attack on rail yards at Montzen at the end of April cost 432 Squadron three of its aircraft, all falling to night fighters which arrived in force as the second wave was going in. Nine men were killed.

Several aircraft were lost in accidents during the spring and summer of 1944, the worse of these involving a mid-air collision between two Halifaxes near Selby as they were flying in close formation. It cost the lives of 14 men from East Moor squadrons, including 415's CO, W/Cmdr McNeill, and one of 432's flight commanders, S/Ldr Wilmot.

The summer and early autumn saw both squadrons operating at maximum capacity as Bomber Command began to tighten the screw. A posthumous DFC was awarded to pilot F/L Woodward who was critically injured in an attack on Bottrop. His bomb aimer, F/O Hay, took over and flew the damaged aircraft back to England, the injured pilot helping him to crash-land at Woodbridge. F/L Woodward later died of his injuries.

Members of the ground and air crew of 415 Squadron's A-Able at East Moor, 1944. (Yorkshire Air Museum via Peter Green)

The worst of the losses were now behind them, but occasionally fate dealt the young Canadians from East Moor a cruel hand in the night skies over Europe. Two almost-new Halifaxes from 432 Squadron failed to return from a raid on Stuttgart and two more were lost in an attack on Duisburg, one in a mid-air collision with a Lancaster. 415 Squadron lost two of its aircraft in a day-light raid on Hamburg in the spring of 1945, both falling to Me 262 jet fighters. Two aircraft, one from each squadron, failed to return from an attack on Chemnitz, one of them shot down by British anti-aircraft gunners as it flew over Walton-on-Naze in Essex.

One of the final casualties at East Moor was a 415 Squadron Halifax, LV941, which was badly damaged in the raid on Heligoland on 18th April 1945 and was later written off. The aircraft was over a year old – a real veteran in Bomber Command terms – and had already seen much service with 433, 425 and 429 Squadrons.

The final operation of the war, the attack on gun emplacements on the island of Wangerooge, was completed from East Moor on 25th April with 19 Halifaxes of 432 Squadron and 18 of 415 Squadron all returning safely. Three weeks later both squadrons were disbanded at East Moor, by which time 54 OTU had moved in to train night fighter pilots. The unit, which flew Mosquitos, remained at East Moor until the summer of 1946 when it moved to Leeming. It had shared the airfield briefly with 288 Squadron, which brought its Vengeance aircraft from Hutton Cranswick and was disbanded within a month of its arrival.

This marked the end of flying at East Moor and within a matter of days the airfield formally closed and the site eventually returned to agriculture.

13
ELVINGTON

There is no finer memorial in the whole of Yorkshire to the thousands of RAF men and women who served in the county during the last war than the Yorkshire Air Museum at what was once RAF Elvington. Run by a band of dedicated volunteers, many of the wartime buildings, including the control tower, have been restored and a new hangar completed containing a magnificent collection of aircraft.

Pride of place amongst this collection is a replica of the most famous Halifax of them all, 158 Squadron's *Friday The Thirteenth*. It was rebuilt by volunteers at Elvington, with the help of British Aerospace apprentices using fragments from the Halifaxes recovered from as far afield as Australia, France and the Isle of Lewis.

There are archives, displays of memorabilia and a chapel and memorial garden which commemorates the squadrons which flew in 4 and 6 Groups from Yorkshire during the Second World War. All this combines to make Elvington one of the best of all wartime bomber airfield museums.

There was nothing remarkable about the airfield's origins. The site, then known as Scotch Farm and Gypsy Plantation, was selected for a bomber airfield soon after the war began. Work commenced in September 1940 on laying out the airfield with grass runways. However, by early 1941, these were clearly going to be unsuitable for the heavy bombers then going into service and three asphalt runways were laid on the land between Grimstone Woods and Black Plantation.

The airfield was officially completed on 8th October, three days after 77 Squadron began arriving from St Eval in Cornwall where it had been on detachment to Coastal Command. It was a welcome return to Yorkshire after three months of unrelenting boredom for the squadron's Whitley crews, particularly as they were told that as soon

Flying control at Elvington during 77 Squadron's time. This control tower has now been fully restored and is open to the public. (Edith Kup)

as they arrived at Elvington they would be converting to Halifaxes.

A quick survey of their new home found it far from suitable for its new use. One of its main shortcomings was that among the numerous Nissen huts erected – most of the huts intended for accommodation were along Elvington Lane and Wheldrake Lane – there wasn't one big enough to use as a briefing room. This problem was solved by the RAF's 5006 Airfield Construction Squadron at Sherburn-in-Elmet which located a suitable building at Leconfield, dismantled it and re-erected it at Elvington. Conditions were rudimentary, as they were on most wartime RAF airfields, although life was made a little easier for those at Elvington by an unofficial tea-and-wad bar run by an enterprising local woman from an old railway coach just beyond the end of the main runway.

Training began on the Halifaxes almost as soon as they were flown into Elvington. Ground crews were sent to Pocklington to work alongside the engine and airframe fitters there and 77 Squadron pilots flew on operations with 102 Squadron to gain experience. Among the pilots who went was 77's CO, W/Cmdr Embling. He flew as the second pilot with one of 102's flight commanders, S/Ldr Walkington, in a raid on Frankfurt early in December. The Halifax was shot down over France by a night fighter, killing three of the crew, including the pilot. W/Cmdr Embling, however, was one of two from the crew who evaded capture. By early 1943 he had made his way to Spain and then via Gibraltar back to England, only to find another man at his desk at Elvington. That man was W/Cmdr Arthur 'Lofty' Lowe, the first air gunner to command a bomber squadron. His appointment had created hostility in some quarters but Lowe quickly won his doubters over and was to become a very popular figure, playing a major part in making Elvington a particularly happy station.

The training period at Elvington cost the squadron two aircraft and the lives of twelve men, but 77 finally became operational on its Halifaxes on the night of 4th February 1943 when W/Cmdr Lowe flew as mid-upper gunner in F/Lt Butch Bainbridge's aircraft in an attack on U-boat pens at Lorient. Bainbridge's aircraft landed at Docking with an engine problem but the remainder made it back to Elvington. It was a good start which was to continue, 77 Squadron flying operationally a further nine times that month without a single loss.

All that was to come to an end on the night of 9th-10th March when two of the four aircraft sent to attack the Dornier works in Munich failed to return. P/O Huggard's aircraft was shot down by flak, falling into Lake Constance with the loss of all on board. The second aircraft was flown by S/Ldr Bobby Sage. It suffered a glycol leak, possibly after being hit by flak on the outward journey, and was then shot down by a night fighter after it had drifted off track in strong winds near Mons. S/Ldr Sage ordered his crew to jump and all managed to escape except the rear gunner, whose parachute failed. Three of the crew evaded capture and the remaining three, including Sage, became prisoners.

There was a remarkable escape for Sgt Williams, the rear gunner in F/Lt Kendrick's Halifax, which was attacked and damaged by a night fighter over Dusseldorf. The pilot ordered the crew to jump and Sgt Williams prepared to do just that, swinging his turret to enable him to fall clear. But as he pushed his way out his foot became trapped and he was left hanging in the slipstream of the aircraft. Somehow he managed to climb back into his turret where he found the order to jump had been rescinded – although the navigator had already left by this time. Then the damaged Halifax was attacked by three Me 109s and Sgt Williams managed to shoot one down and drive away the other two. The damaged aircraft later landed at Stradishall and Williams was immediately awarded a DFM.

110

77 lost another Halifax in a raid on Berlin at the end of March, the start of a period of terrible losses for the squadron. Eight aircraft and the lives of 46 men were lost in April, three failing to return from a single raid on Essen. In May six aircraft were lost and 37 aircrew from Elvington killed. One of these losses was particularly tragic. Halifax KN-C flown by Sgt Rees exploded in mid-air during a raid on Dusseldorf, possibly when the bombs were detonated by cannon shells from a night fighter. The force of the explosion also brought down two Stirlings, one from 7 Squadron and the second from 15 Squadron, which were flying nearby. There were no survivors from the 21 men on board the three aircraft.

Six aircraft were lost in June, one killing three Belgian civilians when it crashed after being shot down on its way home from Dusseldorf. Six of the crew survived. Three were lost in an attack on Krefeld and one over Mulheim. During this raid, KN-P was damaged by flak over the target and lost two engines and a lot of fuel. The aircraft was then

Halifax HR723 IIa of B Flight 77 Squadron, November 1943. Pictured are (l to r) F/Sgt Paddy Jackson (bomb aimer), F/Sgt Gerry Angell RCAF (rear gunner), W/O Cecil Manson (pilot), F/Sgt John Diffley (wireless operator), F/Sgt Clifford Smith (navigator), F/Sgt Jack Whitley (mid-upper gunner) and F/Sgt Jim Shirley (engineer). (Gerald Myers)

further damaged by a night fighter, which was shot down by the rear gunner, Sgt Bill Speedie. The pilot, Sgt Francis Mathers, ordered everything possible jettisoned and managed to land his damaged aircraft at Martlesham Heath. He was later awarded a Conspicuous Gallantry Medal. His aircraft, P-Peter, was repaired and survived the war but Mathers and his crew were killed a few weeks later in a raid on Mulheim.

July saw losses drop to just three aircraft but a three week period in August cost 77 Squadron twelve Halifaxes and the lives of 65 men. One of the aircraft was lost on the Peenemunde raid while six failed to return from two raids on Berlin, the second of which was on the night of 31st August-1st September. Another eight aircraft failed to return in September and 50 men were killed. October saw the departure of W/Cmdr Lowe, replaced by W/Cmdr Roncoroni, who turned out to be another popular commanding officer, flying whenever possible on operations. His arrival, however, brought little respite for 77 Squadron, whose Halifax IIs were providing relatively easy prey for the German night fighters. One of the survivors from two Halifaxes lost over Kassel on the night of 22nd -23rd October was navigator F/O Bower, who was later to become an air vice marshal and finally retired from the RAF in 1975.

An attack on Berlin on 22nd-23rd November cost 77 Squadron another Halifax while a second was lost when it collided with a 102 Squadron Halifax in the Pocklington circuit, killing all 14 men on board the two aircraft. This type of accident, happening so close to home, held a particular kind of horror for air crew, as did another incident at Elvington on the night of 26th November. 77 Squadron had been stood down because of fog but Lincolnshire-based Lancasters were involved in a raid on Berlin. When they returned fog had affected some of their airfields and a number were diverted. One of these, from 619 Squadron at Woodhall Spa, arrived in the circuit at Elvington and was given permission to land. The aircraft overshot but lost power and crashed just beyond the airfield boundary. As it did so it exploded, probably because of bombs which had 'hung up', and caused widespread damage to nearby buildings.

By this time 77 Squadron had begun converting to Halifax Vs and one of these crashed during a fighter affiliation exercise, the aircraft vibrating violently before turning on its back and crashing. Two of the crew managed to bale out. Clearly, all the problems with the Halifax had still not been resolved.

Air Commodore Gus Walker (centre left) with 77 Squadron air crew at Elvington, 1944. Handing him the mascot (which went by the name of F/Sgt Wakey-Wakey) is the bomb aimer, Sgt Harry Clayton. Others are (l to r) G/Capt Bertram, Bob Johnson (wireless operator), Jack Waddilove (air gunner), F/Lt Sidney Wodehouse (pilot, killed 16th June 1944) and F/Lt Peter Cadman, who was to be killed while instructing at an OTU late 1944. (Harry Shinkfield)

The squadron lost two more aircraft over Frankfurt on the night of 20th-21st December. One of these was flown by S/Ldr Herbert Bickerdyke, who had taken over from S/Ldr Derek Duden, who had just completed his tour. The aircraft was shot down over Belgium with just two men surviving. Among those who died were the squadron's gunnery leader and the rear gunner, who had won a DFM with 76 Squadron. It was a mixture of Halifax IIs and Vs which took off for Berlin on the afternoon of 29th December, an operation which resulted in nine of the 22 aircraft returning early for one reason or another. Eight of the Halifaxes were the new Mk Vs and the high number of early returns was perhaps an indication of their unreliability. The pilots who turned back early included the squadron commander. One aircraft – a Mk II – failed to return from the raid.

Among the men who flew to Berlin that night was S/Ldr Farmery, who had just arrived at Elvington as a replacement for S/Ldr Bickerdyke. He was to survive just one operation, being killed on

21st January 1944 in one of four 77 Squadron aircraft shot down in a raid on Magdeburg, an operation which cost the squadron the lives of 20 men. Eight nights later the squadron went to Berlin once more and again four aircraft failed to return, three falling to flak and the fourth to a night fighter. This time 21 died and six men became prisoners. One of the aircraft lost – F/Sgt Walker's KN-R – was found 15 years later in one of Berlin's many lakes. On 15th February the squadron was involved in another major raid on the German capital and this time three aircraft were lost and there were no survivors at all.

Two more aircraft were lost by 77 Squadron in an attack on rail yards at Amiens on 15th March. It was spared the slaughter of Nuremburg – its aircraft were out mining that night – but a second raid on rail yards at Laon cost the squadron a single aircraft, that flown by S/Ldr Kenneth Bond, which was attacked by a night fighter. He ordered the crew to bale out and managed to jump himself before the aircraft crashed. However, when he was found by the Germans he was severely wounded and died later in Beaujon Hospital. One of his crew, the rear gunner F/O Bill Jacks, who had been a librarian in Edinburgh before the war, evaded capture and arrived back at Elvington on 5th June. Ironically, the flight engineer, Sgt Victor Clare, was released from his PoW camp in time to return to Yorkshire at the end of the war only to be killed when his Halifax crashed. It was one of the aircraft being flown for scrapping to Clifton, near York, when it hit the spire of Clifton Catholic church and crashed into the car park of a nearby pub.

There was an incident-filled mining operation to Rostock later in the month. P/O Ian Robertson won a DFC and both his gunners were awarded DFMs after shooting down one night fighter and claiming a second as a 'probable'. Two other aircraft were lost on the same operation, four of the crew of one of the aircraft escaping to Sweden.

The squadron's days at Elvington were now numbered and 77 was to depart in mid-May for the new airfield at Full Sutton, leaving Elvington to 346 and 347 Squadrons of the Free French Air Force. Before the change, several French pilots had flown with 77 Squadron crews to gain experience of Halifax operations, while a few crews and members of the admin staff remained behind at Elvington for a few weeks to help the French units settle in to their new role.

First to form was 346 (Guyenne) Squadron which came into being on 16th May. All its officers and air crew – with the exception of the squadron adjutant – were drawn from the FFAF and most had previously served in North Africa. They were commanded by Lt Col G.

E. Venot and quickly settled into their new surroundings. They flew operationally for the first time on the night of 1st-2nd June when twelve aircraft formed part of a force of 101 Halifaxes from 4 Group which attacked the radio listening site at Ferme-d'Urville on the Normandy coast, eleven bombing the markers and one returning early with a faulty Gee set. 347 (Tunisie) Squadron formed early in June and between them the French squadrons were to fly over 2,700 Halifax sorties before the war ended, each squadron losing 15 aircraft.

Life in Yorkshire was very different to what the French air crews had enjoyed in North Africa but they were determined to make the best of it. One of the traditions they brought with them was the right of every man to enjoy a glass of wine with his meal, even though circumstances demanded the wine originated in Algeria.

347 Squadron became operational on the night of 27th-28th June when eleven aircraft attacked a V1 site at Mont Condon. In the meantime, 346 had suffered its first loss, one of its Halifaxes being badly damaged by both flak and a fighter during a raid on rail yards at Amiens. The crew managed to get their aircraft back to the emergency strip at Carnaby where it crash-landed. 347 Squadron suffered its first

Halifax NP763/N of 346 Squadron on a daylight raid from Elvington in the autumn of 1944. It was delivered to the squadron in September that year and survived the war. (Yorkshire Air Museum via Peter Green)

loss and casualties when an aircraft crashed near Thorne in South Yorkshire during a training exercise early in July. It was the last Mk V Halifax to be lost on operations. 346's first casualties came during the early hours of 13th July when two of its aircraft collided at 2,000 feet in the Elvington circuit following an attack on a flying bomb site. One aircraft made it back safely with superficial damage but the second crashed and burnt at Dunnington, close to the airfield, killing all those on board.

Just one aircraft was lost in August – it was shot down over a V1 site in northern France – and two in September, although a third was destroyed when a 1,000lb bomb, which had 'hung up' during a raid on German army positions around Le Havre, exploded as the aircraft touched down at Elvington, killing six of the crew. During the month both squadrons were involved in the operation by 70 Halifaxes from 42 Base – Pocklington, Elvington and Full Sutton – to fly petrol in jerry cans to Melsbroek in Belgium to help keep the British army supplied with fuel.

A raid on Cologne at the end of October saw two Halifaxes from 347 Squadron fail to make it back. One suffered flak damage and landed at Brussels while the second ditched in the North Sea after three engines failed, the crew later being picked up.

346 Squadron suffered its worst night of the war when it lost five aircraft in a raid on Bochum with the loss of 23 lives. It was a bad night all round for 4 Group, its Halifaxes getting a severe mauling by night fighters, while the Lancaster force escaped mainly unscathed. The squadron was to lose two other aircraft during the month, one in a daylight raid on Dusseldorf and a second in an attack on the refinery at Sterkrade.

347 Squadron suffered no losses in November, but there were two in December, one over Osnabruck and the second in a daylight attack on Essen on Christmas Eve. A third aircraft was destroyed and 13 members of the squadron's ground staff, nine of them French, killed during an accident at the end of the month. One of the squadron's Halifaxes was being bombed up when it appears a bomb fell from the aircraft. It exploded and detonated the rest of the bomb load. Damage was caused over a wide area and a further five men were seriously injured in one of the worst wartime accidents on a bomber airfield.

The squadron lost six aircraft in January, one of them in a mid-air collision during an attack on Saarbrucken. LL590 collided with another Halifax from 51 Squadron and crashed, killing three of the crew. The 51

Squadron aircraft lost ten feet of its nose but remarkably made it back to Snaith. The squadron also lost two aircraft in an attack in support of the advancing British army on Goch early in February, while 346 lost two in a raid on Worms later in the month.

Elvington's French squadrons suffered particularly badly on the night of 3rd-4th March when three of their aircraft were shot down by German intruders as they returned from an attack on Kamen. One crashed at Sutton-in-Derwent, near Elvington, killing the pilot, S/Ldr Terrien. A second was shot down near Cranwell in Lincolnshire, killing all seven on board, while the third was hit by cannon fire and a wing set on fire as it prepared to land at Croft, the diversion airfield for the Elvington squadrons. The skipper, Capt Notelle, managed to retain control of the aircraft as he overshot and he put the aircraft down in a small wood. The trees ripped off the burning wing and the crew managed to extricate themselves from the wreckage.

The airfield itself was attacked by one Ju 88 which struck a house and crashed close to the airfield boundary, the last Luftwaffe aircraft to crash in Britain during the war. It came in at low level and had turned to run into the airfield from the west when a wing tip clipped a tree and the aircraft hit Dunnington Lodge, which stands on the York-Elvington road about a mile and a half from the airfield. The wreckage of the aircraft came to rest at a nearby road junction. Two women in the house, Mrs Helen Mull and her daughter-in-law Mrs Violet Mull, were killed and Mrs Mull senior's husband, Richard, was badly burnt. His son, Fred, rescued his own son, three-year-old Edgar, and then made repeated attempts to get into the burning house to rescue his wife and his mother. Violet is believed to have run back into the house in an attempt to save her parents-in-law. Reports at the time suggested the German aircraft had machine gunned the Lodge and neighbouring cottages before the crash, but this was not confirmed and the story might have arisen from exploding ammunition in the Ju 88 wreckage. A memorial to all those who died now stands outside Dunnington Lodge.

Both Elvington squadrons flew together on 4 Group's final operation of the war, the attack on gun batteries at Wangerooge on 25th April. NP921 of 347 Squadron was hit by anti-aircraft fire on its bomb run and crashed in flames into the sea. There were no survivors.

The French squadrons remained at Elvington until October when they finally returned to France, their Halifaxes being presented to the newly reformed French Air Force. Sadly, one of the aircraft crashed at Deighton, south-west of Elvington, killing two of the crew.

Elvington was retained by the RAF and in the early 1950s was allocated to the United States Air Force and was greatly extended, including the construction of the 9,800 foot runway which was used briefly by jet bombers then being deployed in Britain during the Cold War. The Americans left in 1958 and the RAF began using Elvington and its long runway as a relief landing ground of No 7 FTS at Church Fenton and later No 1 FTS at Leeming. The airfield itself was sold to William Birch and Sons and during 1983 it appeared that most of the wartime buildings would be demolished. However, following an approach from an Elvington resident, Rachel Semlyn, the company agreed to lease part of the airfield at a nominal rent and the Yorkshire Air Museum came into being.

Uncertainty surrounds the future of the runway. At the time of writing, the Ministry of Defence was considering disposal of it and efforts were being made to raise the money necessary to acquire it for the museum. This would ensure the continuation of the popular air shows, which have become one of the major attractions at Elvington.

14
FINNINGLEY, DONCASTER AND FIRBECK

Born in the Expansion Scheme of the mid-1930s, RAF Finningley was to become perhaps the best known of all Yorkshire airfields in the post-war years. It was home to part of the country's mighty V-bomber arm, played host to some of the biggest air displays staged in Britain, and was chosen for the Royal Review of the Royal Air Force in 1977.

However, its wartime career was, but for a brief spell at the end of 1940, that of bridesmaid, albeit a very important one, to Bomber Command. Its role for virtually the entire war was training, beginning with air crew for 5 Group and ending as the Bomber Command Instructors' School.

The airfield lies on the flat plain south-east of Doncaster and close to the boundaries of South Yorkshire with both Lincolnshire and Nottinghamshire. Communications to the area were excellent and this was one of the deciding factors in almost 450 acres of land being acquired early in 1935 for the construction of the airfield.

It was built very much to the pattern of Expansion period airfields with five large C-type brick hangars and substantial technical and accommodation sites, though these still proved insufficient at the height of its use when some unfortunates had to live in tents around the airfield. An advance party moved in on 30th July 1936 and the airfield officially opened six weeks later with W/Cmdr Gallehawk as its first commanding officer. It was then under the control of 3 Group and its first occupants were to be 102 (Ceylon) and 7 Squadrons, the former destined to play a leading role in the air war to come in Yorkshire.

These were expansionist times for the RAF and the B Flights of both squadrons were later detached to form new squadrons, 7's becoming 76 Squadron and 102's 77 Squadron. Both were to operate for much of the war from Yorkshire airfields. Big though it was, Finningley could not accommodate four squadrons and 77 and 102 left for Honiton.

The outbreak of war saw 7 and 76 Squadrons in residence, both recently re-equipped with a mixture of Hampdens and Ansons. They had been given a training role and, with the transfer of Finningley to 5 Group, it was their task to provide crews for the group's front line squadrons. Their wartime stay at Finningley was brief; within three weeks of the invasion of Poland they left, moving to Upper Heyford in Oxfordshire where they reformed as 16 Operational Training Unit.

Their place at Finningley was taken by 106 Squadron, which moved in from Cottesmore, again with a combination of Hampdens and Ansons to continue to provide training for 5 Group's Hampden squadrons. The squadron was to remain at Finningley until February 1941, operating for most of that period in a training capacity. They were to lose some 20 Hampdens during this period, five of them during the early autumn of 1940 when they were briefly used operationally in what became known as the Battle of the Barges.

The first aircraft to be lost came on 24th October 1939 when P/O Dier undershot during night flying training and clipped trees near the airfield boundary, writing off L4175 and suffering a broken leg for his pains. At the time, crews were using a small bombing range near Haxey and another aircraft crashed here after stalling at low level. The crew escaped serious injury.

Finningley's safety record was remarkably good at this period – a reflection of the high quality of airmanship in the pre-war RAF – and it wasn't until the late summer of 1940 that losses began to increase. Four men were killed when their Hampden dived into the ground at Owston Ferry after being dazzled by searchlights during a training exercise; four more died when their Hampden hit a balloon cable over Coventry; another crew were lost when their aircraft blew up in the air over Buckinghamshire. A gunner was killed when his Hampden was mistakenly attacked by Spitfires during a cross-country exercise.

It was on 8th September 1940, when the threat of invasion was very real, that 106 Squadron became operational. Its training role continued, but attacks on Channel and North Sea ports took priority. P/O McGregor and his crew were the squadron's first operational casualties, their aircraft shot down by flak over the Elbe estuary early on 19th September. A week later P/O Huggins was the only survivor when his aircraft ran out of fuel and crashed in Somerset on its return from a minelaying operation. Another crew were lost over Lorient in November and the following month Sgt Sidebotham and his crew died when their Hampden ditched in the North Sea after another minelaying sortie. 106's final operational loss from Finningley was the Hampden of F/Lt Burr-Thomas which failed to return from St Nazaire early in February 1941. Two weeks later the squadron became fully operational and moved to Coningsby in Lincolnshire. It left behind C Flight which provided the nucleus for Finningley's next occupants, 25 OTU.

By this time Finningley was also being used by 1507 BAT Flight, which had arrived in January as 7 Blind Approach Training Flight, the renumbering being part of a change in the organisation of training in Bomber Command. Its Blenheims and Ansons were later replaced by Oxfords for its role in teaching pilots blind landing techniques.

It was during the early months of 1941 that Finningley was bombed on four occasions, the first occurring just before 106 Squadron left, one aircraft being slightly damaged. A second raid nine days later destroyed a hut and injured an airman, although only two of the eight bombs dropped exploded. Two attacks in May left a hangar, part of the married quarters and an Anson damaged.

Overcrowding and the lack of hardened runways led to Bircotes, just south of Bawtry, and Balderton, near Newark being used as temporary satellites. It was the use of Balderton that was to lead to the worst tragedy of the war involving an aircraft from Finningley.

Balderton had been built as a bomber airfield just south of Newark and its runways were being used by the 25 OTU Hampdens for training purposes. Shortly after midnight on 16th August 1941 Sgt Baldachin was on his final approach when a wing tip clipped some tall trees and the aircraft crashed into a house in London Road, Balderton where a Mrs Brompton and her seven children were asleep. Mrs Brompton managed to carry one of her children to safety from the burning house but the other six, aged between 18 and five, died in the flames along with Sgt Baldachin and his observer, Sgt Wood. The air gunner, Sgt David Macdonald, escaped with minor injuries, his attempts to save Sgt Wood being thwarted when the Hampden's fuel tanks exploded. Two other houses were destroyed in the crash but the occupants escaped injury.

Accidents like this were a tragic by-product of war and the wonder was that more civilians were not killed in the numerous crashes involving units like 25 OTU. It lost two aircraft to balloon barrages, the first in Concorde Park, Rotherham Road, Sheffield in April and the second over Weybridge in October. Five airmen were killed but no one on the ground was injured.

25 OTU used a variety of aircraft in its time at Finningley, including Manchesters and Wellingtons, which it used operationally as part of the '1,000' attacks on Cologne, Essen and Bremen in May and June of 1942.

The Essen raid is remembered in particular by Mrs Irene Bennet, then LACW Irene Shaw, a WAAF who spent three years in the signals section at Finningley. 'My job involved working on the teleprinters and the switchboard and on this particular day I was taking messages off the teleprinter. I had to make sure that each of a number of officers received copies, with the top copy going to the operations room, which was next door. I remember reading this particular message because it gave details of an attack that night – the target was to be Essen – and the various squadrons and airfields taking part and it stipulated how many aircraft would be going from each, what their bomb load would be and how much fuel they should carry.

'I took the top copy into the operations room and gave it to a sergeant and walked out, thinking no more of it. The next minute the door opened and I was ordered to come in. I wondered what I had done wrong. I was asked who had taken the message and I said I had and was then asked if I had read it. The officer said that it was a terrible breach of security. No message like this should be sent in plain language, it should be in cipher. I was told that in the circumstances I would be confined to camp until the raid was over as, however innocently, I might let something slip. I told him I had signed the Official Secrets Act but that cut no ice. I had to stay on the camp. I then couldn't wait to get back to read the rest of the message – it was certainly more interesting than the usual messages we got.'

By this time 25 OTU was equipped with Wellington ICs and during the summer and early autumn of 1942 they were used occasionally on Main Force attacks on German targets. The first 1,000 bomber raid, on

Cpl Irene Shaw, Finningley, 1944. (Mrs Irene Bennet)

Cologne on the night of 30th-31st May, cost 25 OTU one of its Wellingtons, P/O Hughes and his five-man crew baling out of their burning aircraft. The following night a second Wellington was lost over Essen while an attack on Dusseldorf on 31st July-1st August saw four of the unit's Wellingtons shot down with the loss of 20 men, all but 15 of whom were killed. Two more aircraft were lost and all ten crew members killed in another attack on Dusseldorf on 10th-11th September with another failing to return from Essen five nights later. Bomber Command could ill-afford to lose so many fledgling crews and seasoned instructors and OTU aircraft were not sent again on Main Force attacks over Germany.

The heavy use of the airfield by the OTU inevitably led to a deterioration of facilities and it was briefly closed for flying early in 1943, a period which coincided with the disbandment of 25 OTU. Its replacement was 18 OTU, which moved in from Bramcote and was also equipped with Wellingtons together with a few Defiants, Lysanders and Martinets, which were used for target towing.

The training routine went on much as before, the cross-country flights and circuits and bumps being augmented by the use of OTU

An 18 OTU Wellington about to land across one of the boundary roads at Finningley. (Ron Barrowcliffe)

aircraft on 'spoof' raids designed to fool German radar. This involved groups of aircraft flying to predetermined points in the North Sea before turning for home, the hope being that these feints would draw the defenders away from the real targets of Bomber Command. Occasionally the Wellingtons would fly across northern France or the Low Countries scattering leaflets aimed at convincing the civilians that freedom was not far away.

1507 BAT Flight left for Warboys in the spring of 1943 and was replaced almost immediately by 1521 BAT Flight, which arrived from Stradishall. Finningley was now earmarked for hardened runways but, before this work could commence, a new satellite airfield at Worksop was opened in the autumn of 1943, Bircotes being down-graded and used only by the 1 Group Communications Flight, which had been a 'lodger' at Finningley since the move of the group's HQ to Bawtry Hall.

Interestingly, the runways at Finningley were laid not by one of the many contractors engaged on this work in Yorkshire and Lincolnshire, but by 5016 Airfield Construction Squadron, one of the units created by the RAF Works Service in 1941 initially to repair bomb damaged airfields. Later, as Luftwaffe attacks decreased, the squadrons were used for other civil engineering projects, the runways at Finningley being one of the largest tackled in Yorkshire.

Finningley reopened in May 1944, 18 OTU moving back in from Worksop. Bomber Command was now approaching the peak of its expansion programme and to keep pace with the demand for more and more crews, the small airfield at Doncaster was pressed into use as an additional satellite.

18 OTU was finally disbanded in the late autumn of 1944 and was replaced at Finningley by the Bomber Command Instructors School, which came into being on 5th December, operating a mixture of Lancasters, Halifaxes and Wellingtons. The school brought together the vast amount of talent and experience in Bomber Command to help further improve the training being given to crews moving up through the heavy conversion units.

Throughout the war, Finningley had proved a popular posting for most who served there. Irene Bennett, whom we have already met, went there in 1940 when she finished a signals course at Cranwell.

'I half expected to be posted to Iceland but I could hardly believe my luck when I was told it was Finningley as my family lived nearby in Sheffield and I was able to nip home two or three times a week without a leave pass,' said Mrs Bennett.

WAAFs in the signals section were accommodated in some of the married quarters, three or four occupying each two-bedroomed house. This was something of a step down from Irene's first night at Finningley – she and a draft from Cranwell were housed in one of the houses used in peace-time by the senior officers and their family.

It was a popular place to be for the WAAFs and particularly for Irene. She worked shifts which meant when she finished work at noon and wasn't on duty until the next morning she could slip out to catch a bus to Rotherham, then a tram into Sheffield city centre and then another tram home to Eccleshall Road where her family lived, all without asking permission. 'Sometimes I used to get a leave chit just to make it official,' she said.

Finningley straddled the boundaries of two licensing divisions, much to the delight of air crew and ground staff alike. 'One pub would close at 10 o'clock, which was the same time as all the pubs in Sheffield, but the other pub in Finningley must have been in a different area so it closed at 10.30. So come 10 o'clock everyone would pile out of one pub into another,' recalled Irene.

Dorothy James of Rawmarsh served at Finningley from late in 1943 until 1945 as LACW Dorothy Atkin. Mrs James was a flight mechanic and worked on Merlins fitted to Wellingtons, Lancasters and Spitfires. The mechanics worked in two 'gangs', one being responsible for the port engines, and the other the starboard engines. She was one of two WAAFs in the 'gangs' and remembers being treated 'just like one of the boys'.

She had volunteered for the job at Insworth. 'I told them I didn't want to be a cook – I could do that at home!' said Mrs James. 'It was a great job and we loved almost every minute of it. It wasn't a feminine job, we wore greasy overalls and had to do the same work as the men, engine changes, carbs, changing plugs, removing propellers and refuelling the aircraft, but we enjoyed it.

'I remember one day we were asked to do an engine change on a Wellington which was needed for an air test at 8 am the following day. It meant working through the night. We were given a break for supper and, as we made our way back, one of the WAAF officers stopped us and asked where we were going. We told her and she said she wasn't going to have her WAAFs working through the night and it was the last time we did.'

'One of the highlights of the job was being invited to go up for air tests in the aircraft. When we did it was our job to keep an eye on the dials for the oil pressure and the like. We also had time to enjoy the flight and I remember going up three times in Wellingtons and twice in Lancasters. It was lovely.'

Mrs James also worked for a while at the old Doncaster airport, servicing Dakotas and working on Oxfords and Ansons. But it is Finningley she remembers as the best place she served in the war. It was friendly and the WAAFs enjoyed themselves, Dorothy helping out as the dresser for a concert party called The Slipstream, which put on regular shows at Finningley and Lindholme

The airfield was still being used by the BCIS when the war ended. That September Finningley staged the first of many hugely successful Battle of Britain air displays. The airfield was to continue in its training role until the mid-1950s when it was upgraded to become the home of two of the RAF's Vulcan bomber squadrons. With echoes of wartime, its operational period was brief and by the early 1960s it began training crews for Vulcans and Victors. When the V-bombers were phased out, Finningley took on a variety of training roles for the RAF until its closure in the mid-1990s.

Aircraft had been using land around Doncaster racecourse since 1909, the Second World War airstrip opening in 1939 when it was used by 7 (Aircrew) OTU, flying a handful of Ansons and Hampdens. The following year 271 Squadron was formed at Doncaster, from the old National Air Communications unit, its task being to provide aircraft for communication duties, flying a mixture of Bombays, Hadrians, Harrows, Sparrows and even a Ford Tri-Motor. It was also to be used briefly by 613 Squadron, flying Curtiss Tomahawks.

The Wellingtons of 18 OTU arrived in June 1943 and later that year facilities at the airfield were used to carry out modifications on newly-arrived Dakotas before they went into squadron service with the RAF.

In 1944 271 Squadron finally departed, leaving behind its Sparrow aircraft to form an Ambulance Flight which operated from Doncaster until the end of the war when the airfield was closed to military flying.

Firbeck was the most southerly of all Yorkshire's wartime airfields. It lay just across the county boundary with Nottinghamshire in the mining area between Worksop and Doncaster and was used between 1940 and 1945 by training and army co-operation units.

The site was laid out early in 1940 with a number of Blister hangars being erected. A grass runway was laid out and some accommodation huts were erected around the airfield and in the grounds of neighbouring Firbeck Hall.

The airfield was first used in the early autumn of 1940 by 613 (City of Manchester) Squadron, which flew its Lysanders in an army co-operation role. It was in residence at Firbeck until April 1942 when it was replaced by 654 Squadron, equipped with Austers. This, too, moved at the end of April 1943 and was replaced by a new Lysander squadron, 659, which formed at Firbeck before leaving in August that year.

For the remainder of the war Firbeck was used as a relief landing ground by the Tiger Moths of 25 (Polish) Elementary Flying Training School, which was based at Hucknall in Nottinghamshire until the end of the war when flying ceased and the airfield was finally closed.

15
FULL SUTTON

Full Sutton, near York, is currently the home of one of the country's top security prisons. More than half a century ago it had the distinction of being the last operational airfield to be built for Bomber Command. It was formally opened in mid-May 1944 and was to be the final wartime home of one of Yorkshire's finest squadrons, 77.

It was to be an operational bomber airfield for just 357 days but in that time 77 Squadron was engaged in most of the key raids staged by Bomber Command in the final year of the war. It also played an important role in keeping the British Army supplied with fuel during the crucial campaign in the Low Countries in the early autumn of 1944. Those 357 days were to cost 77 Squadron the lives of 135 men and some 27 aircraft, seven of them in one dreadful night in June 1944 when virtually a third of the squadron was shot down in a raid on the Ruhr.

The original site selected by the Air Ministry for a bomber airfield in this part of Yorkshire was at Huggate Wold, mid-way between York and Driffield. Before work could start a better site was found at Full Sutton, close to the Saxon battleground at nearby Stamford Bridge, some nine miles east of York. It was to be the final major airfield contract of the war for many of the men engaged on the work of laying three concrete runways and erecting two T2 and a single B1 hangar. The work had begun in the late summer of 1943 and was finished in time for the arrival of 77 Squadron from Elvington.

77 had been flying heavy bombers from the Yorkshire airfields since the summer of 1938 and was about to begin converting to the Halifax Mk III when the order came through to move the few miles from Elvington to Full Sutton. It flew its last operation from Elvington to Lens on 10th May before beginning the move to what was to become its final wartime home. Several crews remained behind for some weeks to

Halifax III of 77 Squadron with crew at Full Sutton, 1944. Pictured are: F/O Gordon Hansen RAAF (pilot), Sgt Morley (navigator), F/Sgt Bairstow (bomb aimer), F/Sgt Knapp (wireless operator), Sgt Forster (flight engineer), Sgt Talbot (mid-upper gunner) and Sgt Smith (rear gunner). (Gordon Hansen)

assist Elvington's new occupants, 346 and 347 Squadrons of the Free French Air Force.

New though it was, Full Sutton looked very much like every other wartime bomber airfield with its collection of Maycrete and Nissen huts, hangars and the ever-present mud. In his wartime history of 77 Squadron, Harry Shinkfield refers to a letter written home by flight engineer Sgt Reg Rose on 17th May, the day after he and his crew arrived on the squadron from 1658 HCU at Riccall. 'This place is out in the wilds, nearest village about two or three miles, I think. It's a good job I have my bicycle. The grub is certainly better, everything brand new.' Within a week Sgt Rose and three of his crew were dead, killed when their aircraft was shot down in 77 Squadron's first operation from Full Sutton, an attack on the marshalling yards at Orleans on the night of 22nd May.

D-Day saw 77 Squadron attacking German troop concentrations around Maisy and St Lô, the only casualty being a Halifax which

Flying control at RAF Full Sutton. (Ron Barrowcliffe)

crashed on take-off, the crew escaping injury. Two nights later, however, P/O Gordon Hyde and his crew died when their aircraft crashed as it was taking off from Alençon. The deaths of seven young men so close to the airfield was a blow for everyone at Full Sutton, but there was much worse to come.

On the night of 16th-17th June the squadron was detailed to provide 25 Halifaxes for an attack on the synthetic oil plant at Sterkrade in the Ruhr as part of a force of 321 aircraft, mainly Halifaxes and Lancasters drawn from squadrons in Yorkshire and north Lincolnshire. The attack was a failure for Bomber Command and a disaster for 77 Squadron. Thick cloud and ineffective marking meant little damage was caused and the routing of the bomber stream close to a German night fighter beacon led to easy pickings for the Luftwaffe crews, who shot down 21 aircraft while the flak gunners brought down another ten.

Quite why 77 Squadron should suffer so grievously was one of those tricks of fate which made the life of a bomber crew so uncertain. There was no hint of what lay in store for the Full Sutton Halifaxes and their crews when the first aircraft, piloted by S/Ldr Welch, lifted off at 10.30 pm on the night of 16th June. He had to return early after excessive vibration developed in the aircraft, dumping his bombs in the sea before landing back at Carnaby. Another aircraft, F/Sgt Currie's E-Easy, failed to take off but the other 23 joined 139 other 4 Group Halifaxes, 147 Lancasters from 1 and 6 Groups and twelve 8 Group Mosquitos as they headed across the North Sea. A second raid that night, by 405 Lancasters, Halifaxes and Mosquitos, on V1 sites in the Pas de Calais region, was expected to draw off some of the night fighters.

That quite clearly did not happen. Instead, the routing of the bomber stream took it within a few miles of the fighter beacon at Bocholt, which had been chosen that night by the Luftwaffe controllers as one of the holding points for their night fighters. At least two of the 77 Squadron aircraft lost are known to have been brought down by fighters – the exact fate of the others has never been determined.

One which fell victim to a night fighter operating out of Schiphol – now Amsterdam's international airport – was NA508, Full Sutton's A-Able, which was flown by F/Sgt R. Blair. Five of the crew, including the pilot, were Australian and there were no survivors. The Halifax crashed in marshy ground near Amsterdam and it was to be another 47 years before all the bodies were recovered from the crash site and finally buried with full military honours.

Another night fighter victim was MZ705. It was attacked over Holland by a Ju 88, which damaged both turrets, part of the fuselage and the port wing. Both engines were damaged, the flaps shot away and a fire was started. The night fighter, in the meantime, was hit by return fire from the Halifax's gunners and was seen to dive away in flames. With the Halifax now on fire, the pilot, P/O Judd made for the emergency airfield at Woodbridge but it quickly became clear he would not make it. The radio had been shattered in the attack along with most of the other instruments and lights, making conditions for ditching very difficult indeed. However, the resourceful wireless operator, Sgt Trengrove, used his trailing aerial to give the pilot a height indication, reeling out the aerial and running it over a pencil laid across the drum. When the weights on the aerial hit the water the pencil snapped and the wireless operator raced back to his crash position shouting "Two hundred feet!", just the length of wire trailing below the Halifax. Helped by this information, P/O Judd put the aircraft down on the water some 20 miles off the Dutch coast and the crew scrambled into their life raft. They were spotted shortly afterwards by a Warwick of Coastal Command, which was out looking for E-boats. It contacted Royal Navy units in the area and MTB 685, commanded by Lt/Cmdr Hughes RNVR, soon picked up the crew and, remarkably considering no SOS had been sent, they were back in Felixstowe later that morning.

There were other survivors that night. P/O Alan Crain's MZ715 was seen to explode in mid-air over Holland, whether as a result of flak or night fighter is unclear, and just the wireless operator, W/O Owen, survived. Six of the crew of MZ711 baled out when their aircraft was hit over Germany and became PoWs. The body of the navigator, P/O Tom Cusson, was later found in the wreckage. All seven on board NA524, including the American pilot, F/O Shaw, were later to be reported as prisoners of war while three men managed to bale out of MZ698 when it was shot down over Holland. The navigator, F/Sgt Bulmer, and wireless operator, F/Sgt Needham, were quickly captured but the Australian bomb-aimer, F/Sgt Jack Nott, evaded pursuit. Three weeks later he was discovered by the Gestapo hiding in a house in Tilburg with a Canadian airman from 431 Squadron at Tholthorpe and an RAF officer from 83 Squadron at Coningsby in Lincolnshire. All three were shot and the Dutch woman in whose home they were hiding, Mrs Coba Pulskens, was taken to the Vught concentration camp where she was executed.

The final aircraft lost from Full Sutton that night was MZ545 which is believed to have crashed in the sea off the Dutch coast. The bodies of five of the crew, including the Australian pilot, P/O Harold Bird, were later washed ashore. Those of the mid-upper gunner, F/Sgt Fred Meeghan and the bomb aimer, F/O Stuart MacKay, were never found and their names are recorded on the Runnymede Memorial.

Another 77 Squadron Halifax, MZ673, suffered a hydraulics failure after bombing and later crash-landed at Carnaby. The crew escaped injury but the aircraft, 77's B-Baker, was damaged beyond repair.

There was little time to grieve at Full Sutton. Replacement aircraft and crews quickly arrived and within a week another major raid was launched, this time on rocket sites in northern France. Just one Halifax failed to return, MZ702 crashing in the Channel after being involved in a mid-air collision with an unidentified aircraft over Laon. Only the wireless operator, Sgt Dade, survived. Two nights later another Halifax was lost in similar circumstances when 77's V-Victor collided with a Halifax from 102 Squadron at nearby Pocklington over Fontaine L'Etalon. All 14 men on board the two aircraft were killed.

A third attack on rocket sites in France resulted in the loss of yet another Halifax from Full Sutton, MZ748 being shot down near the target on the night of 28th-29th June. Three of the crew were killed, two captured and two evaded.

Replacement crews were arriving thick and fast at Full Sutton during the summer of 1944. Stuart Cook was the rear gunner in a crew which arrived in August.

After OTU at Moreton-in-the-Marsh in Gloucestershire, it was found that all the 4 Group heavy conversion units were full so a place was found for them in neighbouring 6 Group at 1666 HCU at Wombleton near Kirbymoorside.

Full Sutton had only been open for around 10 weeks when they arrived, but they were not aware they had been posted to what was to become the last airfield to open in Bomber Command during the war.

'It was pretty much like everywhere else we'd been in the RAF, wide open, spread out and very utilitarian,' said Mr Cook. 'In fact it wasn't until some years ago that I found out a bit more about the very short history of Full Sutton. As far as we were concerned then, it was as cold and muddy as anywhere else.'

Their first operation was a daylight attack on railway yards at Munster on 12th September. 'At the briefing we were told that the flak

A 77 Squadron Halifax en route for the Ruhr seen through the wireless operator's window of another Halifax from the squadron, October 1944. (Stuart Cook)

Party time at Full Sutton, September 1944. Sitting on the barrels are (l to r): 77 Squadron CO W/Cmdr Roncoroni, the gunnery leader and F/Lt Bill Walker RCAF. (Stuart Cook)

was likely to be light and there would be little opposition. When we got there the sky was so full of flak bursts you could have lowered the wheels and taxied across it. Our thought coming back was if that was light opposition, what was the heavy stuff like?' 4 Group lost two Halifaxes from that attack, including one from 77 Squadron at Full Sutton. The pilot, F/O Raymond Cave, was killed along with two of his crew when their Halifax, coded KN-Q, was hit by flak as it left the target area.

Stuart Cook and his crew had completed just three operations when their pilot, who suffered from TB, was grounded and they were sent to Marston Moor to pick up a new pilot, a man who had already done one tour on Wellingtons in the Middle East. Back at Full Sutton, they completed another 17 before their second pilot became tour-expired. The six remaining crew members were then posted to 102 Squadron at Pocklington where they were joined by their third pilot. By this time, however, the war was nearly over and, although briefed for a number of raids, they were not to fly operationally again.

Pocklington, however, was to play an important part in Stuart Cook's life. It was there he met his future wife – in the town's Oakhouse dance hall (later, perhaps inappropriately, the Zillertal). When the war ended they moved to Canada and Stuart was to spend a number of years in the RCAF, with whose members he had trained at Wombleton in 1944. The couple returned to England in the 1970s and Stuart now lives close to the old airfield at Pocklington.

The late summer of 1944 gave 77 Squadron a respite from the scale of losses it had suffered in May and June. The crew of one Halifax died when their aircraft, MZ768, broke up, crashed and burned on the North Yorkshire Moors after the pilot lost control in July, while the only loss in August was MZ347, which failed to return from a raid on Braunschweig. Only the body of the navigator was ever found. A daylight attack on Munster on 12th September, as we have seen, cost the squadron another Halifax and, with it, the lives of three men, including the pilot, F/O Raymond Cave. His was to be the last Halifax

F/O Bob Pont's crew and ground crew at Full Sutton before a daylight raid, March 1945. Pictured are (back row, l to r): one of the fitters, F/Sgt Don Morphew (mid-upper gunner), F/Sgt Jim Watson (navigator), F/O Pont, F/Sgt Stu Cook (bomb aimer), Sgt George Timberlake (flight engineer); (front): a member of the ground crew, F/Sgt Ray Harris RAAF (wireless operator), F/Sgt Pete Matthews (rear gunner) and a third member of the ground crew. (Stuart Cook)

77 Squadron lost for almost two months.

Halifaxes from Full Sutton were involved in a novel but effective operation during late September and early October when they were used to ferry over 430,000 gallons of petrol to Melsbroek airfield near Brussels for the British 2nd Army, which had virtually outrun its own fuel supplies and was in danger of grinding to a halt. The four squadrons which made up 4 Group's 42 Base, which included Full Sutton, were chosen for the task and the first trials were flown in a 77 Squadron Halifax piloted by F/Lt Jimmy Hale. His Halifax was so full of four-gallon jerry cans he had to leave behind his two gunners. It proved to be a success, but the final loads were reduced to permit the Halifaxes to take along their gunners.

Over the next week 435 sorties were flown from Full Sutton, Pocklington and Elvington – 175 of them by 77 Squadron – and a total of 432,840 gallons of fuel delivered for Montgomery's troops.

The day after the petrol runs ended, 77 Squadron was back in action with a raid on the synthetic oil plant at Scholven/Buer. It was the first of eleven raids mounted by the squadron during October, all without loss. An attack on Dusseldorf early in November, however, saw one aircraft, MZ829, fail to return. It was later learned the Halifax had crashed in the Ardennes region of Belgium. There were no survivors.

There was better luck for F/Lt Beadle's crew on 16th November when their aircraft was hit by flak while supporting American troops near Julich. The entire crew managed to bale out and landed behind Allied lines, returning to Full Sutton within a matter of days. It was the same story for F/Sgt Smith's crew when their Halifax was hit by 'friendly' incendiaries over Essen on 28th November. The incendiaries struck while the Halifax's bomb doors were still open and the draught quickly fanned the flames. Despite the efforts of the crew, it quickly became clear that MZ923 was not going to make it back to Yorkshire and, once over the Allied lines, the crew jumped to safety.

December saw 77 involved in 14 raids with the loss of just one aircraft, MZ428 which failed to return from Osnabruck. The bodies of the crew were never found. Another aircraft, MZ336, was wrecked when it hit a hangar at Manston while attempting to land in a strong cross wind following an attack on Duisburg.

77 Squadron was in action almost constantly in January 1945, despite appalling weather. One aircraft was wrecked when an engine cut on take-off for Ludwigshafen on 2nd January and another in a forced landing near Stamford Bridge when the starboard inner failed on take-

off for Saarbrucken. In both instances the crews escaped injury but six members of the crew of MZ360 died when their aircraft failed to return from Hanover. The only survivor was the pilot, F/O Fitzgerald. Another aircraft and its crew were lost when MZ812, KN-U, was lost in a mining operation off Kiel on 12th January.

Thirteen operations in February cost 77 Squadron four aircraft and the lives of 23 men. One of them was F/Lt John Braund, the pilot of MZ924 which crashed in Denmark during a mining operation. He was the twin brother of F/Lt Marwood Braund, who had died just a month earlier in 77 Squadron's U-Uncle.

The end of the war was now very much in sight and numerous operations were scrubbed as possible targets were overrun by Allied troops. Those that did take place still exacted a toll from the attackers. RG507 was brought down by flak in an attack on a benzol plant near Bottrop on 15th March when all but the mid-upper, F/O 'Jack' Frost, survived. The last aircraft to be lost from Full Sutton was RG529, in an attack on Witten on 19th March 1945. All seven men on board were killed.

Operations continued from Full Sutton until 25th April when 19 aircraft from 77 Squadron were part of a large force of Halifaxes which bombed gun batteries on the island of Wangerooge.

On the day that the war in Europe formally ended 77 Squadron, along with many other 4 Group squadrons, was transferred to Transport Command and its Halifaxes were replaced with Dakotas by the beginning of August. Three weeks later 77 Squadron began to move out of Full Sutton and the airfield was put on a care and maintenance basis until November when 231 Squadron reformed there, using a mixture of Lancasters and Lancastrian transports. Its tenure was to be short-lived and by May 1946 the only occupants at Full Sutton were No 30 Aircrew Holding Unit, formed to speed the demobilisation of air crew.

Full Sutton closed in April 1947, reopening in 1951 during the Korean War as the home of 207 Advanced Flying School. It continued in this role until late 1954 when it was allocated to the USAF as a reserve airfield, but it was never used operationally. It was returned to RAF control in 1957 and used to house Thor missiles of 102 Squadron, which had its headquarters at Driffield. This disbanded in 1963 and RAF Full Sutton finally closed. The site was used for a variety of purposes before part of it was acquired by the prison service.

16
HOLME-ON-SPALDING MOOR

Rising above the flat plain which stretches from the Humber towards York is a solitary hill. On it stands the church of All Saints, which looks down on the straggling village of Holme-on-Spalding Moor. Between 1941 and 1945 that church was both a beacon and a hazard to the hundreds of young men who served on the bomber airfield which took its name from the village.

Holme-on-Spalding Moor was among a number of airfields in East and South Yorkshire which were to be used by both 1 and 4 Groups of Bomber Command and in turn by units operating Wellingtons, Lancasters and Halifaxes. But it is through 76 Squadron that the airfield is best remembered, a squadron which was to fly more operations in Halifaxes than any other unit and which lost over 100 aircraft during its time at Holme-on-Spalding Moor.

It was typical of wartime bomber airfields in Yorkshire, cold and uncomfortable, yet it won a place in the hearts of all those who served there and went through so much together. Some, however, remember the comradeship with more affection than the conditions. James Hampton, in his book *Selected for Aircrew*, recalled that most of the wooden furniture had been burnt on the stoves and asbestos shelves had been fitted above beds to prevent any further acts of arson. He wrote: 'On no other RAF station, before or after, did I ever encounter such intolerable living conditions. Outside ... there were muddy paths leading to the ablutions. The washing facilities were primitive and little interest was taken in trying to improve them or even maintain them properly.'

He remembered an almost complete lack of plugs for washbasins, something which was '... endemic in the wartime RAF and appeared to be accepted by a higher authority as a law of nature that could never be changed.' By and large, aircrew accepted these conditions with good humour. He added: 'Those who didn't were usually advised by their fellows that if they couldn't take a joke, they shouldn't have joined!'

The site on Holme Common between the villages of Holme and Spaldington was identified as suitable for a bomber airfield during the summer of 1940 and work began almost immediately on its construction. By the summer of 1941 the airfield was deemed to be ready and officially opened as a 1 Group station on 8th August when 20 BAT Flight was formed, equipped with Oxfords. In the meantime, Holme's first bomber squadron, 458 (RAAF), was on its way from Australia where it had formed in July. It arrived on 25th August and was equipped with Wellington Mk IVs and led by W/Cmdr Mulholland, who already had a DFC to his name and considerable experience behind him. It flew its first operation on the night of 20th October when two aircraft went to Emden and eight to Antwerp, one of which failed to return. Five of the crew were killed, including the second pilot Sgt Crittenden, the first Australian to be killed in an RAAF bomber squadron.

By the end of the year 458 was given notice of its transfer to the Middle East and flew its last operation from Holme-on-Spalding Moor on 9th January 1942 to Cherbourg, one aircraft being lost to flak and another hitting high tension cables as it tried to land in Dorset with flak damage. The two losses cost 458 the lives of ten men with two others seriously injured. The squadron finally left Yorkshire early in February, initially for Malta.

Its short operational life had highlighted a number of shortcomings at Holme and a major expansion programme began in March, including the construction of further hangars – the airfield was eventually to have six as a Base HQ station – and the provision of accommodation for more air and ground crews.

It was to be September before its next operational unit moved in, 101 Squadron arriving from Stradishall where it had flown Wellingtons in 3 Group. In the interim the airfield had been used briefly by 460 Squadron's Conversion Flight, which brought its Halifaxes the few miles from Breighton. It had been planned to equip 1 Group's squadrons with Halifaxes (103 already had them across the Humber at Elsham Wold) but it was around this time that the decision was

Sgt Marcel Fussell, pictured following his posting to 101 Squadron. (Mrs Y. Bartlett)

made at Bomber Command HQ to equip 1 Group with the new Lancasters already in service with 5 Group further south in Lincolnshire. In the meantime some limited operational flying was carried out by the handful of Wellington crews awaiting their conversion courses.

In the early autumn of 1942 a young pilot, 20-year-old F/Sgt Marcel Fussell, was posted to Holme-on-Spalding Moor with his Wellington crew to join 101 Squadron. As he arrived the majority of 101's crews were leaving to convert to Lancasters at Wigsley, near Newark, home of a 5 Group heavy conversion unit. During the short period he was at Holme, Marcel Fussell wrote regularly to his family in Dorchester. Holme, he declared, was 'not at all bad'. The food was good and, for wartime, plentiful and he was issued with a bike. He went on: 'Yorkshire is full of fogs and mists. I bet it will be cold in the winter but we have a very good stove in our room (three of us). Our hut is set in a wood, so there is plenty of fuel.'

F/Sgt Fussell and his crew went to Krefeld where he told his parents he hoped they had hit the target despite the haze. Three nights later it was Aachen but the weather was so bad, Marcel Fussell wrote, that they had to bring their bombs back, the CO at Holme complimenting him on his landing with a full bomb load after a six and a half hour trip. Two nights later, however, the weather cleared sufficiently for the handful of Wellingtons at Holme to join in a raid by 237 aircraft on Osnabruck. 'The town was good and properly hit with some good fires going when we left,' he wrote.

With the bulk of the squadron back from Wigsley with their Lancasters, it was the turn of F/Sgt Fussell's crew to join a conversion course. Instead of the HCU in Nottinghamshire, they were sent a few miles down the road to Breighton where 460 was in the process of converting from Halifaxes to Lancasters. Breighton came as something of a shock to young Marcel Fussell. He and his crew were accommodated in draughty Nissen huts, which were usually cold despite the hot stove in the centre. The weather was miserable with little or no flying and instead, interminable lectures. He wrote to his parents: 'I know just about everything about the Lancaster, except how to fly it!'

When flying was possible, the crews from 101 hardly got a look in. The few Lancasters available were invariably allocated to the Australians of 460 and young F/Sgt Fussel became so frustrated he biked back to Holme to report what was happening to his CO. The 101 crews were immediately ordered back to Holme and the following day a Lancaster and instructor arrived from Breighton to commence a conversion course for the remaining Wellington crews.

On Tuesday, 8th December he wrote home to tell his parents that two nights before he and his crew flew operationally for the first time in a Lancaster. They were heading for Mannheim when an engine failed over Luxembourg and they had to turn for home, dropping their 4,000lb bomb in the Channel, where it exploded 'with a colossal bang'.

On the afternoon of 16th December he wrote excitedly to his parents to tell them he would be coming home to Dorchester on 21st December and did not have to return from leave until the 27th. 'I don't mind where we go for a walk as long as there is a pub to visit en route,' he wrote.

That evening F/Sgt Fussell and his crew were briefed for a mining sortie off the French coast. What happened during that sortie was never established but in the early hours of 17th December, Lancaster W4319 SR-S crossed the English coast near Redcar. There was no signal from its IFF, no firing of the colours of the day. At the time there was a small-scale German raid going on in the North East and the anti-aircraft defences were on full alert. The gunners opened fire on the lone aircraft

76 Squadron crews at Holme-on-Spalding Moor boarding transport for their aircraft prior to a raid on Kassel, 22nd October 1943. (Grace Van den Bos)

143

and, in all probability, cheered as they saw it hit and begin its last plunge to earth. It came down in a field a mile from the town, just alongside the Redcar South Bank road. The seven men on board, Marcel Fussell and Sgts Worsnop, McIntyre, O'Malley, McLean, George and Warren, were all killed instantly.

In a letter to his parents some two months later, W/Cmdr Reddick, the CO and Marcel Fussell's flight commander at the time of his death, said it was likely the Lancaster had been damaged by enemy action and had been off track when it approached the English coast. It was, he said, an unfortunate accident of war and no blame could be attached to the crew or the gunners on the ground.

His was the third Lancaster lost by 101 during its time at Holme. It was to be followed by a further 28 before the squadron left for its new Lincolnshire home at Ludford Magna in mid-June 1943. Six of those

A 76 Squadron crew at Holme-on-Spalding Moor as their Halifax V LK912 was being refuelled, late 1943. They are (l to r): F/O Tony Walker (rear gunner), Sgt Cal Rathmell (bomb aimer), Sgt Jack Bates (flight engineer), F/O Roy Bolt (pilot), Sgt Joe Josey (wireless operator), Sgt Harry Van den Bos (mid-upper gunner) and P/O Fred Hall (navigator). The crew survived their tour but this particular aircraft was lost in a raid on Magdeburg, January 1944. (Grace Van den Bos)

were lost in a single night, an attack on Dortmund on the night of 4th May. The raid cost the lives of 20 men. Seven more were injured and the single survivor of the night fighter attack became a prisoner of war.

101's departure in June – at Ludford they were selected to become Bomber Command's first electronic counter-measures squadron – saw Holme-on-Spalding Moor transferred to 4 Group. It was quickly occupied by 76 Squadron, which moved from Linton-on-Ouse, its partner squadron there, 78, moving at the same time to Breighton.

The move coincided with the height of what became known as the Battle of the Ruhr. 76's first operation from its new home came on the night of 22nd-23rd June when some 557 bombers attacked Mulheim. It was a particularly effective raid but it cost the new tenants of Holme-on-Spalding Moor one of its Mk V Halifaxes, MP-Q, which was shot down by a night fighter over Holland. Flying as second pilot in the aircraft was the new station commander, G/Capt Wilson. He became a PoW along with six other members of the crew – the seventh died when his parachute failed to open.

Raids on Wuppertal and Cologne cost the squadron three more aircraft (and 17 men killed and four more as prisoners) before the end of the month. These were hard times for the Halifax squadrons in 4 Group and in its first six months at Holme-on-Spalding Moor 76 Squadron was to lose over 40 aircraft. Only the introduction of the much-improved Halifax Mk III in the early weeks of 1944 saw the loss rate finally begin to decline and the chances of a crew making it through their 30-op tour improve.

Fred Hall was a sergeant navigator who was posted to Holme in August 1943 after spells at 10 OTU and at 1663 HCU at Rufforth. He was 30 at the time – his pilot was just 19. Their introduction to operations coincided with a series of heavy losses for the squadron. A raid on Munchengladbach at the end of August cost 76 three Halifaxes – one crashing on take-off, another to a night fighter and a third crashing at Bradwell Bay with battle damage – while two more failed to return from Mannheim. Two raids on Hanover at the end of September cost the squadron four aircraft with the deaths of 21 men and worse still was an attack on Kassel early in October when four aircraft were shot down.

By this time Fred Hall and his crew had completed eleven operations and on 3rd November, as he prepared charts for a raid on Dusseldorf that night, his crew, flying MP-A *Hetty the Hefflump*, crashed near Market Weighton during a pre-op air test. Five had been killed

F/O Gordon Greenacre and crew of 76 Squadron, who were killed on the Nuremburg raid, their 21st operation. (Grace Van den Bos)

instantly while the pilot, F/Lt Steele, and 23-year-old Miss Dorothy Robson, a bomb sight expert from the Royal Aircraft establishment at Farnborough, were critically injured. Both died during the next few days. After sorting out his crew's personal kit and attending the funerals of the pilot and rear gunner at Harrogate, he was sent on leave, later joining another crew. He completed a further 22 operations before being screened.

It was during this time that W/Cmdr Douglas 'Hank' Iveson was appointed commanding officer of 76 Squadron. He was born in Hull, where he learned to fly with the RAFVR and had already completed one tour with the squadron at Middleton St George. He was an outstanding character, respected by everyone on the squadron, and believed firmly in leading from the front. Fred Hall remembered him as 'a big man in every way'.

76's worst night over Berlin came on 20th-21st January 1944 when two of its aircraft failed to return. One was shot down by a night fighter near Berlin itself and F/Sgt Parrott and his crew were killed. The second was badly damaged but P/O Whitehead managed to reach France before skilfully crash-landing the bomber. One of the crew died but Whitehead and three others evaded capture and eventually made it back to the squadron. The following night the squadron suffered terribly in a raid on Magdeburg, losing five of its Halifax Vs. One crashed on take-off and the other four were all shot down with the loss of 25 lives.

An attack on Stuttgart on 1st March also cost the squadron two aircraft, one crashing soon after take-off and the second coming down in France. The following day another aircraft suffered rudder failure, an old Halifax problem, and plunged into the ground at high speed near Scunthorpe.

The Nuremburg raid at the end of March brought near disaster to the squadron with three of its Halifaxes shot down – all by night fighters – and a fourth written off after crash-landing at Tangmere. Fred Hall was the navigator in that aircraft.

'We were nearing the end of our tour and I knew how easy it was to relax concentration and knew that this was when crews became vulnerable. There was no question of relaxing that night; I really thought our number was up,' he said.

Shortly after dropping their bombs they had been attacked by a night fighter. Fires were started in the fuselage, starboard wing and bomb bay and the pilot F/Lt Roy Bolt, managed to extinguish them by diving the aircraft. They were then attacked by a second night fighter but mid-upper gunner Sgt Harry van den Bos, spotted it and gave plenty of warning to the pilot. As the fighter closed in both gunners opened fire and it appeared to dive away out of control. The Halifax was now low on fuel but Bolt managed to reach Tangmere where the crew found that the undercarriage refused to come down. The uplocks were jammed and had to be attacked with axes before the wheels finally came down. 'We didn't know whether they would stay down or not,' continued Mr Hall. 'In the event they did but just as we got down a tyre burst and we went across the field at a 90-degree angle. When we got out I was so pleased to be down I kissed the ground.' An inspection the following day revealed their aircraft was damaged beyond repair.

They, however, were the lucky ones. Of the 22 men in the three missing Halifaxes, 13 had died and the remainder were prisoners.

The end of May saw Holme's BAT Flight – now numbered 1520 – move to Leconfield. It was replaced by 1689 Bomber Defence Training Flight, which flew Spitfires, Hurricanes and Martinets on fighter affiliation exercises with 4 Group bombers.

76 was heavily involved in the bombing campaign which preceded and followed the Normandy invasion. Three aircraft were lost in a raid on the rail centre at Trappes on 3rd June. Its task in the early hours of D-Day was to join a 4 Group attack on coastal batteries at Mont Fleury and of the two Halifaxes lost, one was from Holme-on-Spalding Moor, all on board being killed. The next few days were among the most hectic of the war for the Halifax crews as they followed this with further attacks in support of the Allied landings. Many were against railway targets and one of these, to Amiens on the night of 12th-13th June cost the squadron two aircraft, one shot down over the target and the second breaking its back in a heavy landing on the emergency strip at Woodbridge. There was another bad night for the squadron at the end of the month when it lost three of the eleven Halifaxes shot down in an attack on the rail yards at Blainville.

The resumption of the bombing of German targets saw a dramatic drop in losses compared with the same period in 1943. The aircraft were better, more experienced crews were available, navigation had improved and the RAF was finally getting the measure of the German defences. Night fighters in particular still posed a serious threat but there was now a realistic chance of crews completing their tours. Raids on Russelheim, Bochum, Worms and Cologne all claimed the lives of 76 Squadron crews and in the early morning of 4th March 1945 two

Holme-on-Spalding Moor Halifaxes fell to German night fighters which followed the aircraft back from a successful raid on the oil refinery at Bergkamen. One was caught by a night fighter over Lincolnshire and crashed near Brigg, the second force-landing at Carnaby. The aircraft shot down over Lincolnshire was the last to be lost by the squadron on operations. Two were written off with battle damage after returning from a daylight raid on Osnabruck on 24th March, the squadron flying its final operation on 25th April when all 25 Halifaxes attacked the gun batteries at Wangerooge. Tragically, two of the Holme-on-Spalding Moor aircraft collided near the target and there was just one survivor, P/O Lawson, the pilot of one of the Halifaxes, who managed to parachute into the sea and then swam ashore to become one of Bomber Command's final prisoners of war.

76 was to leave Holme-on-Spalding Moor soon after the war ended and by the autumn the airfield had closed. It was reopened during the Korean War as an advanced flying school and was later used briefly by the United States Air Force. In 1957 the airfield was taken over by Blackburn Aviation which was in the process of developing a new aircraft, the NA39, at its nearby factory at Brough. The aircraft was the forerunner of the successful Buccaneer and first flew from Holme-on-Spalding Moor in 1958. It was used for much of the later development work on the Buccaneer and the RAF's Phantoms, many of which were uprated by Blackburn's engineers.

Today, Holme-on-Spalding Moor, like many of Yorkshire's wartime airfields, is an industrial estate. There are, however, many reminders of its past, including impressive memorials erected to those who served with 76 and 458 Squadrons.

17
LECONFIELD

Shortly before 10.30 pm on the night of 3rd September 1939, ten Whitleys began taking off from RAF Leconfield on what was the very first operational sortie of Bomber Command in the Second World War. The aircraft were from 51 and 58 Squadrons, based at Linton-on-Ouse. Earlier in the afternoon they had flown across Yorkshire to load more than four million leaflets and that night began to scatter them across northern Germany.

It was one of several significant 'firsts' for Leconfield which, over the next five years, was to be used by Fighter, Bomber and Transport Commands at one time or another.

Leconfield was one of the first wave of Expansion Scheme airfields in Yorkshire, officially opening as a 3 Group bomber airfield in December 1936. It then passed to 4 Group but had become surplus to requirements by the summer of 1939 and was on a care and maintenance basis when used for that first leaflet drop of the war. The following month it was taken over by Fighter Command and for the next two years was to be used by numerous Spitfire, Hurricane and Blenheim squadrons, all of which were rotated quickly by Fighter Command.

The first occupants were 616 Squadron, which was then joined by 72, which brought its Spitfires from Church Fenton for a brief stay before moving to Drem. Two Blenheim squadrons, 234 and 245, were formed there.

It was 616 Squadron which was to be involved in the only major air battle fought by day fighters from Yorkshire. The squadron was somewhat disheartened at missing out on the developing air battles over southern England when, at lunch time on 15th August, the squadron was scrambled after coastal radar stations picked up the

Spitfire Is of 616 Squadron at Leconfield in the summer of 1940. (Peter Green)

approach of a large number of unidentified aircraft. Over Flamborough Head 616's Spitfires were joined by a flight of 73 Squadron's Hurricanes from Church Fenton and it was then that they first saw some 60 unescorted Ju 88s heading for the coast. During the next few minutes the Leconfield and Church Fenton fighters shot down seven of the bombers and badly damaged another three. However, the survivors of KG30, which were operating from Aalborg in Germany, pressed on with their attack and inflicted serious damage to the nearby bomber airfield at Driffield (see the chapter on Driffield for a fuller account of the raid).

It was to be the first and last time Leconfield's fighters were involved in this kind of action and the new year saw 72 move to Church Fenton and 616 briefly to Catfoss before returning until May when it moved to Rochford. The Blenheims also left for Church Fenton and Drem and were replaced by 249 Squadron's Hurricanes and 74 Squadron's Spitfires. A Polish squadron, 302 (Poznan), was formed at Leconfield in July from remnants of the Poznan Air Regiment and 1/145 Polish Squadron in France. By the end of the month it had been equipped with Hurricanes, moving to Northolt and changing places with a second Polish squadron, 303, which was later sent to Leconfield to rest after recording 26 kills in the air battles over Kent. 303 remained at

Leconfield until January 1941, one of numerous movements in and out of the airfield that winter.

60 OTU was formed in April to provide night fighter training before moving out in June, making way for a new squadron, 129 (Mysore), which was formed that month, its name reflecting the financial support provided by the Indian state. It became operational by the end of July and, during one of the many North Sea patrols flown from Leconfield, two of its aircraft succeeded in shooting down a Me 110. It left for Tangmere at the end of the month with Leconfield's second squadron, 313, moving to Portreath. They were replaced by 610 Squadron, the last of the wartime Fighter Command units to use Leconfield. The airfield was to be returned to Bomber Command and in October, 28 Conversion Flight was formed at the airfield, equipped with a number of the new Halifax BIs. This was the forerunner of the heavy conversion units and a second, 107 CF, was formed at Leconfield in December before both moved to Marston Moor. 610 Squadron took its Spitfires to Hutton Cranswick, leaving 15 (P) AFU as the only resident unit at Leconfield while runway construction began.

Leconfield reopened as a bomber airfield on 2nd December 1942, its first occupants being 466 and 196 Squadrons both of which had been formed on Wellingtons at Driffield. 466 was a Royal Australian Air Force squadron, although its initial complement of Aussie aircrew was just two – the squadron CO, W/Cmdr Bailey, and the gunnery leader. The Australian element was to grow considerably over the years and its use of the pre-war airfields at Leconfield and Driffield was consistent with the gentlemen's agreement which saw a number of Australian squadrons in Bomber Command being allocated big pre-war airfields, all of which had comfortable accommodation for air crew.

Several 466 pilots had already flown 'second dickey' trips from Pocklington before their arrival at Leconfield and they were quickly operational following their move on 27th December, six aircraft taking part in a minelaying operation off the Frisians on 13th January. 466, along with 196 when it became operational, was to become one of the 4 Group experts on 'gardening' trips and it was the second of these, on 14th January, which cost the squadron its first operational loss, Sgt Babington and his crew being killed when their aircraft was brought down by flak off Ameland. The following night the squadron flew its first bombing raid when four aircraft went to Lorient. It should have been ten aircraft but the remainder could not be armed in time for take-off. The squadron's T-Tommy went down in a mining operation off Terschelling and in the early hours of 27th January one of ten Wellingtons sent to Lorient lost power on the return and crashed near Retford, only the rear gunner, Sgt Ferris, surviving.

466's first operation to Germany came on the night of 29th-30th January when two aircraft, flown by F/Lt Simmonds and Sgt Axby, failed to make it back. A week later Sgt Murdoch and his crew had a lucky escape when they brought their load of mines back from an abortive trip to Brest. The aircraft overshot on landing and ran out of runway. The crew had just scrambled clear when the mines exploded.

F/Lt Kirk's Wellington was shot down on a raid on Cologne later in the month, the aircraft crashing with three of the crew still on board near the village of Meerhout in Belgium. Part of the tail fin was recovered by villagers and was later erected as a memorial to those who died. A second aircraft on the raid crashed back at Leconfield, killing the rear gunner.

Several crews returned after extraordinary brushes with death over the night skies of northern Europe. Sgt Rosser's Wellington was attacked by a Me 110 over Wilhelmshaven and set on fire. The bomb aimer baled out and both the navigator and wireless operator were wounded. The flames were brought under control but, as the aircraft headed for home, it was attacked a second time. This time the rear gunner, Sgt Wilcox, shot down the fighter and Rosser and his crew made it back to Leconfield.

196 Squadron had become operational at the end of February 1943 and on the night of 5th-6th March the two squadrons flew together on a raid on Essen. Some 30 miles off the Dutch coast the 'togetherness' became a little too realistic and F/Sgt Tozer's Wellington collided with that of F/O Hope of 196 Squadron. Tozer's aircraft limped back to Leconfield minus a propeller. Hope's aircraft continued its sortie and when it returned from Essen it was discovered that a section of the missing propeller blade was firmly embedded in the fuselage!

On the night of 14th-15th April a 466 Squadron aircraft was badly mauled by a night fighter during a raid on Stuttgart, the rear gunner being killed and three other members of the crew wounded. But the pilot, Sgt Hick, decided to press on with the attack and dropped his bombs on the target before making it back to Ford in Hampshire. He was later awarded a Conspicuous Gallantry Medal, his bomb aimer, P/O Hopkins, received a DSO and there was a DFC and DFM respectively for the navigator, F/O Clayton, and the wireless operator,

Sgt Blair. Hicks was later promoted and was awarded a DFC when he completed his tour.

196 suffered its first losses in a raid on Mannheim on the night of 16th-17th April when one of its Wellingtons failed to return. A second, flown by the squadron CO, W/Cmdr Duguid, was abandoned near Croydon when it ran out of fuel. On the same raid F/Sgt Tozer, who had survived the mid-air collision, was killed when his 466 Squadron Wellington was shot down over the Ardennes. He had been the first Australian to see action with the squadron, flying as second pilot in a 10 Squadron aircraft to Turin the previous December, and was the first Australian on 466 to be killed on operations.

196 was to have a torrid time that spring, losing one over Duisburg, two over Bochum and three in a disastrous mining trip off Langeland. Thirty men died in those five aircraft; the crew of a sixth were more fortunate when they ditched off Grimsby. Both squadrons lost aircraft in raids on Dortmund and Duisburg again early in May while 466 lost three in an attack on Wuppertal and two more over Dusseldorf.

HD-H and crew at Leconfield, 1943. They are (l to r): F/Sgt Jim Hetherington, F/Sgt Aubrey Winston, F/Sgt Jock Cameron, the pilot, F/Sgt Jock Samuels and F/Sgt Geoff Allen. The crew completed their tour on 466's final Wellington sortie in August 1943. Jock Cameron was later promoted and returned to the squadron at Driffield in 1945. (Stan Parker)

This was the period which became known as the Battle of the Ruhr and 196 was to lose another four aircraft before it was transferred to the Middle East in mid-July. Among the last crews lost was that flying with W/Cmdr Owens, a senior officer from 4 Group HQ, whose aircraft, which had been borrowed from 466, crashed during a mining operation off Brest. Astonishingly, five crews from 466 completed their tours during this period and were screened from operations.

The Wellington was reaching the end of its operational life and 466 flew its final sortie with the aircraft on the night of 31st August, attacking an ammunition dump in France. The night before it had attacked Munchengladbach, two of its aircraft collided over Goole shortly after taking off from Leconfield. Both crews were killed along with at least one civilian, several more being injured when the wreckage of one of the aircraft fell into the town.

The squadron's history tells an amusing story concerning one of 466's Wellingtons in those final days. The aircraft was returning from a raid when the crew became lost somewhere over Lincolnshire and decided to land at the nearest airfield. The pilot then spotted the lights of a bomber airfield and found himself in the circuit together with around 30 Lancasters. He called the tower: 'Have only two engines. Can I land?' The duty controller gave him immediate permission to land ahead of the airfield's own Lancasters. It was only when the aircraft was on the ground at RAF Ludford Magna that the controller realised the aircraft was, in fact, a twin-engined Wellington.

The squadron was taken off operations and began converting to Halifaxes. Forty per cent of the aircrew were now Australian and most went to Marston Moor or Riccall for their conversion while ground crews were sent to Riccall to work alongside ground staff with 158 Squadron at Lissett. The squadron was issued with a number of Mk IIs. It was one of these, an ex-158 Squadron aircraft, which crashed off Flamborough on an air-to-sea firing exercise on 3rd November, killing all seven on board.

By the time the squadron was operational, it had begun to receive the first of the new Mk IIIs, becoming the first squadron to be equipped with the vastly improved Halifax. It was also the first in 4 Group to receive H2S ground-mapping radar. The squadron's first operation with its new aircraft was on 1st-2nd December when twelve aircraft went to Terschelling to sow mines. One aircraft suffered a fire and later crash-landed at Catfoss. Its first trip to Germany came on 20th-21st December when two of the 16 aircraft sent to Frankfurt – flown by F/O

Pictured in front of one of the first Halifax Mk IIs delivered to 466 Squadron at Leconfield are: Sgt Joe Brown, Sgt Ron Hayes, F/Sgt Harry Cornwall, the skipper P/O Ted Eagleton, F/Sgt Barney McCosker, P/O Stan Taylor and Sgt Wally Green. The crew went on to complete the tour by which time Ted Eagleton had reached the rank of squadron leader and was A Flight commander. The aircraft, DT559, crashed with the loss of all on board during an air-sea firing exercise off Flamborough in November 1943. (Stan Parker)

Scales and F/Sgt Edwards – failed to return, six of the crew of one of the aircraft surviving.

466 paid its first visit to Berlin on the night of 29th-30th December and was to lose its first crew over the German capital three weeks later, F/Lt Baldwin and his crew falling to a night fighter. A raid on Berlin a week later proved disastrous, three of the 14 aircraft sent failing to return and a fourth crash-landing in Norfolk. One of those lost was flown by S/Ldr McCormick, who was on his 17th operation. He and five of his crew survived, two others being killed. There were three survivors from F/Lt Mack's aircraft while five men survived from the third aircraft, flown by P/O Coombes. Two nights later the squadron was able to provide only twelve aircraft for another attack on Berlin, six of these returning early with mechanical problems.

Early in February surplus crews from 466 together with 158 Squadron's C Flight helped form a new squadron, 640, at Lissett. It was the last wartime squadron to be formed in Bomber Command and quickly moved to Leconfield and was soon in action. It lost three aircraft in a raid on Leipzig, an attack which also cost 466 Squadron two Halifaxes. An attack on Frankfurt in March cost 466 another three aircraft and three crews – P/O Curnow's being on their 18th operation while F/S Richards' and F/Sgt Watson's were each on their sixth.

Thirty-two aircraft, 16 from each squadron, went on the ill-fated Nuremburg raid at the end of March with wildly varying fortunes. All 466's Halifaxes returned safely, one being slightly damaged, and there were no casualties among its air crew. 640, however, suffered very badly. Three of its Halifaxes were shot down and three more were damaged. Two of those shot down fell to night fighters while the third was shot down by a flak ship off Dieppe, the last of the 96 to be shot down over Europe. It was flown by Canadian pilot P/O Burke and all on board were killed. The pilots of the other two aircraft were also Canadian and three men from these two Halifaxes survived to become PoWs.

There was a fortunate escape for the crew of 640's S-Sugar, which was hit by flak during a raid on Aachen on 12th April. The aircraft caught fire, turned over and went into a spin, diving some 6,000 feet before the pilot, F/Sgt Roy Crockett managed to regain control although both he and the flight engineer, Sgt Duff, were wounded. The attack came before the aircraft reached the target and Crockett tried to dump the bombs but only part of the load could be dropped because the bomb bay doors were damaged. By this time the smoke in the cockpit was so thick that at one time the pilot was having great difficulty seeing his instruments. However, the crew got the fire out and Crockett nursed the Halifax back to Pocklington where he landed safely. He was immediately promoted to pilot officer and awarded the DFC.

The switch to railway targets on the run-up to the invasion led to five Leconfield Halifaxes, three from 466, being lost in two attacks on the marshalling yards at Tergnier in April. 640 lost another three in an attack on railway yards at Hasselt on the night of 12th-13th May, a fourth crash-landing at Woodbridge, while five Leconfield aircraft were lost in an attack on railway yards at Trappes on the night of 2nd-3rd June. Three were from 640 squadron while another from 466 was severely damaged. One of those lost from 466, HX242, crashed near the village of Tourville-la-Campagne, Sgt Coleman and his crew being buried in the village cemetery. Thirty years later two streets in the village were renamed Rue des Australiens and Promenades des Aviateurs Allies in recognition of their sacrifice.

This proved to be 466's final operation from Leconfield. They moved on 3rd June to Driffield, leaving 640 as the only occupants.

D-Day saw the Halifaxes of 640 Squadron hitting gun batteries just inland from the invasion beaches, all aircraft returning safely to Leconfield. One aircraft was lost in an attack on railway yards at Versailles two days after the invasion and another nine days later in an attack on the oil refinery at Sterkrade, an attack which cost 4 Group 22 Halifaxes. Targets later switched to V1 sites in northern France, 640 leading an attack on Wizernes on 28th June. One of its aircraft was hit by flak and later crash-landed and burnt out at Hawkinge in Kent. Railway targets were still being hit and 640 lost two Halifaxes in an attack on Dijon in August.

The early autumn saw Leconfield's aircraft back over Germany. Losses by now had dropped dramatically but raids on Sterkrade, Nordstern, Osnabruck and Bochum all led to 640 Squadron aircraft failing to make it back to their East Yorkshire airfield. After an attack in support of American troops at Jülich in November 1944 one Halifax crash-landed at Leconfield after over-shooting.

Two aircraft were lost in the attack on Chemnitz in February 1945 and a second raid on the same target the following month resulted in a 640 Squadron aircraft being abandoned low on fuel over France. Leconfield's final loss of the war was Halifax MZ494 which failed to return from a raid on the Ruhrstahl steelworks at Witten on the night of 18th-19th March.

The squadron had briefly shared Leconfield with 96 Squadron, which reformed at Leconfield within Transport Command at the end of December 1944 and was later equipped with Halifaxes which had been fitted out as troop transports. The squadron lost one of its aircraft in an accident during its time at Leconfield, the Halifax crashing at Brantingham, killing six of the crew. The squadron was to remain at Leconfield until March when it moved to Egypt.

On 20th April 1945, 51 Squadron moved to Leconfield from Snaith and five days later flew its final operation of the war alongside 640 to Wangerooge.

Leconfield was among the Yorkshire airfields included in the RAF's post war planning. Not so 640 Squadron. Despite its proficiency in bombing which saw it top the 4 Group bombing tables, it was disbanded on 7th May some 15 months after being formed. 51 Squadron transferred to Transport Command and moved to Stradishall. Leconfield itself was to revert to a fighter airfield and over the next 20 years was one of the key elements in Britain's air defences, housing Meteor, Hunter, Javelin and Lightning squadrons before being transferred to the Army in 1977, under whose charge it became the Army School of Mechanical Transport. The RAF, however, retained an interest in Leconfield and still operates Sea King air-sea rescue helicopters from the airfield.

18
LEEMING

Few airfields were to play such a significant role in Bomber Command operations in the Second World War as Leeming. It was to see the debut of the first two of the RAF's trio of four-engined heavy bombers, the Stirling and the Halifax, and to become the first centre of operations for the all-Canadian 6 Group. It is perhaps fitting, therefore, that Leeming should today be the RAF's major base in Yorkshire.

Flying had started at Leeming early in 1938 when Yorkshire Air Services established a popular flying club on what was then part of Clapham Lodge and Wilson's farms just south of Leeming Bar and close to the Great North Road. The flying club was to be short-lived for, by the end of the year, the land had been acquired by the Air Ministry for airfield development.

RAF Leeming finally opened on 3rd June 1940 as an Expansion Scheme airfield, complete with five C-type hangars and substantial brick accommodation blocks and technical buildings. Concrete runways were to come a year or so later.

Although the airfield had been built as a bomber station its first occupants were the Blenheim night fighters of 219 Squadron, which was detached from its base a few miles up the Great North Road at Catterick. Leeming, however, didn't have to wait long for its bombers. 10 Squadron began arriving with its Whitley Vs on 10th July from nearby Dishforth, flying the first operation from Leeming on the 20th when nine aircraft set out to bomb an aircraft plant at Wejendorf in Germany. All returned safely and it was another three weeks before the squadron lost one of its Whitleys after an attack on Milan. It had been damaged by an Italian fighter and almost made it back but was forced to ditch off Dymchurch, two of the crew, including the pilot P/O Parsons, drowning. Another ten aircraft were to be lost on operations before the end of the year, three disappearing without trace.

A fine view of Leeming in 1941. Between the C-type hangars is Whitley ZA-G of 10 Squadron. (RAF Leeming)

In the meantime, Leeming had seen the arrival of the first of the new breed of heavy bombers planned for Bomber Command. At the beginning of August, 7 Squadron had reformed as part of 4 Group at Leeming and was destined to become the RAF's first Stirling squadron, although it was to have to wait until its transfer to 3 Group before it began operations on its new aircraft. At this early stage it appears that the Stirling was pencilled in as a replacement for 4 Group's Whitleys, the oldest and slowest of the medium bombers then in Bomber Command service. The Stirling certainly had the range but it was equipped with Bristol engines and 4 Group, whose Whitleys were Merlin powered, had no experience of these engines, and eventually it was decided that the Stirling should go into service with 3 Group, then equipped with Wellingtons. After three months of trials with the early production Stirlings, few at Leeming were sorry to see the aircraft go when 7 Squadron eventually moved to Boscombe Down to complete its trials. The handful of Stirlings delivered to the squadron – they were all built singly by Shorts – suffered numerous problems, one crash-landing near Kirkby Lonsdale and another force-landing at Scampton.

The first of these occurred at Hodge Bridge, Barbon, three miles north of Kirkby Lonsdale. One of the first on the scene was local schoolboy John Priestley whose Sunday lunch had been interrupted by the crash in a field adjacent to his home. When he arrived he found the pilot, Flying Officer T.P.A. Bradley, inspecting the damage to the still-smoking aircraft. Although a keen aircraft spotter, John had never seen anything quite like the very large aeroplane in the field near the house and it wasn't until recently he learned that it was, in fact, one of the very first Stirlings to see service with the RAF.

By the time the Stirlings left at the end of October the first Merlin-engined Halifaxes were coming off the production lines, destined for 4 Group and Yorkshire airfields. 35 (Madras Presidency) Squadron had been reformed at Boscombe Down, where it became the first to be equipped with Halifaxes. These it brought to Leeming when it arrived in 4 Group on 20th November 1940. It remained for a little over a fortnight before it moved on to Linton-on-Ouse from where it was to fly the Halifax operationally for the first time in the spring of 1941.

Leeming briefly housed 102 Squadron, which moved in from Driffield where it had suffered badly in a bombing attack. It remained for a few days before moving to Linton. 10 Squadron, in the meantime, was operating whenever the weather and the condition of the grass runways at Leeming permitted (concrete runways were laid the following year). Losses early in 1941 were light but among them was Sgt Hoare's crew following a raid on Cologne on the night of 1st-2nd March. Their Whitley crashed into the North Sea and no trace was ever found of the crew. The navigator was P/O Floringy and, by a tragic

Whitley Z6942 ZA-W of 10 Squadron about to be bombed up at Leeming during the summer of 1941. The aircraft was lost in a raid on Hüls in September, the entire crew becoming PoWs. (RAF Leeming)

coincidence, his brother was killed the same night when his 102 Squadron Whitley ditched off the Norfolk coast. Both men are commemorated on the Runnymede Memorial which lists all aircrew who have no known grave.

Another 10 Squadron crew was lost after ditching in the North Sea on its return from a raid on Bremen on the night of 8th-9th May. Five weeks later another crew from Leeming whose aircraft ditched following an attack on Schwerte owed their lives to the pilot of a Luftwaffe He 111. Its pilot spotted the Whitley's crew clinging to their upturned dinghy in bad weather and later found an RAF ASR launch which it successfully guided back to the dinghy. P/O Littlewood and his crew were landed at Yarmouth having changed their views somewhat on the Luftwaffe.

Bremen was raided twice in July 1941 by the Leeming Whitleys. The first raid cost 10 Squadron one aircraft and its crew, the second four Whitleys and the lives of 15 men. Three came down near the target while a fourth was abandoned by its crew after being set on fire, four of those baling out later being picked up by the Germans in Kiel Bay. Losses were now beginning to increase as the bombing campaign gained momentum and the German defences improved. A raid on Duisburg on 30th-31st July cost 10 Squadron another Whitley while a second was shot down by an intruder over Norfolk. Two were lost in an attack on Hanover, all ten on board being killed. Two raids on Cologne in August cost the squadron five Whitleys with 15 men being killed and ten becoming PoWs, while a raid on Hüls early in September saw two aircraft fail to return while a third was wrecked during a pre-ops air test, four of the crew being killed when it hit power cables near Acklington in Northumberland.

10 Squadron had by now been joined at Leeming by 77 Squadron, which moved in from Topcliffe after a spell on detachment with Coastal Command. The Hüls raid saw 77 operational again but it lost three of its Whitleys, two being shot down with the cost of nine men while the third crash-landed at Cromer. Three crews from Leeming, two of them from 10 Squadron, were to be rescued from the North Sea in the coming weeks, one by a destroyer, another by a trawler and a third by one of the new high speed launches based at Grimsby and deployed in the North Sea for just such emergencies. Many men from Lincolnshire and Yorkshire airfields were to owe their lives to these launches and those who crewed them.

10 Squadron lost its last Whitley on 12th December when an aircraft

The ops room at Leeming, August 1941. (RAF Leeming)

crashed at Pateley Bridge following a raid on Cologne, one of the crew being killed. It then began converting to Halifax IIs, operating its new aircraft for the first time on 18th December in a daylight attack on the battlecruisers *Scharnhorst* and *Gneisenau*, then berthed in Brest. The raid proved inconclusive and a second attack was mounted on 30th December. Again little damage was done to the warships and one 10 Squadron aircraft was badly damaged by a fighter and its rear gunner, F/Lt Roach, killed. The Halifax later ditched off the Cornish coast and the remainder of the crew were rescued.

77 Squadron was still operating its Whitleys and lost two in crashes following a raid on St Nazaire on the night of 15th-16th February. There was just one survivor, P/O James Spalding, who baled out moments before his aircraft came down near Warwick. It was to be a brief reprieve as he was killed a month later when flying as second pilot in one of two 77 Squadron Whitleys lost following an attack on Emden. The squadron remained at Leeming until 6th May when it left for a second spell with Coastal Command.

In the meantime, 10 Squadron was still involved in the battle between 4 Group and the German navy. Its Halifaxes flew out of Lossiemouth to attack the battleship *Tirpitz*, then hidden in Asenfjord.

A reflective moment for an air gunner in the Sergeants' Mess at Leeming. (RAF Leeming)

Two of the squadron's aircraft were lost, F/Lt Pools and his crew being killed when their aircraft crashed near Trondheim. The second, flown by the squadron CO, W/Cmdr Don Bennett, was hit by anti-aircraft fire and crash-landed at Stjordal in Norway. W/Cmdr Bennett was one of three members of the crew who escaped to Sweden and he was back at Leeming early in June. Shortly afterwards he left 4 Group to take command of the new 8 (PFF) Group.

10 Squadron itself was to spend most of the summer at Leeming, taking part in numerous attacks on German targets, one of them being Essen. The squadron lost three aircraft during these attacks, one of which had been borrowed from 78 Squadron. Another ditched off the Dutch coast and six of the crew were picked up by a German warship. The squadron's departure for Melbourne in August marked a major change for RAF Leeming, which was about to be transferred to the Royal Canadian Air Force.

6 Group was not due to come into being until 1st January 1943 and in the meantime the RCAF squadrons at Leeming would fly as part of 4 Group. The first of these to arrive was 419 (Moose) Squadron – its name came from the nick-name given to its first CO, W/Cmdr 'Moose' Fulton – from Mildenhall where it had flown its Wellingtons in 3 Group. Its stay was brief, just three days, before it moved to Topcliffe. It was followed by 408 (Goose) Squadron, which transferred from 5 Group, where it had flown Hampdens from Syerston and Balderton, and immediately began converting to Halifax Vs. 408 Conversion Flight was formed to carry out this work and this was later joined by 405 Conversion Flight – 405 Squadron left Topcliffe for a spell with Coastal Command before returning to Leeming the following March. The two conversion flights were merged into 1659 HCU and then moved to Topcliffe to begin training Canadian crews.

408 Squadron lost its first Halifax in a training accident when it crashed killing five of the crew near Croft, while its first operational loss came in January 1943 when one crashed near Retford following a raid on Lorient, the crew surviving. Six nights later a second was shot down in an attack on the same target. By early February the squadron was taking its Halifaxes to Germany and began to suffer as a result. One was lost over Hamburg, six of the crew surviving, while four were lost in attacks on Berlin with 20 men killed, two taken prisoner and seven being interned following a crash-landing in Sweden.

405 (Vancouver) Squadron finished its spell in Coastal Command at the end of February and returned to Yorkshire, spending a few days at

Topcliffe before arriving at Leeming. Its stay in 6 Group was a brief one, leaving Leeming on 18th April for the new 8 Group where it was to become one of the first Pathfinder squadrons. Before its departure the squadron lost two Halifaxes in a raid on Essen, an operation which also cost 408 two aircraft with a third written off in a crash on its return to Leeming. Two more 405 aircraft failed to return from a raid on Kiel and a mining trip before the squadron moved to Gransden Lodge in Bedfordshire. It was replaced briefly by 424 (Tiger) Squadron which brought its Wellingtons from Topcliffe in preparation for a spell in the Middle East, leaving again on 2nd May. It, in turn, was replaced by 427 (Lion) Squadron, which moved in from Croft and began converting to Halifax Vs. 427 had been adopted by the MGM studios in Hollywood and took its name from the company's lion symbol. The link entitled squadron members to cut-price cinema tickets during their stay in Yorkshire!

The late spring and early summer of 1943 was to be one of the worst periods for Bomber Command. While 427 worked up on its new aircraft, 408 was in the thick of the action, losing four aircraft in a raid on Pilsen in which all 28 men on board were killed. An attack on Dortmund cost a further two aircraft, including the first all-RCAF crew to be lost in 6 Group (most of its original flight engineers were British).

By the beginning of June 427 was ready for operations and over the next two months the two Leeming squadrons were to lose 26 Halifaxes, all but four of them over occupied Europe, and 15 of them from 408 Squadron. Ninety-eight men from Leeming were to die in those few weeks. 427 lost four in an attack on Mulheim, including P-Pampas whose pilot, P/O Cadmus, was Argentinian. Two nights later 427 lost another three over Gelsenkirchen in a raid which also cost 408 a Halifax and its crew. 408 was to lose two itself in an attack on the same target shortly afterwards and among the eleven killed were two men from 1659 HCU who had gone along to gain experience.

More changes were in store at Leeming and 408 moved out early in August for Linton-on-Ouse where it was due to exchange its Halifax IIs for Lancasters. Its replacement was 429 (Bison) Squadron which moved in with its Halifax IIs from East Moor under the command of W/Cmdr Pattison. 427 and 429 Squadrons were to remain together at Leeming until the end of the war.

A 427 Squadron Halifax was badly mauled by a night fighter on its return from Mannheim on the night of 9th-10th August but in one of those almost superhuman efforts which often went unreported, the crew managed to get their aircraft back to England before finally baling

Halifax III MZ314 of 429 Squadron at Leeming during the summer of 1944. It was to be lost at the end of November that year along with P/O Clark's crew when it was involved in a mid-air collision with another Halifax from 578 Squadron at Burn during a raid on Duisburg. (Yorkshire Air Museum via Peter Green)

out over the south coast. The pilot, F/Sgt Briggs, was recommended for a CGM by the squadron but this was turned down and he, the wireless operator and flight engineer each received a DFM. Later in the month one of the squadron's aircraft was damaged in the Peenemünde raid and later landed at Mildenhall. It proved to be the final operation of their tour for Sgt Schmitt and his crew who were one of the original 427 crews and the first to complete a tour. The squadron lost another Halifax on this raid and two more shortly afterwards on the first of the coming autumn's big Berlin raids. Another Halifax landed at Ford in Hampshire after being damaged. A few days later three of the ground crew were being ferried to Ford to repair the aircraft when the squadron's communications Oxford crashed killing all four on board.

Early in October 429 lost its first aircraft in a raid on Frankfurt, two of the crew being killed when it crashed in Sussex. Another was lost a few nights later over Hanover and this time there were no survivors. Later in the month six aircraft from Leeming, four of them from 427, were all shot down in a raid on Kassel with just seven of the 42 men on board surviving. 429 itself lost three in a raid on Frankfurt, all falling to night fighters. The following night the squadron lost another Halifax, the crew being picked up after ditching off the Sussex coast on their way home from Stuttgart.

The Halifaxes of 6 Group had been spared from some of the Berlin raids but the Leeming squadrons went to the German capital on the night of 20th-21st January, three failing to return. One, from 427, crashed trying to land at Coltishall and caught fire. A farmer and his wife were each to receive a BEM for rescuing four of the crew, all of whom later died from their injuries.

The following night 427 lost four of its Halifax Vs in a raid on Magdeburg and immediately began converting to the much improved Mk III. 429 would have to wait another month for its new aircraft, the conversion beginning after another disastrous night when four aircraft were lost in an attack on Leipzig.

It was during this period that 429's CO, W/Cmdr Pattison, was seriously injured at Leeming. He was watching the squadron preparing for take-off when a canister of incendiaries fell from one aircraft and began igniting. He and another officer tried to kick them away from the aircraft and both were badly burnt.

The first of Leeming's Halifax IIIs were lost in raids on Stuttgart in February and March while the last of the great Berlin raids on 24th-25th March cost each squadron three aircraft on a night when 24 men were killed and 18 more made prisoners. The Nuremburg raid saw five aircraft lost from Leeming, including one from 427 which was involved in a collision with a Lancaster over Luxembourg. Among the squadron's casualties was S/Ldr Bissett, one of the flight commanders.

Both squadrons suffered losses in the run-up to the Normandy invasion, including six of the crew of a 429 Halifax which crashed and caught fire on take-off for Le Mans. A number of firemen were also badly injured when the aircraft's bomb load later exploded. Fourteen men were killed when a Halifax from each of Leeming's squadrons collided over Belgium during a raid on rail yards at Aachen. An attack on Acheres on 7th-8th June saw a 429 aircraft hit by flak over Dieppe, critically injuring the pilot, S/Ldr Anderson. The flight engineer, Sgt Steele, took over the controls and flew the aircraft back to England where all on board, including the pilot, managed to bale out, although S/Ldr Anderson later died of his injuries. A raid on Arras a few nights later cost 427 three aircraft and the lives of 16 men. One of them, Sgt Long, was killed exactly a year after his brother had been killed flying from Leeming with 408 Squadron.

Although the bombing war had reached a new intensity, losses were dropping sharply and more of the men in those aircraft shot down were surviving. Among them was the crew of a 429 Squadron aircraft brought down by the Boulogne flak. The crew were picked up by a Walrus amphibian which was so overloaded it had to taxi on the surface of the sea to meet a rescue launch which took the Halifax crew on board. They returned to Leeming but all were to be killed three months later when their aircraft was shot down over Osnabruck.

Another crew from the same squadron had a double escape in October. P/O Augusta and his crew survived a crash-landing in Norfolk following flak damage over Bochum. Four days later they were back over Germany in a daylight attack on Duisburg when they were again hit by flak. Despite having a wing on fire, they bombed the target before bailing out and spending the rest of the war as POWs.

Four Halifaxes from 429 were wrecked in an accident on 1st November when they were among a number diverted to Spilsby in Lincolnshire. A 207 Squadron Lancaster swung on take-off and crashed into the line of parked Halifaxes, caught fire and later exploded. One of 429's flight engineers, P/O Platt tried to move one of the Halifaxes and was badly injured when it burst into flames, and he later died from his injuries.

Leeming lost twelve Halifaxes in the first two months of 1945, including three in a raid on Chemnitz, but just three more aircraft were to be lost before the war ended. One of these was one of the Lancasters with which both squadrons were re-equipped in March.

Both Canadian squadrons remained at Leeming after the war and were transferred to 1 Group before being disbanded the following year. Leeming itself was destined to play a vital part in the post-war Royal Air Force, housing first a series of training units before being extensively redeveloped in the mid-1980s and becoming the home of Tornado and Hawk squadrons.

19
LINDHOLME

Bomber airfields in Yorkshire will always be associated with 4 and 6 Groups. But one airfield, which lay close to the county's boundaries with both Nottinghamshire and Lincolnshire, was to serve 5 and 1 Groups during the war in both an operational and training role.

RAF Hatfield Woodhouse opened as a 5 Group bomber airfield in June 1940 and within a matter of weeks was renamed RAF Lindholme, an easier name for W/T operators and one which would avoid confusion with Hatfield airfield in Hertfordshire.

The site on the edge of Hatfield Moor, the flat peaty area east of Doncaster, had first been earmarked in the mid-1930s as a location for an Expansion Scheme airfield and work began on construction in the summer of 1938. It progressed at a fairly leisurely pace, so much so that when war was declared on 3rd September 1939 there was still much to be done. This explained in some way the mixture of pre-war solidity and wartime austerity many of those who served at Lindholme remember. The airfield had its five large C-type brick hangars, built alongside a mixture of concrete and wooden buildings which were to serve the many thousands of airmen who were to pass through Lindholme during five years of war.

The airfield finally opened within 5 Group on 1st June 1940 when G/Capt E. F. Wareing became the first commanding officer of RAF Hatfield Woodhouse. Within a matter of days the Hampdens of 50 Squadron began arriving from Waddington, just south of Lincoln. They were in action within three weeks of their arrival, eleven aircraft taking part in an attack on Hamburg on 14th July.

The arrival of a squadron of Hampdens caused quite a stir in the rural community of Hatfield Moor and the neighbouring Isle of

Axholme. Dennis Prosser of Epworth remembers the period when he lived with his family on Hatfield Moor, close to the airfield. His father drove the big steam engine at the peat cutting works on the moor and the flat landscape meant just about every take-off and landing could be observed from the family house. He recalls during 1940 cycling along the Bawtry-Thorne road and seeing a row of Hampdens parked up on the airfield, all with their tails neatly lined up against the hedge.

There were no concrete runways at Lindholme in those days and landing directions depended on the wind. But the Prossers lived north-east of the airfield and, in normal conditions, this meant the Hampdens coming in right over their house. On one occasion a Hampden crash-landed on the moor not far from his home. By climbing to the top of the peat mill, young Dennis could see the sun glinting on the Perspex of the bomber, which had made a near-perfect wheels-up landing on the peat moor. Curiosity later got the better of him and he walked across to see the aircraft at close quarters. It was being watched over by a solitary guard from Lindholme, who looked both lonely and hungry. When he got home, Dennis told his mother about the guard and she immediately took pity on him, baked a rabbit pie and sent young Dennis back with it to give to him!

Among the early visitors to the airfield was the Air Officer Commanding 5 Group, Air Vice-Marshal Arthur Harris, who looked round his group's newest airfield and gave a pep talk as only he could to the aircrew of 50 Squadron during July 1940. The squadron was to lose almost 50 aircraft during the year it spent flying operationally from Lindholme, the first being Hampden P1321 which crashed in the sea off the Norfolk coast early in the morning of 26th July 1940 after suffering flak damage over the Ruhr. The Cromer lifeboat was launched together with a motor boat crewed by two brothers which put out from Happisburgh beach. Between them they found the wreckage of the Hampden and recovered the bodies of its crew, P/O Mulloy, P/O Taylor and Sgts Watt and Stewart, the first men to be killed flying from what a few days later would become RAF Lindholme.

Two weeks later another Hampden and its crew were lost in the North Sea, Sgt Thomas and his crew being killed when their aircraft was believed to have ditched returning from a raid on Mannheim. The Hampden was notorious for its fuel problems and 50 Squadron was to leave several more of its aircraft on the bed of the North Sea in the months to come.

A raid on Berlin at the end of August cost 50 Squadron two more

Hampdens, both in somewhat bizarre circumstances. P/O George Potts managed to nurse his damaged aircraft most of the way back across the North Sea before finally ditching in the sea within sight of the beach at Scarborough. The crew was quickly picked up, and then followed a race amongst local fishing boats to tow the still-floating Hampden ashore, presumably in the hope of claiming salvage. The aircraft, however, sank while under tow.

In the meantime P/O Wawne and his crew had become lost after leaving Berlin and, almost out of fuel and after coming under inaccurate AA fire, landed at an airfield they thought was in Scotland. It was only after addressing a welcoming ground crew in English and hearing replies in German that the unfortunate Wawne discovered his mistake. He had landed at a Luftwaffe airfield in southern Germany. He later told his captors he was used to being fired on by anti-aircraft gunners when he returned to England!

50 Squadron was to be involved in most of the major bombing raids of the coming winter and was to pay the price for it. Not all crews were as fortunate as S/Ldr Willans whose Hampden was shot down on a raid on Hamburg. Wireless operators picked up a brief message: 'Jumping for it' and later it was learned that all four men were in a PoW camp. Bomber operations were made more hazardous by the weather and the rudimentary navigational aids then available to crews. Early in October P/O Thwaites lost an engine over Hamburg but managed to bring his aircraft back across the North Sea where a flare path was spotted. The aircraft was almost out of fuel but it was only as he was about to land that the pilot realised the 'airfield' wasn't all it was supposed to be. It was a decoy site near Dunbar in Scotland, the Hampden hitting a tree before coming to rest. Fortunately, the only casualty was the rear gunner who suffered a broken leg. An attack on Berlin at the end of the month ran into problems from the start with severe icing affecting most of the attackers, including Hampden X3000 of 50 Squadron. P/O Walker and his crew also ran into a severe snow storm 50 miles from the target. They finally made it back to England after a ten-hour flight, surely one of the longest ever in a Hampden, only for both engines to cut, the carburettors blocked by ice. The crew managed to bale out, landing safely near Linton-on-Ouse.

The crew of X2908 were not so fortunate, their Hampden crashing into buildings in Dunhill Road, Goole following engine failure on their return from Hamburg in November. There was only one survivor.

Mining operations also proved costly for 50 Squadron. In February

1941 P/O Tunstall successfully laid his mine in the Gironde estuary. His aircraft also carried two 250lb bombs and the pilot decided to attack what he thought was a water tower. It turned out to be a flak installation, the aircraft was hit and crash-landed close to the estuary, killing the pilot and the navigator, Sgt Barclay. The wireless operator/ air gunner, Sgt Fred Bailey, suffered broken ribs but still managed to drag gunner Sgt Dixon, who had broken both of his ankles, clear before trying to wave away other Hampdens which were preparing to attack the 'water tower'.

A similar operation also cost 50 Squadron another experienced and highly decorated pilot. At the end of April 1941 S/Ldr Goode and his crew failed to return from a minelaying operation off Lorient. It was later determined the aircraft had simply flown into the sea in thick fog. The year before, on another mining operation off Oslo, Goode had received an immediate DFC after being badly wounded by flak. It was only when the crew noticed the erratic behaviour of the aircraft that they had found Goode covered in blood from wounds to both arms and face. Fortunately, another pilot, P/O Gardiner, was flying as bomb aimer and as the crew managed to ease Goode out of his seat, was able to take the controls. Gardiner also received an immediate DFC and survived the war. S/Ldr Goode's body was never found. On the same night another Lindholme Hampden, flown by Canadian F/O James Whitecross, suffered engine failure over Brittany. Whitecross and another member of the crew baled out, the pilot climbing out onto the starboard wing to avoid hitting the tail plane. Whitecross managed to evade capture and made his way to Spain and back to Lindholme, only to be killed soon afterwards when his aircraft crashed on an air test near Finningley just before the squadron left its Yorkshire base.

Not all aircraft were lost over enemy territory. One crashed in Co. Wicklow, Eire killing the crew, who had become lost on their way home from Berlin. Another hit a house near Leicester, killing two of the crew and a civilian on the ground. The pilot had been stunting to impress his girl friend.

In June 1941 Lindholme saw the formation of 408 (Goose) Squadron, the second RCAF bomber squadron to be formed overseas. It worked up at Lindholme before moving to Syerston in Nottinghamshire a month later. Its move coincided with major changes at Lindholme. 50's CO, W/Cmdr Gus Walker, a man destined to become a 4 Group legend, was replaced by G/Capt Sanderson and the squadron moved to Swinderby. Lindholme itself was then transferred from 5 to 1 Group

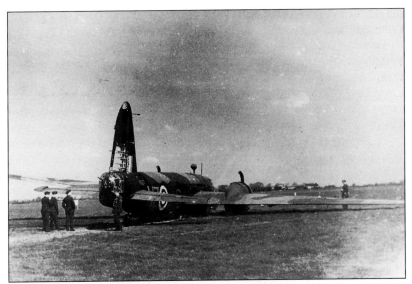

Wellington Ic R1697 of 304 Squadron following a wheels-up landing. Note the battle damage to the rear of the aircraft. (P. Brych via Peter Green)

and became the new home for two Polish squadrons, 304 (Silesian) and 305 (Ziemia Wielkopolska), which moved in from Syerston. They had both been formed a couple of months earlier, mainly from Poles who had joined the French Air Force before finally moving to Britain after the fall of France.

They were to spend some ten months at Lindholme, flying their Wellington Ics and IIs, on over 90 operations in which they lost more than 30 aircraft. 304 remained at Lindholme until April 1942 when it was transferred to Coastal Command and moved to Tiree in the Hebrides. 305 stayed until July that year before moving to Hemswell and then Ingham in Lincolnshire, where it continued as a 1 Group bomber squadron before being transferred to the 2nd Tactical Air Force. Before 305 left Lindholme, it provided 13 of the 1,000-plus aircraft which raided Cologne at the end of May 1942, losing the station CO, G/Capt Krzyztyniak, three weeks later in a raid on Bremen. His Wellington had suffered flak damage and ditched some 40 miles off Yarmouth. The rest of the crew were picked up by an MTB but the body of the pilot, who was one of Poland's most distinguished pre-war flyers, was washed ashore some weeks later on the Dutch coast.

It was during the Poles' occupancy of the airfield that the legend of

'Lindholme Willie' was born. This was the ghost which was, the story goes, to haunt the airfield for more than two decades.

Alan Hollingworth, a post-war CO at Lindholme, recalls that the airfield was surrounded by soft, marshy land, much of which was still waiting to be drained. One night a Wellington crash-landed in this inaccessible bog and all on board were killed, some of the crew drowning in the marsh. The aircraft could not be recovered and the tail-fin could be seen sticking out of the peaty mud, still visible two years later. One of those killed was a young officer who had been billeted in the CO's house. Some time after that started the sightings of a ghostly figure wearing flying clothes, appearing at various parts of the airfield – including the WAAF quarters. Mechanics working late at night in hangars would often claim they were offered a spanner by a man in flying clothes, only for him to disappear as they reached for the proffered tool. The story persisted long after the war, and during his time as CO, Alan Hollingworth called staff together in an attempt to persuade them there was nothing in the legend of Lindholme Billy. However, the CO was to change his mind one night when he and his

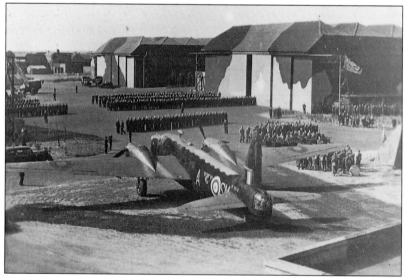

A formal occasion at Lindholme in the spring of 1942. The aircraft in the foreground is a Wellington II, W5590 of 305 Squadron. It was to be lost a few weeks later when it ditched 146 miles off the Lincolnshire coast following a raid on Hamburg. The crew was later picked up by a warship. (P. Brych via Peter Green)

176

wife were awoken by the sound of their piano being played downstairs. When he went to investigate, he found the doors locked and the ground floor deserted. It was only after he left Lindholme that Alan heard that during reclamation work on Hatfield Moor the body of a young Polish officer had been found alongside a partly deployed parachute. He was later given a military burial in a nearby churchyard ... and Lindholme Willie vanished, although stories persist today of an apparition which is still seen occasionally close to the site of the old No 4 hangar.

The departure of 305 heralded a major change in life at RAF Lindholme. The airfield was closed for runway construction and when it reopened in October it was at the centre for training within 1 Group. 1656 Heavy Conversion Unit moved in from Breighton where it had been formed to prepare 1 Group crews for the change to Lancasters. Initially, crews were trained on Manchesters and then completed their course on the unit's Lancaster flight before going on to squadrons then re-equipping with Lancasters in 1 Group. 1656 was to be joined in November 1942 by 1481 Target Towing Flight, which moved from Binbrook to provide training for observers and gunners. Two months later 1503 BAT Flight arrived to provide blind landing technique training for pilots. In June 1943 a second conversion unit, 1667, was formed at Lindholme with Halifaxes and Lancasters.

Aircraft from 1656 were occasionally used in Main Force attacks and on 17th-18th January 1943 the Lancaster flown by instructor F/Lt Hood was lost along with its seven-man crew in an attack on Berlin.

The creation of the Base system within Bomber Command saw Lindholme become the 11 Base HQ in August, with its sub-stations at Blyton, near Gainsborough, and the still-to-be completed Falding-worth, near Market Rasen. In October the whole of 1667 moved to Faldingworth, relieving pressure on the grossly overcrowded facilities at Lindholme. The shortage of Lancasters led to the Lancaster flights from Faldingworth and Blyton joining Lindholme's to form the 1 Group Lancaster Finishing School which, in January 1944, moved to Hemswell. In the spring of 1944 the new airfield just across Hatfield Moor at Sandtoft opened as a sub-station of Lindholme, with 1667 moving in from Faldingworth.

The Halifaxes operated by Lindholme and its sub-station were, certainly in the early days, hand-me-downs from 4 Group squadrons or from the 1 Group squadron conversion flights formed before the conversion units came into being. This, together with the inexperience of crews and the unforgiving nature of early versions of the Halifax, inevitably led to losses. 1656 was to lose in excess of 30 aircraft in crashes, the vast majority of them Halifaxes, including three in the space of little more than an hour on the night of 20th November 1944. The first hit a tree and crashed at Dunscroft, killing five of the crew, when the pilot raised the flaps instead of the undercarriage. Just twelve minutes later the second lost height after take-off and crashed and burned at the end of the runway. This time six of the crew were injured. The third incident occurred 55 minutes later and it was believed the pilot was distracted by the fires still burning from the first two accidents as he selected flaps up instead of undercarriage after take-off and crashed at Lings Farm, Dunsville. Six men died in this crash.

It was at conversion units like Lindholme that crews were finally assembled. Dave Fellowes, a rear gunner who went on to serve at Binbrook with 460 Squadron, recalls he went to Lindholme with five of his crew from 30 OTU at Hixon and it was there that they were joined by a flight engineer.

'The crews were assembled at the back of the room and the flight engineers were brought in to be paraded in front of us. I saw one who looked old enough to be my dad and I remember thinking: "I bet we get that doddery old so-and-so." And we did. It was the best thing that happened to us. He was a first class engineer who had also been a master baker in Goole before the war, so he knew the area.'

During the month or so his crew were at Lindholme they were accommodated in wooden huts, all the brick-built accommodation being allocated to the station staff. They flew 21 hours by day and 15 hours 30 minutes by night, including one trip to drop leaflets over Marseilles and another windowing around Bordeaux, before they went to the LFS at Hemswell.

His crew's experience of operations during their time with 1656 was nothing new. In January 1943 one of the unit's Lancasters is recorded as being lost with its crew on a raid on Berlin.

In his book *Aircrew* Bruce Lewis describes his time at Lindholme and remembers how fortune smiled on some and not on others. He and his crew completed a six-hour cross-country exercise in one of Lindholme's ageing Halifaxes. On landing, the machine was refuelled and a fresh crew took off for another navigational exercise but no sooner had they become airborne than the Halifax simply tipped over and dived into the ground, killing everyone on board.

He also recalls a time when his Halifax landed at Fulbeck in south Lincolnshire, then being used by American transport aircraft preparing for the Normandy invasion. GIs came from all quarters to examine this strange aircraft which had landed in their midst and insisted on entertaining the crew to lunch which consisted of a huge steak covered in peanut butter, pineapple chunks and sugar!

Lindholme's training role was to continue after the war, first as home to 1653 HCU and later the No 5 Air Navigation School and Bomber Command (later Strike Command) Bombing School. Flying ended in the early 1970s but the runways continued to be used for a number of years as a relief landing ground by aircraft from nearby Finningley. During the 1980s much of the site was redeveloped as a prison.

20
LINTON-ON-OUSE

Few would argue that Bomber Command's spiritual home in Yorkshire is to be found at RAF Linton-on-Ouse. This big pre-war airfield, which stands just off the A19 a few miles north of York, was operational from 3rd September 1939 until the very last bombing raid from Yorkshire; it was used by ten heavy bomber squadrons which between them flew Whitleys, Halifaxes and Lancasters; and it also served briefly as headquarters of both 4 and 6 Groups.

Linton was one of the biggest of a number of major Expansion Scheme airfields built in Yorkshire in the mid-1930s. Five brick-built C-type hangars were among the many buildings completed by the time the airfield opened on 13th May 1937. Unusually, its construction included the provision of a concrete runway which was later extended and added to. It was used initially as the headquarters of No 4 Group, which opened there on 28th July and was to remain at Linton until April 1940, when it moved to Heslington Hall, now part of York University. Construction continued until April 1938 when Linton's first squadrons, 51 and 58, moved in from Boscombe Down. Linton was to continue almost exclusively as a two-squadron airfield until the late spring of 1945.

On the first night of the war ten Whitleys from Linton's squadrons scattered leaflets over Hamburg, Bremen and the Ruhr in the first incursion by Bomber Command over Germany, three of the 58 Squadron aircraft later force-landing in France. Several aircraft from 58 were then sent to northern France where they operated briefly from Rheims on leaflet raids, writing off two Whitleys in the process, before being loaned to Coastal Command and moving back to Boscombe Down. 51 Squadron, which lost three Whitleys in those early leaflet operations to the vagaries of the weather and mechanical problems, left

Linton for Kinloss in November to begin a short spell with Coastal Command. It was replaced by 78 Squadron, with 58 returning in late February 1940. The German invasion of Norway saw 4 Group aircraft involved in attacks on airfields and one Whitley from 58 failed to return after one of these on Stavanger on 30th April.

In the meantime, 78 Squadron was still working up on its Whitleys but the invasion of the Low Countries and northern France saw its aircraft flying a number of reconnaissance missions, one of which led to the squadron's first loss on 24th May. It flew its first bombing operation early in July, when four aircraft went to Gelsenkirchen. Soon afterwards 78 Squadron moved to Dishforth and was replaced by 77, which was itself replaced in October by 102 Squadron. It was to remain at Linton for just five weeks, losing one aircraft, a Whitley which was abandoned by its crew near the airfield after being hit by flak over the German coast. Among 102's pilots at the time was a young man destined to become one of the legendary figures in Bomber Command, Leonard Cheshire. He won a Distinguished Service Order on the night of 12th-13th November when his Whitley was hit by flak and set on fire over Cologne. Cheshire, showing all the qualities which were later to earn him a Victoria Cross while commanding 617 Squadron, brought the badly damaged aircraft under control and nursed it back across the North Sea to Linton.

During 77's brief stay one of its aircraft ditched in the sea following an attack on Berlin in late September and the crew were later spotted in their dinghy some 100 miles east of Hartlepool. The weather was deteriorating and it was to be another four days before a destroyer finally located the Whitley's dinghy. By that time only one of the crew, Sgt Riley, was still alive.

At the end of November 102 moved to Topcliffe and was replaced a week later by 35 Squadron, which had been reformed a month earlier at Boscombe Down. The squadron, commanded by W/Cmdr Collings, had been selected as the first to be equipped with the new four-engined Halifax. It was to spend the next three months working up on the new aircraft before becoming operational. During that time 35 lost just one aircraft, F/O Henry and his crew being killed when their aircraft caught fire and crashed near Dishforth.

58 Squadron was still using its Whitleys and was to lose several aircraft that winter, some to enemy action and others to the elements. One of the more bizarre losses occurred early in December when Whitley T4207 was written off when the pilot tried to land at a K-site –

a dummy airfield intended to fool German reconnaissance aircraft – at Cold Kirkby, Yorkshire, only to overshoot and collide with a wooden Whitley! The only casualty was reported to be the crew's pride.

Navigational aids were still elementary and many Bomber Command aircraft were lost that winter simply by becoming lost. 58 suffered two such losses in a single night, 11th-12th February 1941, when several aircraft strayed off track on their return from Bremen. One was abandoned by its crew near Glasgow and the second near Nottingham.

The Halifax Mk Is of 35 Squadron finally became operational on the night of 10th-11th March when W/Cmdr Collings led the first of six aircraft off for Le Havre. Four of the Halifaxes bombed the primary

The rear turret of a 78 Squadron Halifax Mk II at Linton-on-Ouse, 1942. The distinctive D-shaped fin was later to be replaced by a rectangular one following tests suggesting it contributed to numerous accidents involving early versions of the Halifax. (Sir Guy Lawrence)

target, a fifth attacked Dieppe, while the sixth was unable to locate the target and was forced to turn back because of lack of fuel. As the bombers returned across southern England one, F-Freddie, was attacked and shot down by a British fighter. The pilot, S/Ldr Gilchrist and his flight engineer managed to bale out but the other five members of the crew were killed when the Halifax crashed in Surrey. It was the first of almost 1,900 Halifaxes to be lost on operations over the next four years. The second came a little over a month later when Sgt Wally Lashbrook's Halifax was badly damaged by flak in a raid on Kiel and hit a tree and crash-landed near Linton, the crew escaping serious injury.

Meanwhile, 58 Squadron was still soldiering on with its Whitleys and two nights after the loss of 35's second Halifax, the Whitleys were over Berlin. One of them, the aircraft of P/O Law and crew, was damaged by the Hamburg flak on its way home and lost an engine. The second caught fire over the North Sea and Law was forced to ditch, getting off a Mayday just before the bomber went down. The crew managed to get into the dinghy but it was another two days before they were spotted by a searching Hudson. They were eventually picked up by an air-sea rescue launch after spending 64 hours in the sea. They were found to be remarkably well in spite of their ordeal, returning to operations later in the summer. P/O Law had another lucky escape at Linton on 7th August when his Whitley overshot and struck one of the hangars. His luck finally ran out a month later when his Whitley was recalled from an attack on Kiel and diverted to Acklington, where it crashed into a field, killing the pilot and three of his crew.

Linton itself was damaged in a raid by the Luftwaffe on 12th May, the attackers setting fire to one of the hangars. During the fire fighting operation which followed the station commander, G/Capt Frederick Garraway, was killed. His son was to be killed while flying with 78 Squadron from Breighton in April 1944. In another nuisance raid on the airfield shrapnel from a bomb pierced one of the mustard gas canisters kept in a special enclosure in the station bomb dump 'just in case'. There was no leak but within days the canisters were removed from Linton-on-Ouse and several other Yorkshire airfields.

Despite the hectic pace, few of those stationed at Linton would have swapped for life on one of the smaller bomber airfields in Yorkshire. Eddie McKinna, who lives in Newcastle, worked in the bomb dump at Linton until the airfield was transferred to 6 Group and remembers it with some affection. The work was hard and unremitting but conditions at Linton were excellent. Initially he and the other armourers lived in the pre-war barrack blocks and later they were accommodated, eight at a time, in the station married quarters. During the first two years of war there were around 80 men in the armament section and, apart from working in the bomb dump, they were often called upon to help bomb up aircraft, a practice which stopped in 1942 when more men were available for the work. Many of the bombs issued to the squadrons in the early days were of a poor quality but had improved considerably by 1942. At the same time better bomb trollies were delivered and tractors supplied to tow them. Mr McKinna also remembers the station armoury was equipped with twelve Lee Enfield .303 rifles and eleven Webley revolvers, which could be issued to commissioned pilots to take with them on operations if they so wished.

The airfield was briefly the home of three squadrons, 76 being formed from 35's C Flight before it moved to Middleton St George. 35 Squadron itself was to lose a Halifax in a daylight raid on Kiel at the end of June, the bomber bringing down one of a number of attacking Me 109s before it fell with the loss of six of its crew. Losses were now beginning to rise and both 35 and 58 lost aircraft and their crews in attacks on Frankfurt and Merseberg, while an unescorted daylight attack involving 35 Squadron on the German battleship *Scharnhorst* at La Pallice cost the Linton squadron two of its aircraft, nine of those on board surviving to become PoWs.

The onset of autumn brought further long-distance raids for the Linton squadrons. 35 lost two Halifaxes over Berlin on the night of 2nd-3rd September with the loss of seven lives; five nights later it was 58's turn to lose two over the German capital, this time six men being killed. Four nights later 58's Whitleys were involved in an attack on Warnemünde, one of the aircraft ditching in the North Sea while a second was abandoned over Harrogate, the stricken aircraft crashing into the grounds of the town's Majestic Hotel. 58 was to lose another two in a raid on Stettin later in the month and two more on the night of 10th-11th October when Essen was the target. One was shot down over Germany, four of the crew being killed, and the second ditched off Skegness, where the crew were rescued by the town's lifeboat. Four aircraft, three of them from 58, were lost on the night of 7th-8th November, two of them over Berlin and the others in a diversionary attack on Essen, while a raid on Hamburg at the end of the month cost

58 four Whitleys. A 35 Squadron Halifax also failed to return, the crew of one of the Whitleys being rescued by a Grimsby trawler.

Two more 58 Whitleys were lost in an attack on Dusseldorf at the end of December. These proved to be the last losses the squadron would suffer until one aircraft failed to return from an attack on Emden on the night of 12th-13th March 1942. By that time the squadron was already on notice that it was to join Coastal Command, 58 finally leaving Linton-on-Ouse on 8th April.

The presence of German battleships in French and Norwegian ports attracted the attention of Bomber Command in the early months of 1942 and 35 Squadron was involved in several attacks on both the *Scharnhorst* and *Tirpitz*. The latter was anchored off Trondheim and proved a tough nut for Bomber Command to crack. A raid on the night of 30th-31st March cost 35 Squadron three Halifaxes and the lives of 21 men. A month later they were back again and this time two of their aircraft failed to return. One was shot down with the loss of all seven on board. The second, Halifax W1048 TL-S, was hit by flak and the pilot, P/O Don McIntyre, managed to put the aircraft down on the ice-covered Lake Hoklingen. The flight engineer broke his ankle and became a PoW but the remaining members of the crew escaped to Sweden. Their aircraft eventually went through the ice. Thirty-one years later the aircraft was recovered and is now on display at the RAF Museum at Hendon. The following night two more aircraft from 35 Squadron were lost in attacks on the *Tirpitz*.

Bomber Command's attention was now switching to the Ruhr and that summer 35 Squadron was to suffer severe losses, including four Halifaxes in a raid on Essen, before it finally left Linton in August to join the newly-formed Pathfinder Force at Graveley. Among the aircraft lost was a Halifax which failed to release its 4,000lb bomb over Duisburg. Frantic efforts by the crew to dislodge the bomb over the North Sea failed and back at Linton they were ordered to bale out rather than attempt to land. This they did, the aircraft immediately rolling over, a manoeuvre which led to the bomb falling out and exploding in fields near Knaresborough.

35's departure – its Halifax Conversion Flight went to Marston Moor – heralded the return of 76 (which was to be commanded by W/Cmdr Leonard Cheshire in his third spell at Linton) and 78 Squadrons, both now re-equipped with Halifaxes. They were given little time to settle in before they were in action, three aircraft, two of them from 78 Squadron, failing to return from a raid on Flensburg on the night of

23rd-24th September. There were no survivors from the 78 Squadron aircraft but five were rescued from the 76 Squadron Halifax, which ditched off the island of Sylt. Among them was Sgt Denholm Elliott, later to become one of Britain's best-known actors.

It was to be a hard winter for the Linton squadrons. Another raid on Flensburg cost the station three more Halifaxes and 15 lives while three failed to return from a raid on Genoa early in November. One was brought down by flak, six of the crew surviving, a second ditched off Newcastle and the crew were picked up, while the third suffered an engine failure over the target and refused to climb. It was eventually ditched off the Spanish coast and the crew briefly interned. An attack on Duisburg shortly before Christmas cost 76 two Halifaxes and the lives of 16 men while five more from 78 were killed when their aircraft crashed in the sea 30 miles off Yarmouth. But this was only a taste of what 1943 had in store for the Linton squadrons.

Germany's industrial heartland was to be the target of Bomber Command in the spring and summer of 1943 and between March and June that year the two Linton squadrons were to lose almost 50 Halifaxes. One of them, which was damaged by the Stuttgart flak, crashed into the home of the High Sheriff of Sussex near Horsham, killing several of his household staff. Four failed to return from Essen on the night of 3rd-4th April with the loss of 14 lives while four more and 26 lives were lost over Pilsen two weeks later.

Among the aircraft lost during April was a 76 Squadron Halifax in which the station commander G/Capt John Whitley was flying as second pilot. The aircraft was shot down by a night fighter. The crew was ordered to bale out and all escaped except the pilot, F/L Hull, who remained at the controls long enough for the others to jump. Three of the crew were injured but the other four, including G/Capt Whitley, evaded capture and the station CO returned to England via Gibraltar on 24th May. Whitley was to command 4 Group in the closing months of the war.

Four raids in May cost the Linton squadrons 13 Halifaxes with 37 men killed, while each squadron lost two aircraft in an attack on Dortmund on 11th-12th June. The following night two more aircraft failed to return from Bochum, each squadron losing a complete crew. These were to be the last 4 Group losses from RAF Linton-on-Ouse – the station was about to be taken over by the Canadians.

Plans had been drawn up in 1942 for the creation of the Canadian-funded 6 Group and its headquarters had been established at Linton-

A fine view of Lancaster OW-J of 426 (Thunderbird) Squadron, August 1943. The aircraft was lost in a raid on Dusseldorf on the night of 3rd-4th November that year. (C. Jones)

on-Ouse on 25th October, moving to Allerton Park some five weeks later. 4 Group was to take over the 1 Group airfields at Breighton and Holme-on-Spalding Moor but these would not become available until the summer of 1943. 76 and 78 Squadrons moved out on 16th June and were replaced by 426 (Thunderbird) Squadron which arrived from Dishforth and immediately began converting to Lancaster IIs. 426 was to fly its new aircraft for the first time on the night of 17th-18th August in the attack on Peenemünde. Two were shot down, one of them flown by the squadron CO, W/Cmdr Crooks, one of his crew being the only survivor from the two Lancasters. W/Cmdr Swetman arrived at Linton on 19th August to take over the squadron.

At the end of the month 426 was joined by 408 (Goose) Squadron, which moved in from Leeming and immediately began a Lancaster conversion programme. 408 was to begin operations in October, losing its first Lancaster in an attack on Kassel at the end of the month. Both squadrons were heavily involved in the Battle of Berlin and each lost an aircraft on the night of 23rd-24th November, the 426 Squadron aircraft crashing near Malton with two of the crew being killed. Three failed to return from Berlin on 26th-27th November, one crash-landing near Lincoln. The 408 Squadron aircraft had been badly damaged by flak and a night fighter and had lost an engine. A second engine failed and the skipper ordered the crew to bale out but it was found the escape hatch had jammed and he opted to crash-land near Fiskerton. All on board survived.

Five aircraft, four of them from 426, were lost on the night of 16th-17th December, a night when many airfields were found to be fog-bound when the aircraft returned. Two of the Thunderbirds crashed on their return, killing eleven of those on board. Another was shot down, while the fourth was abandoned over Sweden after its fuel tanks were ruptured in a night fighter attack. Four nights later each squadron lost two aircraft in an attack on Frankfurt, one of the 408 Squadron aircraft being shot down by another Lancaster. The five men who survived this incident were the only survivors from Linton that night.

Four more raids on Berlin cost the station six more Lancasters while the attack on the German capital on the night of 27th-28th January proved disastrous for the Canadians at Linton. 408 lost three aircraft while four 426 aircraft failed to return. Of the 46 men killed that night three were from 420 Squadron who were gaining operational experience. 408 was to lose four more in an attack on Leipzig on 19th-20th February. Among the 28 men killed was a 19-year-old pilot, F/O Frampton. 426 lost an aircraft with eight men on board on the same night. Raids on Stuttgart and Frankfurt in March resulted in eight more Lancasters being lost along with the lives of 46 men. Among the three bombers lost on the Nuremburg raid were the last Lancasters from 426 Squadron before it began converting to Halifax IIIs, the squadron losing the first of its new aircraft in an attack on rail yards at Haine St Pierre early in May.

Later in the month 408's CO, W/Cmdr Jacobs was killed in a raid on Dortmund which cost the squadron two Lancasters. His aircraft was carrying a crew of nine which included the squadron's navigation and gunnery leaders. His replacement was W/Cmdr McLernon, who was brought in from 425 Squadron at Tholthorpe.

Each Linton squadron lost an aircraft during operations over

A Royal visit to Linton-on-Ouse, in 1944. The Queen is pictured talking to officers between radial-engined Lancaster IIs of 408 Squadron on the left and unidentified Halifax IIIs on the right. (Yorkshire Air Museum via Peter Green)

Normandy on D-Day, both crews surviving. Losses were now starting to fall dramatically, but three from 408 plus a 426 Halifax failed to return from an attack on the rail centre at Cambrai later in the month. This period also saw 426 exchange its Halifax IIIs for the new Mk VII. It lost two of its new aircraft in a raid on Metz at the end of June, 13 of those on board surviving. 408 began to convert to Halifax IIIs at around the same time and lost one, plus three Lancasters in an attack on Hamburg at the end of July. They were the last Lancasters lost before the conversion was completed. These were the final multiple losses until November when four aircraft, three of them from 426, were lost on a raid on Dusseldorf. Three of these came down behind Allied lines and the 17 survivors were able to return to Linton-on-Ouse.

Losses continued into 1945 but by now crews' chances of survival had risen dramatically. Several of the aircraft lost managed to come down behind Allied lines and the crews quickly found themselves on their way back to Linton.

Ironically, it was the weather, that fearsome enemy of the early bomber crews at Linton-on-Ouse, which had a nasty surprise in store for 426 Squadron in the closing weeks of the war. On the night of 5th

March Halifaxes began taking off in mid-afternoon for the long haul to Chemnitz. As 426's aircraft became airborne, its aircraft encountered severe icing and within a few minutes three had crashed. One came down close to the village of Hutton-le-Hole and exploded and a second collided with a Halifax from 425 Squadron, both aircraft falling in flames at Poolspring, near Nun Monkton with just one man surviving. The third was involved in the worst incident. F/Lt Emerson's Halifax began to suffer severe problems shortly after take-off and, as it was flying across York, the aircraft broke up under the weight of ice which had accumulated on it. The fuselage crashed into houses in Nunthorpe Grove in the city while one of the engines hit the nearby secondary school. Six of the crew died along with five civilians while a further 18 were badly injured. The only survivor from the Halifax was the wireless operator, P/O Low, who baled out. He was too low for his parachute to open properly but as the bombs on the Halifax exploded the blast caused his 'chute to deploy.

The last operation of the war for 6 Group resulted in the final tragedy for Linton-on-Ouse, a 408 Squadron and 426 Squadron Halifax colliding on their bomb run to the target killing all 14 men on board.

With the war over, Linton-on-Ouse reverted to RAF control and was used by a number of fighter squadrons until the late 1950s, when it assumed a training role.

21
LISSETT

Of all the Yorkshire bomber airfields none was closer to Germany than RAF Lissett. Today little remains but a scattering of buildings, almost lost in the wave of caravan camps which have engulfed this part of the East Yorkshire coastline south of Bridlington. But as motorists on the Hull-Bridlington road pass through the village of Lissett, it is still possible for them to visualise the impact the Royal Air Force had on this part of the county half a century and more ago.

It was in 1941 that a site close to Lissett village was identified as suitable for an airfield and construction began almost immediately. RAF Lissett was a typical wartime station – three intersecting concrete runways, a pair of T2 hangars and dispersed accommodation sites. The runways were finished late in 1942 and were put to use almost immediately by the Blenheims and Beaufighters flying from 2 OTU at nearby Catfoss.

Lissett's only wartime occupants were to be the Halifaxes of 158 Squadron, which arrived from Rufforth in late February 1943 shortly after completing a raid on Nuremburg. The airfield was still not finished and this helped account for the squadron's first loss from Lissett, F/Sgt Wyllie's Halifax II, NP-H, which hit an obstruction as it took off on a cross country exercise and damaged its undercarriage. The aircraft later crash-landed in Wiltshire, the crew escaping injury.

The first operation from Lissett was mounted on the night of 11th-12th March against Stuttgart, one aircraft failing to return. Sgt Witham and his crew all died when their aircraft crashed near Bar-de-Luc in France. Successive raids on Berlin later in the month cost the squadron two more aircraft and the lives of nine men. But this was only the overture to a terrible summer for the men of 158 Squadron.

A raid on Essen on 3rd-4th April cost Lissett three Halifaxes and the lives of 18 men. Fourteen died in two aircraft shot down by flak and four more in the third aircraft which crashed at Hornsea on its return. Attacks on Duisburg, Dusseldorf, Essen and Dortmund resulted in more losses, with two more aircraft being lost over Bochum. After that raid P/O Robinson was awarded an immediate DFC for bringing his damaged aircraft home following an attack by a night fighter. A week later Robinson and his crew were dead, their's being one of two aircraft lost in an attack on Krefeld.

And so it went on in that terrible summer ... Mulheim, Cologne, Gelsenkirchen, Aachen, Montbellard, Hamburg and Essen again. All cost 158 Squadron more aircraft and more men. Most fell to flak or night fighters, a few struggling back to Yorkshire before crashing. One of these was a Halifax which crashed close to Millingdale House Farm at Lowthorpe near Bridlington in the early hours of 26th July. The aircraft immediately caught fire but this, and the risk from exploding ammunition, did not prevent those living at the farm risking their own lives in the vain attempt to rescue the crew trapped inside the bomber.

There was a particularly poignant tragedy in mid-August when one of three 158 Halifaxes which failed to return from an attack on Nuremburg made it back to England, the pilot giving the crew the order to bale out once they were over Selsey Bill. Unfortunately, a strong off-shore wind blew all eight parachutes out to sea and only three of the crew were picked up.

Another aircraft lost that night was the Halifax carrying W/Cmdr Hope, 158's CO, who was nearing the end of his tour with the squadron. He was one of three survivors and spent the rest of the war as a PoW. The squadron's new commanding officer, W/Cmdr Calder, arrived in time to lead the squadron on the Peenemünde raid, which cost Lissett one Halifax.

The squadron was now operating on a three-flight basis and was able to put up 24 Halifaxes at a time making it one of the biggest in 4 Group. Its losses, however, continued to rise. Five failed to return from a raid on Berlin on 23rd-24th August, 16 men being killed and 19 taken prisoner. Among them was an Australian P/O Frisby, who was to become the 'map maker' at Sagan PoW camp prior to the great escape in March 1944.

Attacks on Nuremburg and Munchengladbach on the following nights saw two aircraft lost and a second raid on Berlin at the end of the month resulted in four more Halifaxes failing to return, bringing total losses to eleven in just eight days. Among the aircraft lost over Berlin was that of S/Ldr Elliott, B Flight's commander. Seventeen men were killed in this attack and ten became prisoners. Remarkably one, Sgt Simister, evaded capture after his aircraft crashed near Berlin and made his escape through Switzerland. For this extraordinary feat he was awarded the Military Medal, a rare award for an airman.

Losses on this scale could not be sustained for long and eventually the Halifax IIs in 4 Group were withdrawn from attacks on Berlin until their squadrons could re-equip with the much superior Mk III. This did not mean, however, a lessening of activity for the Halifax squadrons. 158 was to lose another 20 aircraft before the end of the year, including four on two attacks on Hanover and three in a single night in an attack on Kassel, one of these crashing on take-off. An attack on Frankfurt in late December also cost the squadron two aircraft, one of which crashed after being hit by a shower of incendiaries dropped by a Lancaster flying at a greater height.

Not all losses were due to operational action. One 158 Squadron aircraft crashed near Filey during an air test in mid-September killing the seven man crew along with their WAAF driver Sgt Olive Morse and a member of their ground crew, LAC Perrin, who had been taken along for a joy ride.

The end of 1943 saw C Flight detached to form a new squadron, 640, which formed at Lissett under the command of W/Cmdr Eayrs and flew two operations before moving to Leconfield. The first of these was on the night of 20th-21st January when 4 Group provided 158 Halifaxes for a raid on Berlin. 158 flew its new Halifax IIIs to Berlin that same night; one failed to return, F/Sgt Thompson and all his crew being killed. An attack on Magdeburg late in the month cost the squadron two aircraft with two more being lost a week later in a raid on Berlin, one crashing into the airfield sewage plant as it returned on three engines and the other belly-landing in Holland where the crew were taken prisoner. A third Halifax was written off after crashing on take-off.

An attack on Leipzig in February cost Bomber Command 78 aircraft, including two Halifaxes and their crews from Lissett. One of these, NP-M, was flying between Hamburg and Hanover at 2.20 am when it was attacked without warning by a Ju 88. The only survivor was 19-year-old Sgt George Barrett, the aircraft's flight engineer.

A few hours earlier he and his crew had been waiting to take off when they saw a Halifax which had just left Lissett dive into the ground and explode at Little Atwick, near Catfoss. At the time they

Nineteen-year-old flight engineer Sgt George Barrett, the only survivor of Halifax LW501 LP-M of 158 Squadron, which was shot down by a Ju 88 during an attack on Leipzig, February 1944. (George Barrett)

thought it might have been P/O Peter Jennings and his crew, which included George's friend, Charles Seymour. Then they recalled Jennings' crew was on stand-down. It was only many years after the war that George Barrett discovered it was, in fact, Jennings' crew which had perished in that fireball which lit up the night sky. In 1992 a black marble plaque was unveiled at the site of the crash by the brother of the Halifax's navigator. The plaque lies on a bridleway through the field where the aircraft crashed and was later adopted by 12-year-old Georgina Woods, who came across it while walking her dog. Since then she has regularly left flowers at the spot as a mark of remembrance to those who died.

Two Halifaxes were lost in the final raid of the Battle of Berlin – the crew of one being killed when it crash-landed into a minefield on the Norfolk coast – while the Nuremburg raid proved particularly disastrous with four of 158's 16 Halifaxes lost along with 14 men killed and 12 taken prisoner. Two others evaded and made it back to England. Among those who died was one of the squadron's flight commanders, S/Ldr S. D. Jones, who, together with his crew, was on the twelfth trip of his second tour. Five of his crew did manage to escape from their Halifax, which was hit by flak on its way to the target. S/Ldr Jones' rear gunner died with him.

Another of the Lissett Halifaxes was damaged in the attack but one aircraft which did make it back safely was NP-F LV907, a brand-new Halifax which had only arrived from the factory at Radlett a few days before. It was taken to Nuremburg by F/Sgt Joe Hitchman and his crew, who were by then almost a third of their way through their tour.

Hitchman and his crew were due to go on leave that day and were just leaving the camp (complete with their ration books) when they were recalled and told they were on operations that night. Their usual aircraft was G-Gremlin, which they shared with S/Ldr Jones, who had already put himself on operations for that night. 'We were told we would take a new aircraft on the Nuremburg trip, a replacement for "F" which had been lost a night or two before,' recalls Mr Hitchman.

It proved an eventful night for Joe Hitchman and his men and the new Halifax. 'There were so many fighters about we were taking evasive action nearly all the way there and all the way back. All that corkscrewing meant we just had enough fuel to make it back to England and we had to land at Odiham in Hampshire, which was then being used by the Americans,' he said. When they eventually returned to Lissett they learned of the terrible losses 158 had sustained and that among them was S/Ldr Jones in their trusty G-Gremlin.

The whole crew then went on a fortnight's leave and when they returned there was a new 'G' waiting for them. It was the practice for Lissett aircraft to carry lurid nose-art and they asked a member of their ground crew to name their new aircraft G-Gremlin. But it turned out he was superstitious and one of the crew, who had picked up an American comic at Odiham, came up with the idea of G-Goofey, and so was born *Goofey's Gift*, a Halifax which was to complete 83 operations from Lissett.

Joe Hitchman and crew were to make one more trip in NP-F, to Malines on 1st May. By that time the aircraft had become something of a celebrity in 158, despite being on only its eleventh operation. It flew in the face of every superstition and had been given the name *Friday the Thirteenth*. Its fuselage sported a sickle (the regular companion of the airman's friend, the Grim Reaper), skull and crossbones and inverted horseshoe – all symbols most crews would have crossed the road to avoid. It went on to complete 128 operations, the highest number recorded by a Halifax. When the war ended it was chosen to represent Bomber Command at a display of aircraft in London's Oxford Street. Then *Friday* was unceremoniously scrapped. All that remains is the bomb panel containing that famous name and the symbols of its 128 operations, and that is now on display in the RAF Museum at Hendon.

'The story on the squadron was that everyone was fed-up with F-Freddies and the such and so it was named *Friday the Thirteenth*. We certainly didn't think it unlucky to fly in it. The longer it survived the luckier it got,' said Fred Tunstall, rear gunner in Hitchman's crew. Joe Hitchman recalled: 'Dumbo Smith was *Friday's* first regular pilot. He and his crew prided themselves on not being superstitious and that's why they chose the name. That said, he was called "Dumbo" because he and his crew each flew with a little elephant one of the ground crew had made for them.'

Hitchman's crew completed their tour with a daylight raid on Siracourt, by which time all seven were commissioned and had between them five DFCs and two DFMs. Not so fortunate was *Goofey's Gift*. The Halifax, LK839, crashed killing its mainly Canadian crew at Foston-on-the-Wolds on its approach into Lissett on 17th August 1944.

Rear gunner Fred Tunstall had shown remarkably dogged determination to get into aircrew. He had originally served in RAF rescue launches at Aberdeen and Stranraer before volunteering to fly. A disastrous unofficial flight in a Sunderland, which crashed between the

F/O Derek Waterman and crew with 158 Squadron's Friday the 13th *at Lissett, 1944.*
(Ken Cammack)

Scottish coast and Northern Ireland and left him in the water for four hours failed to deter him, as did the seven days confined-to-barracks he received for being absent from his post. After OTU at Kinloss he went to Marston Moor where his crew was completed before being posted to Lissett where he flew operationally for the first time as a replacement gunner in a raid on Berlin in January, 1944. Joe Hitchman did his first operation as a second pilot, again to Berlin while the crew's first navigator flew as a replacement the same night and failed to return.

Friday had several regular crews during the 13 months the aircraft flew operationally from Lissett. Among them, for 28 trips of their tour, was the crew of F/Sgt (later Flying Officer) Derek Waterman, and in the rear turret for each of those raids was Sgt Ken Cammack, a young gunner from Brigg in Lincolnshire. He remembers *Friday* as a good aircraft to fly in, one which never really gave them any problems. It also kept them out of trouble: they went through their complete tour without being attacked by night fighters and Ken Cammack was never to fire his guns in anger during his complete tour at Lissett.

'We had plenty of scary moments with flak, however,' he said. 'They said not to worry about flak until you could hear it and hear it we certainly did on some of our trips, particularly over the Ruhr. We were always aware there were fighters about. We would be flying along in comparative darkness and then suddenly a fighter flare would light everything up.'

Friday's 100th operation came up on 22nd January 1945 when F/Lt Gordon and crew took her to Gelsenkirchen, and her final trip was to Wangerooge on 25th April, appropriately 4 Group's last operation of the war.

Lissett is remembered by those who served there as a good station with typical wartime RAF accommodation. It was very handy for nights out in Bridlington and it was comforting to know the emergency strip at Carnaby with its FIDO was 'just across the fields'. Aircrew who landed at Carnaby were taken to Lissett for messing and one day Ken Cammack walked into the Sergeants' Mess and met a pal from Brigg, Cecil Johnson, who was an air-gunner on a Lancaster which had been diverted to Carnaby.

Harry Lomas later wrote a book about his experiences at Lissett, *One Wing High*, in which he recalls that the camp was renowned for its good food and lack of bull. He shared a 'dark and gloomy' hut with seven other men, heated by a single stove which had already consumed all the hut's wooden shelves. Rumour had it that one crew had acquired a telegraph pole which they had fed bit by bit into their stove. Fuel was so precious crews were advised to keep their coke under lock and key.

158 Squadron lost a number of aircraft on the run-up to the Normandy invasion, including three in an attack on marshalling yards at Tergnier and five in an attack on Trappes. The squadron was involved in operations around the beach head during June and in the series of raids on flying bomb sites in northern France. The late summer saw 4 Group resume its campaign against German targets. These included two attacks on one day on the city of Duisburg in October. One of the Lissett aircraft taking part crashed on take-off. The aircraft caught fire but six of the crew managed to scramble clear. When the pilot, F/L McAdam realised the rear gunner, F/Sgt Minto, was trapped, he braved the flames to drag the gunner clear. Only then did the aircraft's bomb load explode, wrecking a second Halifax.

One of the squadron's Halifaxes was shot down in the Lissett circuit on its return from Kamen on 3rd March 1945 by one of the many

German night fighters which had followed the bomber stream back from the Ruhr. F/Lt Roger's aircraft crashed in flames near Sledmere Grange and there were no survivors. Harry Lomas recalls that it was probably the same Ju 88 which then strafed the airfield. During the attack the station commander, G/Capt Tom Sawyer, is reputed to have returned fire by using a Bren gun mounted on the top of the airfield's watch office. A number of Halifaxes were on the ground after returning from Kamen and the rear gunners of several of these are also believed to have opened fire on the intruder.

Dorothy Forrester of Axbridge, Somerset, then Dorothy James, was in the WAAFs at Lissett at the time and remembers being in the ablution block at the time of the attack and watching in amazement as bullet holes appeared in the roof.

Lissett's war came to an end with the attack on Wangerooge and VE Day was celebrated in style on the airfield, with a large part of the squadron's stock of flares and signal rockets being fired off before many of the aircrew left to join in the celebrations in nearby Bridlington.

Within weeks of the end of hostilities arrangements were in hand for the closure of Lissett and the site quickly reverted to agriculture. Today only a few scattered buildings and a simple memorial in the grounds of St James of Compostela's church in Lissett village remain to remind visitors of the part the airfield played in Bomber Command's role in the defeat of Hitler's Germany.

22
MARSTON MOOR, RUFFORTH AND RICCALL

In 1644 a bleak spot a few miles west of York earned its place in English history. The monument erected on the moor to record one of the defining moments in the Civil War was to become a familiar wartime sight for the thousands of young men who passed through the airfield which took its name from the battle site. RAF Marston Moor was the centre of heavy bomber training within Bomber Command's 4 Group. It controlled satellite airfields at Riccall and Rufforth, and the relief landing ground at Acaster Mablis, and had responsibility for training crews for Halifaxes, which were the mainstay of 4 Group in the final three years of the war.

RAF Marston Moor officially opened on 11th November 1941. Main contractors for the work were Laings and they laid down three concrete runways and erected six T2 and a single B1 hangar.

From the outset Marston Moor had been intended for Halifax conversion training and the first units arrived on 3rd January 1943 when 28 and 107 Conversion Flights moved in from Leconfield, where they had formed during the final weeks of 1941. Once established at Marston Moor, they were disbanded and reformed immediately as 1652 Conversion Unit which, apart from a period of a few weeks, was to serve at Marston Moor until the end of the war. 1652 was to spend a few weeks at Rufforth and Dalton during the summer of 1942 before returning to Marston Moor where the word 'Heavy' was added to its title. It also absorbed 35 Conversion Flight, which had been operating at Rufforth, and added a handful of Spitfires and Hurricanes to its strength for use in fighter affiliation work.

1652 was by now fully equipped with four flights of Halifaxes, mainly Mark Is and IIs it had inherited from 4 Group Squadrons. The Halifax is still revered by those who flew it but they will be the first to admit that the early variants were unforgiving aircraft. That, allied to the extensive use many of the bombers had before they reached Marston Moor, helped contribute in no small way to 1652 losing over 70 aircraft, most of them in training accidents. At least half a dozen, however, were lost on operations.

In the spring of 1942, 1652 supplied over 20 aircraft on each of the opening 1,000 bomber raids. The first, to Cologne on 31st May, resulted in a former 35 Squadron Halifax and its crew failing to return. The attack on Essen two nights later saw two Halifaxes lost and a fourth failed to return from an attack later in June on Bremen. Other aircraft lost after operating over Allied Europe included BB372 which crashed and burnt at USAAF Molesworth after overshooting in July 1944, and HR748 which crashed at North Dalton on the Yorkshire Wolds.

It was on 1st April 1943 that G/Capt Leonard Cheshire took command of 1652. He was already one of the most decorated pilots in Bomber Command and, at 25, was the youngest Group Captain then serving in the RAF. But the AOC of 4 Group, Air Vice Marshal Carr, feared he was burning himself out as CO of 76 Squadron, and saw the posting to Marston Moor as a way of preserving one of Bomber Command's brightest assets. Cheshire hated it and, throughout his five months at Marston Moor, badgered everyone in authority to allow him to return to operational duty. He eventually got his wish – as CO of 617 Squadron at Woodhall Spa in Lincolnshire, where he was to be awarded the Victoria Cross – but not before leaving some indelible memories on all those who served with him at Marston Moor.

Jean Didlock was a young WAAF MT driver who remembers Cheshire as the finest officer she came across during the time she spent in the RAF. 'He was a real gentleman,' she said, 'a man every one of us respected. We never saw him in anything other than battle dress and when he asked everyone to work through a weekend, we did it without question. Everyone looked up to him.'

She still recalls the day in 1943 when she was summoned before Cheshire after accidentally splashing him when driving through one of Marston Moor's many puddles. She fully expected a dressing down but

MT driver Jean Didlock, who has fond memories of G/Capt Cheshire's time at Marston Moor. (Mrs J. Dudley)

instead remembers Cheshire laughing heartily at the incident.

Despite all his qualities, there was little Cheshire could do to stem the losses of aircraft in training accidents. Many involved relatively simple accidents on take-off or landing, others were more spectacular. In May 1943 an ex-35 Squadron Halifax clipped the roof of the local vicarage before crashing on the airfield boundary after an engine fire; another crashed close to the school at Castle Howard after an error by the pilot. One Halifax pilot made a successful landing near houses at Greaseborough, close to Rotherham after an engine failure; BB285 crashed into the sewage works at Spofforth, near Wetherby. DG230 crashed into a pond in the grounds of the Green Hammerton Hotel near York after an engine failed on take-off, while another came down in the grounds of the Fairfield Sanatorium. All six men on board DG226 were killed when it dived into Wetherby golf course from 1,000 feet after an engine fire.

At least four Halifaxes were destroyed in collisions on the ground while the last aircraft lost by 1652 was a relatively new Mk III, NA153, which disappeared on a cross country training flight on 4th April 1945. Wreckage was later found in the Moray Firth but no trace was ever found of the eight-man crew.

One of Jean Didlock's duties as an MT driver was to take ambulances to the many crashes which occurred, particularly during the early days

WAAFs of the M/T Section at Marston Moor. (Mrs J. Dudley)

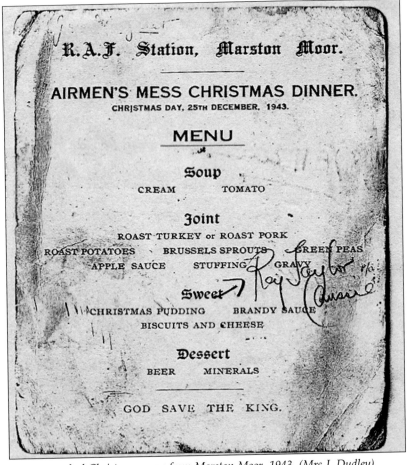

An autographed Christmas menu from Marston Moor, 1943. (Mrs J. Dudley)

of 1652. 'At one of the early crashes I went to I was asked to pick up a flying helmet someone spotted. When I did I found a head inside it. I was horribly sick and I remember someone came up and put a cigarette in my mouth to steady my nerves. It was a long time after that I dared tell my father I had started to smoke. I don't think I ever told him why.'

Jean, now Mrs Jean Dudley of Selby, drove the airfield's ration truck on regular runs to Fulford Barracks in York and to pick up bread from local bakeries. German POWs from a local camp were also brought in to help with the work.

John Taylor was a 19-year-old engine fitter who arrived at Marston Moor in the early autumn of 1944 to join 1652 HCU. It was his job to help keep the Halifaxes, initially early Mk Is and later Mk IIIs, flying almost round the clock as the unit strove to provide its quota of trained aircrew for 4 Group. Marston Moor was, like most wartime airfields, a dispersed site with the accommodation sites a long way from the technical areas. His particular Nissen hut was in a wood a full mile from the airfield with the wash house, NAAFI, canteen, post office and station cinema another half mile away down the road. He remembers that all the staff were issued with Raleigh cycles to help them get around.

He was attached to B Flight as part of a team of six 'erks' – three engine fitters and three airframe mechanics – and their flight lines were on the opposite side of the airfield from the control tower. 'We had to look after six Halifax heavy bombers, DI-ing them [daily inspection] every morning after breakfast. Sometimes this involved changing the plugs, changing propellers and sometimes even changing a complete engine.

'The seven crew members would then come out to the dispersed area in the crew bus and we would watch them check the engines by running them up. If everything was OK, we got the signal and pulled the chocks out from under the wheels to allow them to taxi out from the dispersal pad onto the perimeter track on their way to the end of the runway.

'They would usually take off on a three or four-hour cross country run before returning. Most of them were young sergeants or pilot officers learning to fly on multi-engined aircraft so, as you can imagine, we saw many airy-scary landings which caused the airframe bods to change burst tyres and replace damaged undercarriages.

'As this was a training camp there were no armourers because, as a rule, the aircraft did not carry bombs or bullets. On returning to the dispersal pad, we slipped the chocks back in place and topped up the fuel tanks from the bowser and then topped up the oil tanks before knocking off and going for tea in the canteen.'

It wasn't just Halifaxes which came to grief at Marston Moor. On the night of 28th-29th October 1944, seven 5 Group Lancasters were diverted there following an abortive raid on U-boat pens at Bergen. One of these was PB519 of 49 Squadron based at Fulbeck. The pilot, F/O Ken Lee, landed too far up the runway and the Lancaster Q-Queenie, which still had most of the bomb load on board, careered

Pictured at 1652 HCU at Marston Moor in late 1944 are F/O Clifford Smith (navigator), F/O Jack Bergman (pilot) and F/O Dave Dale (bomb aimer). Bergman and Dale were the only survivors of the crew of Halifax III MZ796 of 102 Squadron which was shot down during a raid on Hanover, 5th January 1945. (Gerald Myers)

through the overshoot area, left its undercarriage in a ditch and came to rest astride a nearby road. The crew made a hasty exit but, fortunately, the bombs failed to explode.

In early December 1944, 1652's veteran Halifax Mk Is began to be replaced by the much-improved Mk IIIs, which were now in plentiful supply. The switch meant a big change for the engine fitters. Instead of the twelve cylinder in-line Rolls-Royce Merlins, they were now working on Bristol Hercules XVI radial sleeve-valved engines.

Apart from its own aircraft, 1652 was responsible for some of the major servicing work for Conversion Unit Halifaxes at both Rufforth and Riccall. Marston Moor had become 41 Base HQ in September 1943 and, on the transfer of all training units to 7 Group Training Command, 74 Base HQ in December 1944.

The end of the war quickly saw 1652 disbanded. Its place was taken for a while by 1665 Heavy Transport Conversion Unit but this moved in November and RAF Marston Moor closed soon afterwards. Today, a few scattered buildings remain close to the village of Tockwith. Unlike the battle of 1644, RAF Marston Moor has no permanent memorial to the part it played in the air war against Germany.

Marston Moor's satellite airfields at Riccall, near Selby, and Rufforth, just west of York, housed 1658 and 1663 Heavy Conversion Units respectively. Of the two, Rufforth was the only one to be used by an operational 4 Group squadron, although 158 Squadron's tenancy was a temporary one until its new home at Lissett was completed.

The site at Rufforth had been selected by the Air Ministry in 1940 and it was decided at an early stage of its construction that it would be used for the training of Halifax crews. Rufforth was built by John Laing and laid out into the familiar pattern with three Tarmac runways, one B1 and two T2 hangars. The runways were in place by the summer of 1942 and were used by 1652 Conversion Unit and both 35 and 158 Squadron conversion flights that summer.

158 Squadron had formed at Driffield in June 1942 and had then moved to East Moor where it began its conversion to Halifaxes. It was earmarked for the new airfield at Lissett, but that was not going to be ready until early 1943 so, as an interim measure, the squadron moved into Rufforth when it officially opened on 6th November 1942.

Two nights later 158 Squadron lost its first aircraft on operations when eight aircraft took part in an attack on Genoa. Only one made it back to Rufforth. The others all suffered from fuel shortages, six landing in the south of England while the seventh, flown by P/O

Beveridge, crash-landed on the Humber foreshore, killing three of the crew. The pilot survived and a week later was involved in another crash, this time while trying to land at what is now Gatwick airport after another raid on Genoa.

158 Squadron was to remain at Rufforth until the end of February 1943 and during that time lost nine Halifaxes, including one which was involved in a mid-air collision with a Wellington of 166 Squadron at Kirmington while returning from a raid on Lorient.

When 158 moved out of Rufforth it had lost 61 aircrew to enemy action and crashes during their brief stay. Twenty of its aircraft were damaged in accidents or lost in action during that time. One of them is remembered in particular by John Dawson, who grew up near Rufforth airfield.

His father worked at the nearby agricultural college and the Halifaxes of 158 Squadron and later 1663 HCU became a familiar sight to John and his family. He was 13 at the time and would often help his father out in the fields around the agricultural college, several of which were studded with concrete posts which had been installed a year or two earlier as a deterrent to a German glider-borne landing.

One morning in January 1943 John was driving some sheep from the field. It was a bitterly cold morning and there was a thick covering of snow but this was not preventing a number of Halifaxes taking off from Rufforth on a mining operation. One of the aircraft immediately lost power and John watched as the pilot put the aircraft down in the very field in which he was standing. The big bomber made a wheels-up landing almost parallel to the nearby York-Tadcaster road, not far from the Buckles Inn. It snapped off a series of the concrete posts before finally coming to rest in a shower of snow.

'Everything was quiet for a moment and then one of the crew climbed out followed by the others,' said Mr Dawson. 'He came across and asked me where he could find a phone to call the airfield.' John was to have another brush with a Rufforth Halifax later in the year, and this time it almost cost him his life.

On 1st March 1663 Heavy Conversion Unit was formed with a strength of 32 Halifaxes, divided into four flights. This resulted in almost round-the-clock flying from the airfield as crews were put through an exacting training course prior to joining 4 Group squadrons. The attrition rate was to be high – more than 60 Halifaxes from 1663 were involved in crashes over the final 26 months of the war. One of the first to go was DG413 on 6th April 1943. It was involved in an exercise with a pair of Hurricanes when the starboard wing folded and broke off during a tight turn, the aircraft spinning into the ground near Driffield from 6,000 feet, killing all those on board.

John Dawson's brush with death came on 19th August 1943 at eleven o'clock on a beautiful sunny morning. He was on holiday from school and was riding on a tractor driven by Matthew Atkinson, who lived in nearby Bilborough and also worked for the agricultural college. They were in a field near Copmanthorpe Lane end and they could clearly hear the roar of Halifaxes from Rufforth when tragedy struck.

'I remember looking up and seeing this Halifax coming over the tops of the trees straight at us,' said Mr Dawson. 'The gentleman I was with stopped the tractor and told me to run for it. We both jumped down and ran but we couldn't run far enough. The bomber came down only yards from us and both of us were showered with burning petrol. All my hair was burnt off and I was burnt on the back of my legs but Mr Atkinson caught the full force of it. He was badly burnt from the waist up. He just seemed to be on fire. I grabbed a sack and tried to beat out the flames as we had been shown how to do with grass fires. It was only later I was told I shouldn't have done that, I should have rolled him in the sack. But I wasn't to know.'

Help arrived quickly and both John and Matthew Atkinson were taken to the old County Hospital in York where John remained a patient for three months, with another three months as an out-patient. Mr Atkinson spent many months in hospital recovering from his burns and John remembers him being ill for many years afterwards. John's father later tried to get compensation from the Air Ministry for his son's injuries. He was told the only compensation they could consider was for his damaged clothes.

The Halifax that almost ended young John's life was a six month old aircraft, DG420, which had been issued new to the conversion unit when it was formed in February that year and had had a spell on operations with 76 Squadron before returning to Rufforth a few weeks before the crash. There were no survivors. It had collided in the circuit with a second Halifax, R9497 or 1658 HCU, which was based at nearby Riccall. It was a real 4 Group veteran, almost 18 months old with operational service with 10 and 102 Squadrons before being pensioned off to 1658. Again, there were no survivors.

Aircraft from heavy conversion units were occasionally used in spoof attacks and mining operations, and it was from one of these that DG412 was lost by 1663 at the end of August 1943. It was returning from a sortie to the Biscay ports when it was reported to have broken up due to flak damage and crashed near Great Torrington in Devon.

High ground in the Pennines and the Yorkshire Moors accounted for numerous Halifaxes, and 1663 suffered its share of losses. DG404 hit high ground near Pateley Bridge in July 1943 and a few weeks later DG402 crashed and burned at Keys Beck, Low Mill on the moors. In February 1944, DK192 flew into Garrowby Hill killing those on board.

Several accidents were caused by mechanical failure in the unit's Halifaxes, many of which were squadron hand-me-downs which had led a brief but hard life before arriving at Rufforth. On 7th September 1943 DG415 was being flown over the Flamborough area when the starboard inner propeller flew off taking part of the engine cowling with it. The aircraft crashed and burned close to Bempton village.

Landings and take off were a particularly hazardous time for the student crews and resulted in numerous accidents, one of the more spectacular occurring on 16th November 1944 as JP128 was attempting to land in bad weather. After several failed attempts, the pilot appeared to pick the wrong approach and the aircraft hit Grasslands Farm, killing both the farmer and his wife. The wreckage then careered across the airfield, hitting another Halifax, badly damaging the station fire engine and finally hitting a hangar where a third Halifax was destroyed. All six men on board JP128 were killed.

In November 1944 Rufforth, along with all other HCU airfields, passed to the control of 7 Group Training Command. 1663 HCU was disbanded within three weeks of the war ending but the airfield was retained and was used by No 23 Gliding School and 64 Group Communications Flight. There was some limited use of the runways and technical sites until the early 1950s when the RAF finally moved out and the land reverted to agriculture.

The airfield at Riccall was laid out on a large flat site east of the A19, spanning part of what were then Riccall and Barlby Commons, land which now falls within the Selby coalfield. A variety of contractors were used for the work, which included the laying of three concrete and asphalt runways and the erection of six T2 and a single B1 hangar.

Although not officially opened until December 1942, the Halifax conversion flights of 76 and 78 Squadrons moved into Riccall early in September that year and, on 7th October, formally merged to form 1658 Heavy Conversion Unit. A few days later 10 and 102 Squadron conversion flights were merged into 1658 and on 1st November they were joined by 158 conversion flight, which immediately reformed as C

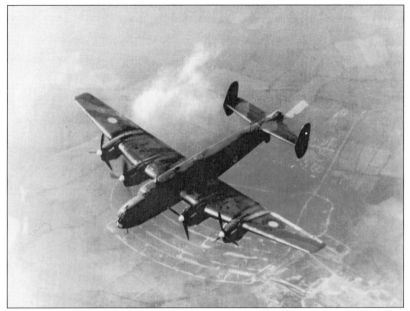

Halifax II of 1658 HCU at Riccall pictured from another of the unit's aircraft over Selby in 1943 while flying on one engine. At the controls at the time was S/Ldr Dobson. Note the white-painted propeller bosses. 1658 had four flights and each had different coloured prop bosses. (Sir Guy Lawrence)

Flight of 1658. This brought the unit up to full strength – 32 Halifaxes in four flights – and this is how 1658 was to remain at Riccall until the end of the war.

Over the next two and a half years 1658 was to complete sterling work, preparing thousands of young men for service in 4 Group's Halifax squadrons. But it was achieved at a high price, the unit losing some 72 aircraft in its time at Riccall.

The first recorded crash involving a Halifax from Riccall came on 9th October 1942, just two days after 1658 came into being. L9574, an ex-76 Squadron aircraft, spun into the ground near Lodge Farm, Thorganby on its approach to the airfield, killing all those on board.

A little more than a week later the conversion unit lost its second Halifax, a tyre bursting on R9366 as it came in to land, the ex-10 and 76 Squadron aircraft ground looping and losing its undercarriage. It was to be a familiar way to write off a Halifax but at least the crew walked away from it.

Engine failure was a familiar cause of accidents and that seems to have been the reason why DT524, which was being flown by P/O Caplan, spun into Newsholme Plantation, a couple of miles from the main runway at Riccall. Smoke had been seen trailing from an engine as the aircraft dived into the ground, killing all ten men on board.

That September was one of the worst periods of the war for 1658 with ten aircraft damaged or lost in accidents. Most were minor and at least one of the aircraft was repaired, only to be destroyed in a fire after hitting the station wind sock early in 1944. Three men were killed when an engine fire caused Halifax JB905 to crash in flames near Finningley. That aircraft had left Riccall earlier in the evening shortly after BB245 had left on a cross country flight with Sgt Wilson in the pilot's seat. Four hours later, as the aircraft was preparing to approach Riccall, it is believed a blade on the port outer propeller broke away, damaging the engine. The Halifax crashed into a row of houses in Darrington, near Pontefract, killing the crew and four people on the ground. At least two other 1658 Halifaxes are believed to have been lost in similar circumstances. The death toll was a grim reminder of what the people of Yorkshire were having to bear for having so many heavy bombers in their midst.

The worst of all crashes involving aircraft from Riccall occurred on the night of 10th May 1944 when Halifax JB789, a veteran which had seen considerable operational service with 158 Squadron at Lissett before being allocated to 1658, hit the spire of St James' church in Selby.

The aircraft had taken off shortly before on a night bombing exercise and was being flown by an Australian, Sgt John Roper. Five of his crew were also Australians, F/Sgts Noel Knight, Bernard Storer, Thomas Laver and Sgts Derrick McDermott and Peter Rockingham. The seventh member of the crew was British, F/O John Dixon.

The port wing clipped the top of the spire as the Halifax banked over the town. The aircraft spun in, an engine from the shattered wing crashing into the roofs of a row of nearby houses. The right wing broke off and hit a food storage warehouse while the fuselage careered along a street before embedding itself in a house. All seven men on board died instantly while eight civilians, the youngest six years old, the oldest 65, were to lose their lives. Three were the members of one family.

One man who remembers the crash vividly is Len Spray, who was then a schoolboy living in Portholme Drive, Selby, some 30 yards from the scene of the disaster.

'I was fast asleep at the time,' he remembered, 'when suddenly there was an enormous crash. There were flames everywhere and I remember there was the sound of exploding ammunition for some time afterwards. The food warehouse caught fire and one bullet came through my bedroom window and embedded itself in the ceiling.

'There was a night watchman on duty in the warehouse at the time and I remember that he came staggering out with his clothes ablaze and seemed to walk down the street on fire before collapsing. It was an awful sight.

'One of the men who lived in the houses was named Calvert and he was working nearby on the railway when the aircraft came down and rushed over the road only to find his wife had been killed with their nine year old daughter in her arms. Another of his daughters was blown out of the house onto the lawn, still in her bed. She survived.'

St James' church itself was badly damaged in the crash. The spire was demolished and much of the roof and the interior destroyed. Restoration work began exactly five years to the day after the crash and when it was completed in December 1950 a plaque was unveiled commemorating the disaster and naming those who died. Listed alongside the seven aircrew are James Mather (63), William Henry Osbourn (37), Doris Osbourn (36), Patricia Osbourn (6), Edith Eleanor Calvert (42), Jean Calvert (9), and James Sayner of Hambleton, who was aged 65.

Not all the losses from Riccall were due to accidents. On the night of 12th-13th September 1944, JD380 was one of 138 Halifaxes and Lancasters from conversion units involved in a diversionary sweep across the North Sea to draw night fighters away from two large raids mounted on Frankfurt and Stuttgart. The route for the diversionary force took it close to the Dutch border and it was believed the Riccall Halifax could have fallen prey to a night fighter.

A German intruder, one of the force involved in Operation Gisella, is believed to have been responsible for attacking another Riccall Halifax, NA566, during a training flight over Yorkshire in the early hours of 5th March 1945. The Halifax lost an engine but managed to crash land on the emergency strip at Carnaby.

Other losses were more bizarre: the pilot of LW445 swung his Halifax on take-off on 1st March 1945, shearing off the undercarriage and wrecking the ex-51 Squadron veteran. Later he explained he had been blinded by an Aldis lamp being shown for another aircraft. The crew of a Mk III, MZ697, had an alarming experience during a cross country flight in October 1944 when suddenly their aircraft flipped onto its back. The pilot managed to right the aircraft and landed it at Pershore in Worcestershire where it was written off with an over-stretched air frame.

1658 HCU was disbanded three weeks before the war in Europe came to an end. Riccall itself then passed to the control of Transport Command and became the home of 1332 Transport Conversion Unit, which flew Avro Yorks and Stirlings converted for freight work. By November this unit had moved north to Dishforth and Riccall was closed for flying. The airfield was used briefly for storage purposes before being sold off for agricultural use. At the time of writing, it is being considered as the site of a cattle incinerator plant.

23
MELBOURNE

On the night of 19th November 1943 a Halifax Mk II of 10 Squadron was returning from a raid at Leverkusen in the Ruhr when the crew picked up a radio message. Their home base, at Melbourne, near York, was fog-bound and F/Sgt Holdsworth and his crew in K-Katy were advised to divert to Tangmere. At 9.35 pm that night as the Halifax tried to land, it struck a hangar and all the crew were killed as the aircraft crashed and caught fire.

A little over an hour later at nearby Ford airfield, a second Halifax from 10 Squadron overshot and crashed as it, too, returned from Leverkusen, where it had been damaged by flak. This time the crew was more fortunate. Four of them, including the pilot, P/O Lucas, were injured and were to spend some time in hospital before returning to the squadron.

The events of that night were nothing new for the crews of 10 Squadron, nor indeed for those of any other 4 Group crews whose airfields in the Vale of York were blighted by autumnal fogs. The irony, however, was that as the Halifaxes had taken off late that November afternoon for the Ruhr, workmen were busy installing the equipment which would have prevented the diversions of the 10 Squadron aircraft. Earlier that year Melbourne had been selected as the 4 Group airfield to be fitted with FIDO – the acronym for Fog Investigation and Dispersal Operation. It was to be the most northerly of the operational airfields to receive the equipment and the second in Yorkshire (the other was the emergency landing strip at Carnaby). Compared with some airfields further south, FIDO at Melbourne was to be used sparingly, with some 120 take-offs and landings being recorded as FIDO-assisted, half of them in the last week of December 1944. The truth was that FIDO came a year too late for the bomber squadrons in

Yorkshire and even when it did finally come into operation, many aircraft from the county opted to use airfields further south.

Work had started on the FIDO installation in August 1943. Main contractors were George Wimpey and the equipment was officially handed over to the RAF on 15th January the following year. FIDO consisted of lengths of burners on each side of the main runway, the heat from which was sufficient to disperse all but the thickest of Yorkshire pea-soupers. It was hugely expensive in petrol – the first 'burn' at Melbourne consumed some 102,000 gallons of petrol – but had a dramatic effect on visibility. Used on the night of 27th-28th May for aircraft returning from a raid on Bourg Leopold, visibility was raised from 300 to 1,400 yards. It was a dramatic sight for those living near the airfield. When the system was tested for the first time at night in February 1944 for a visiting group of senior officers some 30 NFS fire appliances from all parts of Yorkshire were despatched to what was believed to be a major disaster at Melbourne.

On the few occasions it was used, FIDO proved remarkably effective although the crews found landing could be an alarming operation. On 18th November 1944 thick fog blanketed airfields around York. Melbourne was the only one open and nine of the 10 Squadron's aircraft got down safely. F/O Daffey and his crew were in the tenth, F-Freddie. They were an experienced crew having already completed one tour with 77 Squadron but this was their first experience of FIDO. The heat from the burners appeared to keep the aircraft airborne for too long and when it finally got down it was at least half-way down the runway, the Halifax overshooting and losing its undercarriage before finally coming to a halt, the crew scrambling out uninjured.

Melbourne was unique in Yorkshire in that it was in use from 1940 to 1945 and was the home of a single squadron, 'Shiny 10'. In 1940 a temporary airfield had been hastily laid out on a large, flat area of farmland between the villages of Melbourne and Seaton Ross, close to the Pocklington canal. Some temporary buildings were erected on the site and 10 Squadron, by then at Leeming, used the airfield occasionally during the winter of 1940-41 when the runways at their home base were unusable. The squadron was to fly a number of operations from Melbourne before finally moving out early in 1941 when work began on constructing a more permanent airfield.

It was built with three concrete runways and three hangars and reopened on 19th August 1942 when 10 Squadron returned from a short detachment in the Middle East. By now the squadron had converted to Halifaxes and brought with it its own Conversion Flight from Leeming, which remained at Melbourne until moving to Riccall in October to help form 1658 HCU. Melbourne was far from finished when 10 Squadron arrived and for the first few weeks bombs and fuel had to be acquired at nearby Pocklington.

10 suffered its first loss from Melbourne on the night of 6th-7th September when P/O Morgan's aircraft failed to return from Duisburg. This was the first of over 120 Halifaxes to be lost on operations or destroyed in accidents while operating from Melbourne over the next two and a half years. Four of them were lost in a single night at the beginning of October when 27 Halifaxes from 4 Group attacked Flensburg and twelve were shot down. Of the four from 10 Squadron, one crashed in the sea off the Danish coast, another came down over the target. There were just seven survivors from the four aircraft. Despite the losses, there was to be no respite for the Melbourne crews. The following night they attacked Krefeld in the Ruhr and left behind the wreckage of another Halifax and the bodies of the seven young men on board.

A fortnight later the squadron lost its popular commanding officer, W/Cmdr Wildey, who was one of three to die when the Halifax he was piloting was shot down in an attack on Cologne. He was replaced within a matter of days by W/Cmdr Carter. Empty places, whether they be in the cockpit or behind the desk in the CO's office, were never left vacant for long in 1942.

Losses were relatively light that first winter at Melbourne, with almost as many aircraft lost in accidents as on operations. One crashed with the loss of the entire crew near the airfield in November and another came down just outside Seaton Ross the following March, again with all the crew being killed.

The spring and summer of 1943 saw 10 Squadron in the thick of the Battle of the Ruhr. Five men were killed when a Halifax crashed into Sutton Bank after being diverted to Leeming on its return from Dortmund early in May. A second raid later in the month on the same German industrial city resulted in three aircraft being lost with the deaths of all 22 men. On board one of the aircraft was Sgt Ian Inglis, who was on a 'second dickey' trip, gaining experience before his own crew, fresh from 1663 HCU at Rufforth, began operations. The remainder of his crew had to return to Rufforth to pick up a new pilot and were then posted to 76 Squadron at Linton-on-Ouse, their stay at Melbourne a tragic interlude for them.

The Ruhr campaign continued with two raids on Essen early in March, the second of these costing 10 Squadron two aircraft and the lives of 14 men. There was a narrow escape for a third, which was caught by the master searchlight over Essen and then coned by between 20 and 30 more lights. The pilot managed to escape, only for the aircraft to be caught again. By now it was the target for just about every AA gun in the Essen area. The rear gunner, F/Sgt Jacques Barsalou, was badly injured but continued firing at the lights in an effort to put them out. When the aircraft finally made it back to Melbourne it was found to have been hit 18 times. The wounded rear gunner later recovered and was awarded a well-earned DFM.

The Ruhr wasn't the only target of Bomber Command during this period. The Baltic port of Stettin was badly damaged in a heavy raid on the night of 20th-21st April at a cost of 21 aircraft, one of them from 10 Squadron. It was the Halifax flown by Sgt Percy Glover and was claimed by the German naval flak battery at Tjaerborg in Denmark. The crew survived, although all were injured. It seems they did not give up without a fight as several members of the flak battery were wounded

A 10 Squadron Halifax II touches down at Melbourne following an attack on Stettin on the night of 20th-21st April 1943. (C. Jones)

by machine gun fire from the Halifax, whose gunners included the squadron's gunnery leader F/Lt Baker.

The squadron was to lose 13 aircraft in May and June 1943 as the Ruhr raids continued, with two lost in one night over Cologne. The survival rate was low – just one man escaped from the five aircraft lost in June. More fortunate was Sgt Ray Smith, the wireless operator in S/Ldr Hartnell-Beavis' crew. Their aircraft was attacked by fighters on its way home from Essen on the night of 25th July and the crew ordered to bale out. Smith was one of only two to get out before the bomber broke up and crashed. He landed in woods near Tilburg in Holland and was quickly picked up by the Dutch Resistance. After being hidden for most of the summer, he began a perilous journey through France in October, part of which was undertaken hanging onto the underneath of a troop train as it headed south. Finally he and his fellow escapees managed to cross the border and by the end of October he was back at RAF Melbourne.

The three raids on Hamburg at the end of July and in early August saw the introduction of 'window', thin aluminum strips which, when dropped, blinded the German defensive radar. 10 Squadron flew 84 sorties on these raids, all its aircraft returning safely. For some reason, 10 Squadron opted to have the window dropped by its mid-upper gunner, which meant him being out of his turret at critical periods. This may have contributed to an attack on F/Lt Jenkins' aircraft on the third of these raids. The aircraft was badly damaged but the Canadian rear gunner, Sgt Dick Hurst, shot down the attacking Ju 88. Jenkins managed to get his badly damaged aircraft back to Melbourne, a feat which earned him a DFC and his rear gunner a DFM.

Six weeks later Jenkins and his crew were in trouble again when they were attacked over Hanover by a night fighter. Despite the serious damage sustained by their Halifax, which had only arrived from the factory a few days earlier, the crew completed their bomb run but found to their dismay that their 4,000lb 'cookie' refused to move from the bomb bay. When they arrived back at Melbourne they found the hydraulics were damaged and the undercarriage would not lower. It was impossible for them to crash-land with a live 4,000lb bomb on board and they were ordered to return to the coast and then bale out, which they did over Patrington, near Hull, their aircraft later crashing harmlessly in the sea. Jenkins and his crew all landed safely – one in the middle of a coastal minefield – and they went on to complete their tour at Melbourne the following January.

The squadron went to Hanover again four nights later and on this occasion lost three of the 14 aircraft sent. All three were shot down close to the target, three men surviving from the first two to go down. The third crew, all of whom were sergeants, had just begun their tour with 10 Squadron. Their average age was just 20.

On the next occasion Bomber Command visited the city, on 8th October, all the 10 Squadron aircraft made it back but one had to be written off after being damaged by flak and then hit by a bomb dropped by a Lancaster.

An attack on Kassel resulted in three more aircraft failing to return with just one man surviving and then, on 3rd-4th November, Dusseldorf was the target. One 10 Squadron Halifax was shot down in the target area, three of the crew managing to bale out. A second aircraft was badly damaged and eventually crashed trying to make an emergency landing at Shipdham in Norfolk. Six of the crew were killed but the rear gunner, Sgt Winstanley, was rescued from the burning aircraft by Ernest Bowman, who was on duty at the time with the local Home Guard. Mr Bowman received the BEM for his bravery but Sgt Winstanley died from his injuries.

A third aircraft from Melbourne, ZA-D, was attacked several times by night fighters but eventually made it back with three wounded men on board. The wireless operator, Sgt Bisby, was one of those injured and received the Conspicuous Gallantry Medal for his bravery during the struggle to get the badly damaged aircraft back to Yorkshire. There was also a DFC for the Australian pilot, F/Lt Trobe, and DFMs for the other wounded men, Sgts Trowett and Bridge.

10 Squadron was to lose ten of its aircraft on the Berlin raids that winter, two of them on the night of 22nd-23rd November 1943. Three nights later there was a double tragedy at Melbourne when a number of Lancasters belonging to 50 Squadron were diverted north from their airfield at Skellingthorpe, near Lincoln because of fog following an all-Lancaster attack on Berlin. One of these hit a van on the runway as it was landing, killing the driver instantly. The aircraft then slewed across the runway and collided with a second 50 Squadron Lancaster which had become bogged down after running off the runway. Both aircraft were wrecked but the crews survived. Not so lucky were the crew of a fourth 50 Squadron Lancaster which was attempting to land at nearby Pocklington and struck a farmhouse at Hayton, near Market Weighton, killing five of the crew in addition to the two occupants of the house, Mrs Paulcey and Mrs Gertrude Bird.

The squadron lost one of its most experienced crews at the beginning of December in an attack on Leipzig. The aircraft of P/O Walker, who was close to completing his tour, was attacked by a night fighter and the pilot ordered the crew to bale out. Only two managed to escape before the bomber exploded in mid-air.

Four days before Christmas three Halifaxes from Melbourne were lost in an attack on Frankfurt while another aircraft was lost over Berlin on 29th-30th December. During this raid F/Sgt George Burcher won a DFM after bringing his badly damaged 10 Squadron aircraft home. It had been hit by flak on its bomb run, losing an engine. Then the Halifax was hit by incendiaries which left the pilot with no instruments. And then the crew had to struggle to release a 'hung-up' 2,000lb bomb. Finally, as they were crossing the coast, a second engine failed, but F/Sgt Burcher managed a perfect landing at Swanton Morley in Norfolk.

The squadron was due to convert to the Halifax Mk III early in 1944 but had to soldier on for a time with its Mk IIs and Vs as pressure was stepped up on Berlin, losing one aircraft on 21st-22nd January and four in a single night at the end of the month. One of these was flown by F/Lt Kilsby, whose aircraft was attacked by a night fighter on its bomb run. Cannon shells set fire to the aircraft's overload fuel tank in the bomb bay and the skipper immediately ordered his crew to jump. Five managed to do so – including the rear gunner P/O Shipley who was trapped in the slipstream for a time when his right leg became stuck in the turret – but the pilot and wireless operator died when the aircraft crashed. They were among 18 men from 'Shiny 10' to die that night.

The squadron's final loss over Berlin occurred on the night of 15th-16th February when F/O Clarke and his crew were killed when their Mk V (Special) was shot down over the German capital. The crew are all buried in the British military cemetery in Berlin.

Despite the casualties being suffered by the Halifax squadrons, they continued to be thrown into the cauldron over Germany night after night. 10 Squadron was to lose more aircraft in attacks on Magdeburg, Leipzig and Essen – including its first two Mk IIIs – before the end of March when it provided 13 of the aircraft which took part in the catastrophic attack on Nuremburg. The squadron was one of the more fortunate in Bomber Command, losing only one of its aircraft, that of P/O Regan, a Yorkshireman on his fifth operation from Melbourne.

April saw the switch of targets from Germany to France in

preparation for the invasion and this brought some respite for the hard-pressed crews at Melbourne. Losses did continue but not on the scale of 1943 and, with the Mk III Halifax now fully operational, there was a feeling that an important watershed had been reached. The run-up to the invasion saw 10 Squadron lose two aircraft in an attack on the railway yards at Trappes. All the squadron's aircraft returned safely from the attacks on Normandy batteries just before and after the invasion but two Halifaxes from Melbourne were lost in a series of raids against airfields in northern France. Two more failed to return from an attack on marshalling yards at Blainville at the end of the month while the targeting of flying bomb sites in July cost 10 Squadron another Halifax.

German sites were soon back on the target maps in the 4 Group briefing rooms and a pin-point attack on the synthetic oil plant at Bottrop in the Ruhr cost 10 Squadron two more aircraft. Just one aircraft was lost from an attack on Brunswick on the night of 12th-13th August but its loss was deeply felt by the crews back at Melbourne. F/O Saynor and his crew were on their 38th operation and were due to be screened on their return to Yorkshire. It later transpired that all the crew had become PoWs and that their aircraft had been shot down by another Halifax.

Many of the aircraft which did make it back bore the scars of battle. A daylight attack on Munster early in September saw one Halifax from 10 Squadron badly damaged by flak. The pilot made a successful landing at the emergency strip at Woodbridge in Suffolk, but the aircraft was later written off. Another ditched in the Humber off Immingham after suffering flak damage over Essen, while a raid on the same target late in November saw a Melbourne Halifax belly-land near Calais.

The squadron was in action on Boxing Day bombing German positions near St Vith in support of the British Army, one aircraft crashing in the sea off Margate with the loss of all the crew.

The final months of the war saw Melbourne's Halifaxes being used on a number of mining operations in the Baltic and these cost the squadron two aircraft and their crews, both crashing off the Danish coast. One of the squadron's aircraft fell to the Luftwaffe intruders which swept across Yorkshire during the early hours of 4th March 1945 as 4 Group's aircraft were returning from Kamen. The Halifax was caught near Knaresborough as it was being diverted north and shot down in flames by a long-range fighter.

Melbourne's final casualty of the war was a Halifax which returned from a daylight attack on Heligoland on 18th April with flak damage and was written off as 'damaged beyond repair'. The squadron's last operation of the war came on 25th April when all 20 Halifaxes sent to attack the gun batteries at Wangerooge returned successfully.

'Shiny 10' Squadron left Melbourne on 7th May when it was transferred to Transport Command. The airfield was used briefly by another transport squadron, 575, and by the 1552 Radio Aids Training Flight but both units had moved on by the spring of 1946 and the airfield closed. Today a number of buildings still remain and sections of a runway are used for drag racing.

Apart from the 10 Squadron memorial close to the old station gates there is another lasting memorial to the men who served at Melbourne. Their favourite pub, The Blacksmith's Arms in nearby Seaton Ross, has now fittingly been renamed The Bombers.

The magnificent memorial to 'Shiny Ten' at Melbourne. (P. Otter)

24
MIDDLETON
ST GEORGE

The most northerly of all of Bomber Command's airfields, Middleton St George was to see almost constant action from the day it opened in January 1941 until the very last bombing raid from Yorkshire late in April 1945. In the intervening period it served within both 4 and 6 Groups and was used by five heavy bomber squadrons which, between them, lost some 297 aircraft to enemy action or in accidents. It was the only 6 Group airfield from which a Victoria Cross was won, awarded posthumously to P/O Andrew Mynarski of 419 (Moose) Squadron RCAF. Today, Middleton is better known as Teesside International Airport. Many of the original buildings are still in use and the brick-built officers' mess is now the three-star St George Hotel, standing close to the airport terminal building.

The site close to the village of Middleton St George was among those selected in Yorkshire and the North East in the mid-1930s for airfield construction as part of the RAF's Expansion Scheme. Middleton, when it was finally completed towards the end of 1940, had a mixture of pre-war and wartime buildings.

The airfield officially opened on 15th January 1941 within 4 Group and 78 Squadron moved in from Dishforth early in April with its two flights of Whitleys. It was in action by the end of the month and early in May one of the squadron's Whitley Vs, Z6483, became the first to be lost from Middleton, the crew abandoning the aircraft over Abingdon on their way home from Cologne. Twelve days later the squadron suffered its first casualties at Middleton when an aircraft failed to return from an attack on the same target.

In June, 78 was joined at Middleton by 76 Squadron, which brought its new Halifax BIs from Linton-on-Ouse. 76 quickly became operational and lost its first Halifax in a raid on Kiel on 24th June.

78 Squadron, in the meantime, was still operating its Whitleys and during an attack on Hamm on 8th July, one of these, flown by Sgt McQuitty, was damaged over the target and lost an engine. It was then attacked by a night fighter over the Dutch coast, the Me 110 breaking off its assault after a few minutes. The damaged Whitley struggled back across the North Sea but was forced to ditch some nine miles from the Norfolk coast. The aircraft's dinghy was launched but had been damaged either by the Hamm flak or the 110 and quickly sank. The Whitley's observer, Sgt Haffenden, somehow managed to swim ashore and raise the alarm but the remainder of the crew drowned.

The first daylight operation from Middleton was mounted by 76 Squadron on 24th July when it provided seven of the 15 Halifaxes from 4 Group involved in an attack on the German battlecruiser *Scharnhorst* at La Rochelle. 35 Squadron provided the remainder of the force and

78 Squadron's Whitley V Z6577 F-Freddie pictured against a dramatic North Yorkshire sky at Middleton St George, spring 1941. Freddie was then the aircraft of Sgt Harry Drummond and crew. (Sir Guy Lawrence)

together the Halifaxes approached the French port at low level to avoid detection. But as they prepared to attack, the bombers met fierce opposition from fighters and two Halifaxes were shot down before the small force reached the target area. Then they had to run the gauntlet of the formidable flak defences, but their bombing was concentrated and *Scharnhorst* suffered five direct hits and was to be out of action for four months. Three more Halifaxes were shot down as the bombers left the target area and the survivors all suffered varying degrees of damage. Three of the Halifaxes lost were from 76 Squadron, two crashing in the sea and the third near Aiguillon in France.

A raid on Berlin the following month cost the squadron three more Halifaxes. One of the two lost over Germany was flown by F/Lt Christopher Cheshire, whose brother Leonard was then with 35 Squadron. He and four other members of the crew survived and became PoWs. The third loss occurred in the circuit at Middleton when Sgt McHale's Halifax dived into the ground close to the airfield from 500 feet while preparing to land. All seven men on board were killed.

Preparations were under way for 78 Squadron to convert to Halifaxes and it flew its last Whitley operations in October, losing its final aircraft in a similar manner to its first loss from Middleton, the crew abandoning the aircraft, which was almost out of fuel, over Kent as it returned from Nuremburg in bad weather. At the end of the month the squadron moved to Croft to begin conversion and was to return in June 1942 with its Halifax Mk IIs. 76, in the meantime, was involved in two further daylight operations against its old adversary, the *Scharnhorst*, and the battle cruiser *Gneisenau*, which were together in Brest, losing one aircraft to flak in the second of the raids.

The Middleton squadron was to lose another Halifax on 30th January 1942 in an inconclusive attack on the *Tirpitz* at Trondheim. Most of the small force of Halifaxes and Stirlings, which were operating from Lossiemouth, turned back because of bad weather, one of the 76 Squadron aircraft ditching a couple of miles off Aberdeen when it ran out of fuel. A second aircraft was lost in another attack on the *Tirpitz* at the end of March, the aircraft crashing off the Shetlands. Only the body of the pilot, S/Ldr Burdett, was ever found.

The spring of 1942 saw 76 Squadron operating mainly against German targets, one attack on Bremen in June costing the squadron three aircraft and the lives of twelve men. Two attacks on Emden later in the month each resulted in a Halifax being lost. On the second of these, 76's F-Freddie was hit by flak and then attacked by a night fighter. The skipper, P/O Norfolk, ordered his crew to jump. The rear gunner, F/Sgt Salway, had left his parachute in the damaged turret and jumped while clinging to the mid-upper gunner, Sgt Smith. However, when Smith's parachute deployed, the unfortunate rear gunner lost his grip and fell to his death. Two other members of the crew, including the pilot, also died.

In June 1516 BAT Flight began moving to Middleton from Llanbedr, but within days of arriving one of its Oxfords was involved in a tragic mid-air collision with a 76 Squadron Halifax which was on an air test. All seven on board the Halifax and the Oxford's instructor and pupil were killed. The following day one of 76 Conversion Flight's Halifaxes was destroyed in an accident at Middleton when a load of incendiaries ignited and a few hours later six men were killed when a second Halifax crashed during an air test.

In the meantime, 78 had moved back to Middleton from Croft with its Halifaxes and began operations with an attack on Bremen on 25th-26th June, one of its aircraft failing to return along with a second 76 Squadron Halifax. 78 was to suffer particularly badly that summer and lost four aircraft in a raid on Mainz on 11th-12th August, 17 men being killed, eleven becoming prisoners and one evading capture. It lost two more in an attack on Frankfurt on 8th-9th September. On the same night a 76 Squadron aircraft had taken off and was near York when the photo-flash exploded in the bomb bay, igniting the aircraft's bomb load. All the crew died and the wreckage of the aircraft came down over a wide area. A Board of Inquiry later decided that photo-flashes should no longer be carried in bomb bays.

Plans were now being finalised for the transfer of Middleton to 6 Group, which was due to be formed at the end of the year and late September saw 76 and 78 moving out, both squadrons going to Linton while their conversion flights went to Riccall. The first of Middleton's Canadian squadrons arrived with its Wellington IIIs from Skipton-on-Swale on 15th October and operated that night, one of its aircraft being lost without trace from a raid on Cologne. It lost a second a month later over Hamburg.

In November 419 (Moose) Squadron arrived from Croft while still in the process of converting to Halifaxes and flew operationally for the first time in the new year, losing one of its new aircraft on a mining trip on 9th-10th January. All seven on board were killed. The squadron operated with 420 for the first time at the end of the month in a raid on Lorient, 420 losing two Wellingtons while a 419 Halifax made a wheels-up landing at Middleton and was written off.

The arrival of so many Canadians put pressure on the facilities at Middleton and, in the early days of 6 Group, many airmen had to be billeted in Darlington while Dinsdale House on the banks of the nearby River Tees was taken over for use by air crew.

Mining trips were still a regular occurrence for the fledgling crews with 419 and cost the squadron another two aircraft in February. The crew of one Halifax was picked up by the Royal Navy after spending 22 hours in a dinghy.

The two squadrons operated in tandem until May when 420 left Middleton for the Middle East. They were replaced almost immediately by 428 (Ghost) Squadron, which moved in with its Halifaxes from Dalton. 419 and 428 were to operate together at Middleton St George until the end of the war.

The Battle of the Ruhr proved costly for 419 which lost a dozen aircraft in a six-week period in April and May. There was little respite in June with three aircraft from 419 going down in a single night over Wuppertal. One of them was being flown by a crew from 428, the second lost in this fashion.

428 lost its first aircraft to the Gelsenkirchen flak on the night of 9th-10th July and with it went one of its most experienced airmen. S/Ldr Bowden, who already had a DFC and Bar, remained at the controls of the stricken Halifax while the other seven men on board baled out, but he was to die as the bomber plunged out of control. Four nights later the squadron lost three Halifaxes in an attack on Aachen, which also cost 419 one of its aircraft. A 419 Halifax was involved in a mid-air collision over Essen a few nights later with an unidentified aircraft.

Two of the Hamburg raids cost Middleton four aircraft, three from 428 Squadron, while both squadrons lost three aircraft in the raid on Peenemünde. Thirty-seven men were killed and just five survived.

One of 428's Halifaxes on an attack on Nuremburg at the end of the month was that of Sgt Alec Mitchell's crew. Mitchell was an ex-Edinburgh policeman and his crew included three Canadians and three Englishmen, one of whom was the wireless operator, Sgt Charles Lott. They were one of the original 428 Halifax crews and Nuremburg would have been their 18th operation, a night they were carrying a new pilot on his 'second dickey' trip.

Their aircraft had no front or mid-upper turret and the spare gunner was given the job of laying on the floor and keeping an eye out for fighters through a Perspex blister. Just before midnight, Charles Lott

The Caterpillar Club membership card awarded to Sgt Charles Lott for his escape by parachute during his time at Middleton. (Charles Lott)

later recalled, 'all hell broke loose'. Tracer tore through the aircraft, wrecking the radio and most of the electrics. There were flames in the fuselage and through a hole Sgt Lott could see both port engines on fire. The pilot immediately ordered his crew to bale out.

Charles Lott remembers leaving the aircraft at just below 20,000 feet and landing on a hillside alongside what appeared to be a forest. He had lost his right boot but, after hiding his parachute, he decided to try to escape from the area and was about to help himself to a battered cycle in a farmyard when he passed out with delayed shock. When he came to, the farmer was standing over him and he was taken to a nearby house where he found his navigator, Sgt Stuart Brown, and bomb aimer, Sgt Cliff Lunny, the only other survivors of the Halifax. Sgt Lunny was badly injured and was lying on a stretcher. All three were collected by an ambulance which took them to a nearby hospital, Lott and Brown being given a quick examination while Lunny was taken to an operating theatre for emergency treatment.

After being interviewed, Sgt Lott was taken by two high-ranking Luftwaffe officers to the site of their crashed aircraft. Only the rear turret was in one piece. He was asked to identify the bodies of the crew, some of which were laid out in a nearby orchard while the body of the rear gunner, Sgt 'Stu' Hamer, was still in his turret. Later Sgt Lott was taken to a nearby Luftwaffe base where, after a rest, he was kitted out in British army boots, trousers and greatcoat (but deprived of his prized flying jacket) and then marched to a local station and taken by cattle truck to Stalag IVB, where he remained until released by the Russians in May 1945. Two other members of the crew survived. Those who died were identified at the scene by Sgt Lott following his capture.

Back at Middleton there was no respite for the Canadian crews. Sgt Ashton won an immediate DFM the following night for putting out a fire in the fuselage of his Halifax following a night fighter attack over Munchengladbach.

The next night saw the opening of what was to become known as the Battle of Berlin. It proved a disastrous one for the Middleton squadrons, 419 losing three – one of them in a collision with a night fighter – and 428 two.

Lancasters of 419 (Moose) Squadron at Middleton in March 1944. In the foreground is KB711 VR-C which was built by Victory Aircraft of Canada and had just been delivered. It was shot down by a night fighter on the night of 1st-2nd May 1944 in an attack on St Ghislain, the first Canadian-built Lancaster lost on operations. All but two of the crew survived. (RAF Leeming)

428 lost its CO, W/Cmdr Smith in September when his aircraft was hit by incendiaries over Montlucan. The following night one of 419's most experienced officers, F/Lt Kenyon, the squadron's gunnery leader, also became a PoW when his aircraft was shot down in an attack on Modane. Kenyon was on his 44th operation. Remarkably, four members of the crew also managed to evade while the remaining four became prisoners.

It was to be an autumn of heavy losses at Middleton as the bombing campaign reached a new intensity and the limitations of the early models of the Halifax became evident. Four were lost – two from each squadron – over Mannheim, five in a raid on Hanover, all from 428, and four more in a raid on Kassel, three of them from 428.

Replacements were quickly brought in, new aircraft arrived and life went on very much as before at Middleton St George. Raids on Mannheim, Leverkusen, Berlin, Frankfurt and Stuttgart each claimed two aircraft. One of those lost on the Stuttgart raid collided with a Lancaster from 103 Squadron at Elsham close to Middleton. The Lancaster was one of a number of 1 Group aircraft which had been diverted north because of fog. All 14 men in both aircraft perished.

By the early autumn it had been decided to convert both Middleton squadrons to the new Lancaster Mk X, production of which had begun in September at the Victory Aircraft plant at Malton, Ontario. The first two arrived at Middleton on 12th December followed by a third, named the *Ruhr Express*, on the 20th but they were not to be used operationally for some weeks. In the meantime, both squadrons soldiered on with their Halifaxes and they were still in use on operations until April 1944 and for training purposes into the summer. The records show the very last Halifax lost from Middleton was 428's JN953, which suffered an engine failure on 12th June. The crew baled out and the pilot successfully crash-landed the aircraft close to Claxton Hall in Yorkshire.

The Lancasters, in the meantime, were now fully operational. 428 had already lost one aircraft in a training accident in February while 419 lost two in similar circumstances in May. Both squadrons used their new aircraft in support of the D-Day landings.

A week after the Normandy landings 16 Lancasters from 419 were part of a 6 Group low-level attack on a rail junction at Cambrai. Among the crews was that of F/O Art de Breyne in KB726 A-Apple. They had been flying operationally together since April and had already more than a dozen ops to their credit. Close to the target Breyne's aircraft

Andrew Mynarski, VC. (C. Jones)

was attacked by a Ju 88, which raked the Lancaster with cannon fire, knocking out both port engines and setting fire to the mid-section of the fuselage and the port wing. The rear turret was badly damaged and the gunner, F/O George Brophy, was trapped. In the meantime the pilot had ordered his crew to bale out. The mid-upper gunner, Andrew Mynarski – who, unbeknown to him, had been promoted to pilot officer the day before – was about to jump when he realised the rear gunner was still trapped. He climbed through the burning section of the fuselage and tried to free the turret by hand. By this time his flying clothes were soaked in burning hydraulic oil but he continued to try to free the jammed turret. Inside, Brophy could see Mynarski's clothing was on fire and, realising how close the aircraft was to the ground, shouted to him to jump. Reluctantly Mynarski gave up his attempts and moved to the escape hatch. Before he jumped, he turned, stood to attention and saluted the trapped gunner, a magnificent gesture from a man who must by then have been in agony. Then he leapt, trailing flames from his burning clothing and parachute. The damaged parachute did little to slow his descent and Mynarski died from his horrific injuries shortly after being found by some French civilians.

The damaged Lancaster, in the meantime, crashed in flames and exploded. The rear turret remained intact and, by some miracle, P/O Brophy survived as did the remainder of the crew. They were quickly captured but, on their release the following year, told the full story of Andrew Mynarski's incredible courage. On 11th October 1946 he was posthumously awarded the Victoria Cross.

A-Apple was one of three 419 Squadron aircraft which failed to return from that raid and three weeks later the squadron lost another three in a similar raid on Villeneuve St George, an attack which also cost 428 a Lancaster and its crew.

The autumn and winter saw both Middleton squadrons in action over Germany. Losses dropped but both squadrons lost aircraft in mid-air collisions. A Lancaster from 428 collided with a Halifax of 426 Squadron, based at Linton, over Warwickshire as they were returning from Soest on 6th December and two months later a 419 Squadron aircraft collided with another Lancaster over the Ardennes following a raid on Bonn. The 'night of ice' on 5th March 1945 claimed two Lancasters from Middleton, both crashing soon after take-off, on a night which saw nine 6 Group aircraft lost in similar circumstances.

A raid on Kiel on the night of 3rd-4th April 1945 saw one Lancaster lost, KB866 VR-M of 419 Squadron, the last operational loss from

Middleton St George. Both squadrons made their final raid of the war on the gun batteries at Wangerooge on 25th April – the very last aircraft to land being 428's D-Dog flown by F/O Walsh – and shortly afterwards began preparing to return to Canada where they were to be part of Tiger Force, intended for duty in the Pacific.

Middleton St George was retained by the RAF after the war and used by Fighter and Training Command until the late 1950s when the airfield was briefly closed for expansion work. It later housed 226 Operational Conversion Unit for the introduction of the supersonic English Electric Lightning into front line service with the RAF. 226 OCU remained at Middleton until 1964 when the airfield was deemed to be surplus to requirements. It was quickly purchased by the Teesside local authorities, who had long seen its potential as a regional airport.

25
POCKLINGTON

Drive round the little market town of Pocklington and take particular notice of the names of some of the newer streets: Murray Close, Comrie Drive, The Owens, Florent Court. They bear the names of some of the men who gave their lives flying from the wartime airfield which is still clearly visible on the south-western outskirts of Pocklington.

The site just off the main Hull-York road was first earmarked for a new RAF airfield in the 1930s as part of the expansion programme but the war had begun before work commenced and there were to be no brick-built hangars at Pocklington. Instead it was constructed in typical wartime fashion, with wooden huts, Nissens and Maycrete buildings. But it did get concrete runways along with an eventual complement of six hangars.

It was on 20th June 1941 that the first of the two squadrons which were to use the airfield, 405 (Vancouver), arrived with its Wellingtons from Driffield. The squadron suffered its first loss shortly afterwards, a Wellington with an all-RAF crew crashing in the North Sea on its return from Cologne. It was the first RCAF loss in Bomber Command. The squadron's aircrew was initially a mix of Canadians, British and New Zealanders. It was with one of the latter that John Searby – later to become one of the outstanding figures in Bomber Command – flew on his 'second dickey' trip to Hamburg soon after he joined the squadron in November 1941. His pilot was Sgt Williams who was a particularly determined type and dropped to 4,000 feet to get an accurate fix in thick cloud and heavy rain. He was greeted with a barrage of heavy and light flak but this did not deter Sgt Williams who went round the target again at an even lower altitude to make sure his bombs went where they were supposed to.

Searby might have been impressed with the aircrew, but he was far from happy with RAF Pocklington. Writing after the war, he described it as a 'dreary camp', which was cold and uncomfortable and he continued: 'I slept in a wooden hut where draughts from the cracks between the floor and the walls caused my jacket, which was hung on a peg, to swing gently to and fro until I plugged the gaps with newspaper.'

Edith Kup has happier memories of Pocklington. She served as a WAAF officer in the operations/intelligence section and was posted to the station at the end of 1941. Initially, the WAAFs lived in billets in Barmby but then moved into the new WAAF site at Allerthorpe, about half a mile up the road from the airfield. 'Our quarters were good – single rooms for each officer with bath etc under the same roof. Each room had a stove which was lit 24 hours a day during the cold winters. The girls had Nissen huts and separate ablutions.' There was also an unofficial gate in the camp fence which was used by men returning late from a night out in York.

The WAAFs were to play a key role at Pocklington – as they did at virtually every other airfield in Bomber Command. Mrs Kup recalls that the officers in her section each covered a watch with the help of hand-picked WAAF sergeants, working one day from 0900 until 1300, from 1300 to 0900 the next day followed by 24 hours off and then back to 0900 to 1300. 'The idea was to have one night in bed in three and we also had to get up for debriefings if required,' she remembered.

Their work included handling all operational information which came from 4 Group headquarters with details of targets, bomb loads, routes, marking etc. This workload increased still further when Pocklington became a Base HQ. Once the information had been received, all sections were informed of their particular role. Her section had to handle inquiries and arrange for the shut down of the station, stopping private phone calls and ensuring all air crew were confined to camp. Later the WAAFs would often assemble on the roof of the watch tower as the aircraft took off. 'We felt it helped the boys to know we were there,' she said. 'I have always felt one of our most important functions was to provide a shoulder to cry on and a sympathetic ear to any member of the air crew wanting to get something off his chest. It was always highly confidential and no one ever breathed a word to anyone else about it.'

This was a two-way relationship. The WAAFs were protected fiercely by the men in the squadrons at Pocklington. No one insulted them and got away with it.

Ops centre at RAF Pocklington. Standing is S/Ldr David Harris while station commander W/Cmdr Carter and Base Commander Air Commodore Gus Walker busy themselves for this posed photograph. (Mrs E. Kup)

405 Squadron was to continue operating its Wellingtons until mid-April 1942 before it began converting to Halifaxes. It lost some 20 Wellingtons during its time at Pocklington, including an aircraft which crashed during an air test over the town on 18th September 1941. The bomber, which was also carrying two of the ground crew, went out of control after the dinghy broke loose and wrapped itself around the tail, the Wellington coming down close to Northfield Farm. The squadron's final Wellington operation was on 14th-15th April when three of its aircraft failed to return from Dortmund, two crashing in Germany and the third in England.

By this time a Halifax Conversion Flight had been formed – this was before the formation of the heavy conversion units – and 405 flew them for the first time in the first 1,000-bomber raid against Cologne at the end of May, losing one aircraft. It lost another the following night over the Ruhr and nine before the end of June, including three in one night over Essen when one of the few survivors was F/Sgt MacLean, later to become Canada's Minister of Fisheries.

S/Ldr Lashbrook and members of 102 Squadron's Halifax Conversion Flight, Pocklington 1942. (Mrs E. Kup)

In August the squadron swapped places with 102 Squadron at Topcliffe. 102 Squadron brought with it its own Halifax conversion flight. This included a number of the vastly experienced men at its disposal, men like the much-decorated Wally Lashbrook who, during a distinguished wartime career, was to serve at no fewer than nine Yorkshire airfields. But he always considered Pocklington his natural wartime home. When the 102 Conversion Flight was disbanded he went with a number of its members and aircraft to the new 1663 HCU at Rufforth but was to return to Pocklington as C Flight commander later in the year.

102 began operations almost immediately and lost its first Halifax from Pocklington in a raid on Osnabruck on 9th-10th August, five of the crew surviving to become PoWs.

The squadron lost its popular CO, W/Cmdr Bintley, when aircraft returning from Genoa were diverted to Holme-on-Spalding Moor and his was in a collision with another Halifax on the ground. An attack on Frankfurt on 2nd-3rd December led to three Pocklington aircraft being shot down by night fighters. It was 102's worst night until 12th-13th March 1943 when three failed to return from Essen, with the deaths of 15 men. One of those was pilot Sgt Charlebois, whose aircraft was hit by flak over the Ruhr. He remained at the controls while five of his crew managed to bale out, one of the many supreme acts of courage which came to light when the war ended.

During 1943 Pocklington became 41 Base HQ and 31-year-old Air Commodore Gus Walker was appointed Base CO. Whilst serving as CO at Syerston in 1942, he had lost an arm when a bomb accidentally fell from a 106 Squadron Lancaster and exploded. Despite this handicap, Walker was back at his desk two months later. He was an extremely popular commander at Pocklington and later served as Senior Air Staff Officer at 4 Group HQ. He was to become an air chief marshal and Inspector-General of the RAF.

On the night of 29th March 1943 ten Halifaxes from 102 Squadron took off to join 386 other heavies in a raid on Berlin. One of the Pocklington aircraft was in the air for little over a minute before disaster struck. G-George, loaded with high explosive and incendiary bombs and some 2,000 gallons of fuel, appeared to flip over as it flew across the town and crashed onto open land at West Green, opposite Pocklington School. There was an enormous explosion and it was some time before the local fire brigade managed to get the blaze under control and recover the bodies of pilot F/Sgt Bill Comrie and his crew. Eyewitnesses were certain that Comrie managed to haul his aircraft clear of the town centre before crashing.

Another aircraft which took off from Pocklington that night was Q-Queenie, the oldest Halifax on the squadron and which was generally regarded to be clapped out. Tom Wingham was a member of Queenie's crew that night and this is how he remembers it.

'We had been to Berlin two nights before and Harris was determined to get in another raid on the Big City before the light evenings. The weather forecast at briefing was ghastly and our station Met Office unofficially predicted a certain "scrub". Came take-off time and the weather was on the deck with heavy rain from the occlusion running north to south over Yorkshire and Lincolnshire. Cloud was solid up to 15,000ft with severe icing predicted.

'Take-off was put back and we knew there had to be a "scrub". But Harris would not cancel and eventually we took off. The occlusion trailed back over Yorkshire and almost as soon as we lifted off we were in cloud as we set course over the North Sea.

'Queenie was notorious for its lack of climbing agility and poor ceiling. We flogged our way upwards through the occlusion and at 15,000 feet we were still in cloud and were unable to climb another foot. Our climb had been so slow, we had taken the whole of the North Sea to reach this height. Now straight and level and still in cloud, we found ourselves with an iced-up windscreen and turrets and a maximum IAS of 135 knots.

'At this point we must have been somewhere near Flensburg for we suddenly became the object of some heavy AA fire. Even the Germans didn't seem to believe any aircraft could be flying so low since most of the bursts seemed to be ahead of us. With everyone operating "blind" because of the icing, discretion now had to be the better part of valour. We dropped our bombs, hoping against hope they might give the German gunners earache, but more in the hope of getting a bit more speed from the lightened aircraft.

'Thankfully, we turned for home and managed to recross the inclusion without any further icing. As we reached the end of the runway, we had to feather the starboard outer as the oil pressure dropped off the clock. At dispersal we got out and walked around the aircraft to where one of the groundstaff was getting rather excited. A steady flow of glycol was being shed by both inner engines. From one of the wing bomb bays two 4lb incendiaries were protruding and the other 88 were lying loose on the bomb bay doors. The IFF aerial had also disappeared.

'Had we gone on to Berlin it seems certain we would have either run out of engines, had a wing on fire or, as a last resort, have been shot down by Fighter Command. Sometimes it was easier to fight the Germans!'

One of the perils of Pocklington was the proximity of other airfields and their overlapping circuits. The danger of this was brought home to everyone at Pocklington on the night of 22nd-23rd November as aircraft were taking off for a raid on Berlin. A Halifax from 102 collided over Barmby Moor with another from 77 Squadron at Elvington. Both aircraft crashed in flames near Newlands Farm on York Road at Barmby. All 14 men on the two aircraft were killed and later 14 oak trees were planted at the spot, each bearing the name of one of those who died that night.

During 1944, 102 Squadron was to play a leading role in the bombing campaign, losing 16 aircraft on Berlin raids, including seven Halifax IIs on the night of 20th-21st January, two of them after crash-landings.

A wonderful crew photograph at Pocklington in 1944. Astride 102 Squadron's S-Sugar is rear gunner Eric Creasey and others are (l to r, standing): Ken Jones (flight engineer), Steve Dooley (mid-upper gunner) and Mick Macey (wireless operator); front: John Stephenson (navigator), Bud Budden (pilot) and Doug Ryder (bomb aimer). (Ken Jones)

Eight nights later Halifax JD165 ditched off Montrose after suffering flak damage over Berlin. Four of the crew, the pilot F/Lt Pugh, wireless operator Sgt Cohen, mid-upper gunner Sgt Williams and the navigator F/Lt Graham, spent three days in an open dinghy before being picked up, Graham dying shortly after the rescue. The other three crew members, Sgt Purkiss (flight engineer), Sgt Campbell (bomb aimer) and Sgt Burgess (rear gunner) all drowned when the aircraft ditched. The pilot suffered severe frostbite and spent eight weeks in hospital. He later returned to 102 as a ferry pilot.

The squadron was not included in the disastrous Nuremburg raid – it had ten Halifaxes out on mining operations that night – but it was heavily involved in operations in support of the D-Day landings. An attack on railway yards at Blainville on 28th-29th June cost the squadron five aircraft. Eighteen men were killed, eight became prisoners and a further eight evaded capture. Another five aircraft had been lost in an attack on the Sterkrade refinery a few nights earlier with the loss of 33 men. Just two survived.

By the autumn of 1944 the survival rate among crews at Pocklington had begun to increase dramatically. Sheffielder Ken Jones was the

Halifax III LW178 DY-E of 102 Squadron at Pocklington pictured during a daylight raid late in 1944. The aircraft survived the war and was scrapped in 1947. (Stuart Cook)

flight engineer in a 102 Squadron crew which completed a tour of 34 operations in January 1945, most of them in C Flight's S-Sugar, NA559. It was in this aircraft that they took part in their 28th op, a raid on the Krupps factory at Essen on the night of 28th-29th November 1944. Ken takes up the story: 'We had completed our bombing run and turned for home, the angle of change of course being ever so slight and, I suppose, due to an oversight by our skipper, we did a complete circle and found ourselves alone over Essen, the main force having long departed.

'We were attacked by German fighters, coned by searchlights and received several hits from shrapnel, but we somehow managed to escape and made it home on three engines with many holes in the aircraft.

'Some little time later, while I was home on leave, my father asked me where I was on a particular Tuesday at a particular time. It turned out that my dear grandmother, who was a devout Christian, had asked as she had been awakened with an overwhelming need to pray for me. It was precisely the time we were over Essen.'

Ken was in the crew of F/Lt Bud Budden, which had come together at 1658 HCU at Riccall at the end of April 1944. Their rear gunner was F/O (later F/Lt) Eric Creasey, who was on his second tour. He went on to complete 60 operations and thoroughly earned his DFC. Their tour included 18 daylight and 16 night operations and no fewer than 19 were to the Ruhr. At the end of September, along with many other 4 Group crews, they flew five trips to Melsbroek airfield, near Brussels, ferrying petrol supplies for the army. Ken, who was only 20 when he completed his tour remembers that fear was their constant companion on those 34 operations.

Superstition was rife on 102 and Eric Creasey was particularly prone. 'He always insisted that the pilot stopped at the end of the runway before take-off so that he could pop out and place a piece of chewing gum from his mouth on the RAF roundel on Sugar's fuselage,' recalled Ken.

Chewing gum was among the items issued to aircrew before take-off and helped ward off dry mouths during hazardous moments – although on one occasion, when their Halifax was coned by searchlights and attacked by fighters, Ken used up two full packets but his throat was still as dry as a bone.

By the time Ken completed his tour, losses at Pocklington were the exception rather than the rule. But an attack on the German frontier town of Goch on the night of 7th-8th February 1945 in support of a

British army attack cost the squadron two aircraft. One was shot down by a Ju 88 near the target, the crew baling out, while the second, NA175 DY-Q, was on its return home when it was attacked by a night fighter and set on fire. It soon became clear this could not be contained and the captain, W/O Smith, gave the order to abandon the aircraft. All six members of the crew escaped but Smith failed to get out in time and his body was found in the wreckage of the aircraft after it crashed near Lille. He is now buried in the Leopoldsburg War Cemetery in Belgium. He was one of the final casualties suffered by 102 at Pocklington.

When the war ended the airfield spent some time as No 17 Aircrew Holding Unit before finally closing in September 1946. Part of the site later became an industrial estate while the Wolds Gliding Club still uses the airfield itself.

In 1985 a splendid memorial to 405 and 102 Squadrons was unveiled on the airfield by Air Chief Marshal Sir Gus Walker. Sadly, he was to die the following year.

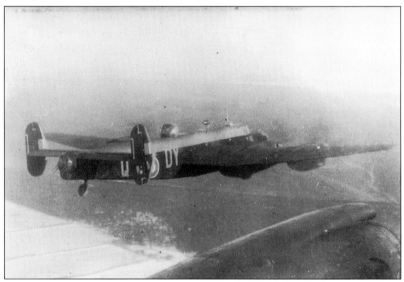

102 Squadron's Q-Queenie pictured during the winter of 1942-43. (Yorkshire Air Museum via Peter Green)

26
SKIPTON-ON-SWALE

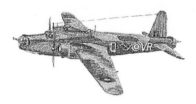

Among the sites selected for airfield development in the early days of the war was one just off the road linking Thirsk with the Great North Road. Nearby was the pleasant village of Skipton-on-Swale and this was the name adopted by the RAF for the new bomber airfield, part of which was ready for use by the summer of 1942.

Over the next three years the airfield was the home of four bomber squadrons, all of them Canadian. They lost around 100 aircraft in that time, most on operations. And, although the Canadians left Skipton soon after the war in Europe ended, memories of their time at the airfield live on. On the village green a simple stone memorial marks the spot where, on 5th August 1944 a Halifax of 433 Squadron crashed, killing two of the crew and five-year-old Kenneth Battensby, who died when he was hit by debris from the aircraft. This single incident united the village and the RAF station in mutual grief. In May 1984 it was Kenneth's brother who unveiled the memorial in front of some 200 RCAF veterans and their families, who had gathered together on the village green at Skipton to remember the events of 40 years earlier.

RAF Skipton-on-Swale was built as a typical wartime bomber airfield, with three Tarmac runways and three hangars. The site was bounded on one side by the Swale and on the other by the Northallerton road, with the village of Skipton itself forming a third boundary. It opened in August 1942 as a satellite of RAF Leeming within 4 Group and its first occupants were 420 (Snowy Owl) Squadron, which had been formed the previous December at

Accommodation and ablution blocks at Skipton-on-Swale. (Michael Parry)

Waddington in Lincolnshire in 5 Group, flying Hampdens. By the summer of 1942 plans were already well advanced for the formation of the all-RCAF 6 Group and 420 was moved north to prepare for this, converting to Wellingtons on arrival at Skipton.

The squadron's new airfield was far from complete when 420 arrived. Many of the accommodation blocks were unfinished and those that were, were scattered around the area, necessitating long treks to 'work' for squadron personnel, something they were unused to at pre-war Waddington. Once settled at Skipton, the Hampdens quickly gave way to Wellington Mk IIIs and the squadron flew its first operation in its new aircraft on 5th-6th October, 420 making its debut alongside 425 Squadron for a raid on Aachen. A week later 420 was on operations again, this time the Wellingtons being flown from Skipton to Leeming where they were bombed up before a raid on Kiel. Two of the aircraft failed to make it back, one crash-landing in Norfolk with no injuries to the crew while the second hit a house on its approach to Leeming, killing the pilot, F/Sgt Croft, and his crew. The crash also claimed the life of five-year-old Barbara Huggins, who was asleep when the Wellington force-landed in a field, crashed through a fence and hit the back of her family's home in Greengate Lane, Londonderry, near Bedale. The cottage collapsed and caught fire but rescuers managed to save her parents, who were in the front bedroom at the time of the crash. Barbara's body was recovered once the fire had been extinguished. Two days later the now operational 420 Squadron left Skipton for Middleton St George.

Skipton-on-Swale was left without a resident unit for over six months, during which time the station was transferred to the control of

6 Group. The period of inactivity also gave contractors the opportunity to complete the work on the airfield, laying new dispersals and completing the perimeter track. On 1st May 432 (Leaside) Squadron – it took its name from the town in Ontario which adopted the squadron – was formed at Skipton, the first to be formed within 6 Group. It was equipped with Wellington Xs and flew operationally for the first time on the night of 23rd-24th May when the squadron CO, W/Cmdr Kerby led 15 aircraft from Skipton as part of a force of some 826 aircraft which attacked Dortmund. All the 432 Squadron aircraft returned safely but they were not to be spared for long. Three nights later P/O Taylor – an experienced bomber captain who had won a DFM with 420 Squadron two months earlier – and his crew were lost without trace. They were the first men to die on operations from Skipton-on-Swale.

Two nights later another Wellington was lost in a raid on Wuppertal while a second aircraft crashed at Reeth in Upper Swaledale, killing two of those on board. This was the period of the Battle of the Ruhr and in the coming weeks 432 Squadron was to suffer badly, losing two aircraft in a second raid on Wuppertal, another over Dusseldorf and four in a single night in a raid on Cologne. Two of those were shot down with the loss of ten men near the target while the remaining two both crashed near Gravesend in Kent. In one incident three of the crew died and two others were injured as their aircraft struck some houses when trying to make an emergency landing, while one man died in the second aircraft, which was abandoned by its crew because of severe flak damage.

It wasn't just operations that proved costly in lives for the Leaside men. On 16th July a Wellington being air tested prior to operations broke up in flight and crashed near Malton, killing the six men on board. Three days later another aircraft suffered engine problems during an air test and crashed at Sowerby, hitting a row of trees. The crew was fortunate enough to walk away from this one.

A raid on Essen on 25th-26th July ended for one Skipton crew as their aircraft ditched off the Norfolk coast. They managed to get into their dinghy and were picked up soon afterwards by the Cromer lifeboat.

W/Cmdr Kerby, a former fighter pilot, became the first of a number of squadron commanders at Skipton-on-Swale to fail to return from operations on the night of 29th-30th July. His Wellington was shot down by a night fighter during one of the Hamburg raids, the aircraft crashing near Luneberg, killing four of the crew. W/Cmdr McKay arrived within a few days to take command of the squadron. Two nights later 432 lost another Wellington on what was the fourth of the 'Battle of Hamburg' raids, the aircraft crashing in the sea. The tail gunner was Sgt Tom Kirkham of Vancouver, whose elder brother, F/O Ernest Kirkham, was killed on the same raid in a 5 Group Lancaster.

432 was to lose two more aircraft, one on a mining trip and the second over Gelsenkirchen, before it moved out of Skipton-on-Swale for East Moor in mid-September. The squadron's departure heralded the advent of heavy bombers at Skipton-on-Swale. On 25th September 433 (Porcupine) Squadron – it was adopted by the towns of Tisdale, Timmins and Whitney in the Porcupine district of Northern Ontario – was formed at Skipton and immediately began working up on the new Halifax IIIs then about to go into service. On 6th November, it was joined by 424 (Tiger) Squadron, which had been on detachment in the Middle East after spells at Topcliffe and Leeming, and it, too, began converting to Halifaxes.

There was a tragic accident at Skipton on 19th December when a 433 Squadron aircraft rolled onto its back and crashed seconds after take-off, killing all six men on board. The aircraft crashed into a second Halifax, killing one of the ground crew working on the bomber and badly injuring two more.

433 Squadron became operational on its new aircraft on the night of 2nd-3rd January 1944 when the three aircraft sent to lay mines off the Frisian islands all returned safely to Skipton. Eight aircraft took part in the squadron's first Halifax bombing raid, to Berlin on the night of 18th-19th January, and once again all returned safely. Three nights later two aircraft were lost in a raid on Magdeburg, one of them flown by the squadron CO, W/Cmdr Martin. The following night 424 lost its first aircraft, the Halifax crashing into the River Swale after an over-shoot during a night exercise, killing one of the crew. A raid on Berlin on the night of 28th-29th January cost 433 three more Halifaxes, but the crews were more fortunate. One of the aircraft had lost fuel after being hit by flak and the pilot, F/O Gray, successfully ditched 15 miles off Hartlepool, all those on board being picked up by a rescue launch at the end of their first op. The second aircraft had been damaged by a night fighter and ran out of fuel soon after it reached Yorkshire. The crew baled out near Thirsk, the rear gunner being killed when his parachute caught on the tail of the aircraft as he jumped. The third Halifax which failed to make it back crash-landed at Catfoss and the pilot was killed. The squadron was to lose another aircraft two nights

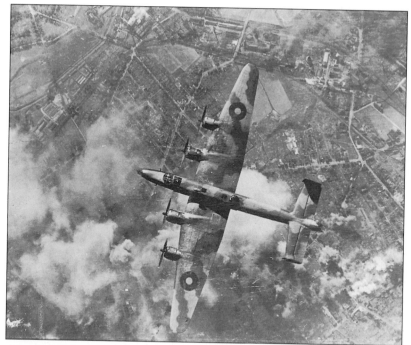

A bomb aimer's view of Wanne Eickel, 12th October 1944. Below is another 6 Group Halifax III. (Via G. Smith)

later in its third attack in the month on Berlin.

In February 424 Squadron joined the fray in its Halifaxes and lost one over Berlin on the night of 15th-16th February. It was flown by one of the squadron's flight commanders, S/Ldr Reilander and he and the other seven men on board were all killed. 433 lost three aircraft and their crews during February, two in one night in an attack on Schweinfurt and the third in a raid on Leipzig.

Both squadrons each lost an aircraft in a raid on Frankfurt in March while a week later the final raid on Berlin of the winter cost Skipton four Halifaxes, two from each squadron. Both 433 Squadron aircraft were brought down on the return leg, all on board F/Sgt Lossing's aircraft being killed. Five of F/Sgt Russell's crew survived although the rear gunner later died in a PoW camp. Of the two lost from 424, one crashed near Berlin with just one member of the crew surviving, while the second was written off after hitting a tree at Brandesburton after overshooting at Catfoss.

Three nights later Skipton lost another three aircraft on the Nuremberg raid, two of them from 424 Squadron. A 433 Squadron Halifax flown by P/O Christian Nielson, an American whose crew had been one of the first five to join the squadron when it was formed, was shot down on its bombing run near Nuremburg by a night fighter – the Luftwaffe's 86th victim that night. Nielson and two others survived but five men died, among them the flight engineer, P/O Christopher Panton, the son of a Lincolnshire gamekeeper. Many years after the war one of his brothers visited his grave and was so moved by the experience that he decided to create a lasting memorial to Christopher and the other 55,000 men of Bomber Command who died in action. This led to Harold and Fred Panton acquiring part of the wartime airfield at East Kirkby in Lincolnshire and restoring it to how it would have looked in wartime. The brothers have also partly restored a Lancaster bomber, which now regularly taxis along part of the old perimeter track much to the delight of thousands of visitors.

A second 433 Squadron Halifax, flown by P/O Ronald Reinelt, was damaged by a night fighter and lost part of its wing but still made it back to Skipton. The two aircraft lost from 424 Squadron included that of S/Ldr Metzler, who died along with his crew when they fell victim to flak near Schweinfurt. There was a single survivor from F/Lt Doig's Halifax, which was shot down by a night fighter.

The Nuremburg raid was to mark a watershed for Bomber Command. The emphasis now switched from the bombing of cities deep in Germany to railway targets in support of the coming invasion. 433 Squadron lost two aircraft in an attack on the yards at Noisy-le-Sec, near Paris, an attack which went horribly wrong, many bombs falling on nearby residential areas, killing some 464 French civilians. Four nights later there was a brief return to Germany with a raid on Dusseldorf which was to lead to the loss of five aircraft from Skipton, three from 433 and one from 424 being shot down while the fifth, a 433 Squadron aircraft, was written off after a heavy landing. Two nights later an attack on Karlsruhe cost 424 two Halifaxes.

Three more aircraft – all from 424 – were lost during the build-up to the invasion in May and early June while D-Day itself saw both squadrons hitting the coastal batteries at Houlgate. The first post-invasion losses came in an attack on rail yards at Cambrai on the night of 12th-13th June when two aircraft were lost to night fighters.

Nine aircraft were lost from Skipton in July, four of them in an attack on rail yards at Villeneuve-St-George on the night of 4th-5th July. Of

Halifax III MZ910 pictured during its time as 'Y' of 433 Squadron at Skipton-on-Swale, when it was the mount of S/Ldr Pierce and crew. It later went to 420 Squadron at Tholthorpe and failed to return from a raid on Witten on 19th March 1945. (Yorkshire air Museum via Peter Green)

the two lost in an attack on Hamburg at the end of the month, one was flown by W/Cmdr Don Blane, who had succeeded W/Cmdr Martin back in January. He, in turn, was succeeded by W/Cmdr Roy, who arrived at Skipton-on-Swale in mid-August and was then shot down in a raid on Bochum in early October and spent the rest of the war in a prison camp.

Early August saw the Skipton Halifaxes hitting V1 storage sites, including one at Bois de Cassan. One 424 Squadron aircraft was shot down near the target while a second, BM-H of 433 Squadron, crashed onto Skipton-on-Swale village green with tragic results. F/O Jimmy Harrison and his crew had left Skipton with a spare rear gunner as Sgt Ray Beaudette had still not fully recovered from injuries he received in a motor-cycle accident, in which his pilot had also been injured. The Halifax had been damaged by flak over the target and had suffered engine damage. As the aircraft attempted to land, the pilot was having difficulty maintaining power and decided to overshoot. At that point a second engine failed and the aircraft banked towards the village, brushing tree tops and hitting the roof of Skipton Hall before crashing into a large elm tree on the village green. The pilot and the flight engineer, F/Sgt Dennis Whitbread, were killed along with five-year-old Kenneth Battensby, whose house and garden were showered with debris. Among the people who witnessed the crash was Sgt Beaudette, who was waiting for an ambulance outside the telephone kiosk on Skipton green when the Halifax crashed. In 1982 he joined survivors of the crew at the unveiling of the memorial on the village green

That August marked a turning point in the fortunes of the Skipton squadrons. In September not a single aircraft was lost on operations, the only casualty being a 424 Squadron aircraft which swung on take-off in fog and lost its undercarriage before coming to rest in a hedge on the airfield boundary. Three aircraft failed to return in October as the bombing campaign reached a new intensity. A raid on Cologne at the end of the month was the second operation for 433's F/Lt MacLean and his crew and they returned safely to Skipton where they omitted to open the bomb doors as their aircraft taxied into its dispersal pan. The following morning the pilot was ordered to return to the dispersal while the bomb doors were opened by a member of the ground crew. As he watched, a 500lb bomb, which unbeknown to the crew had 'hung up' over Cologne, fell out, landing at his feet. Everyone scattered but, fortunately, it failed to explode.

Three aircraft, including W/Cmdr Roy's, were lost in October and seven in November, two in an attack on Dusseldorf. Both were from 424, one being shot down near the target and the second landing safely at an Allied airfield in France with severe flak damage.

Just three more Halifaxes were to be lost from Skipton – a fourth being destroyed when it crashed and blew up on take-off – as both squadrons began to convert to Lancasters early in January 1945. Unlike some other 6 Group squadrons, 424 and 433 were equipped with British-built aircraft, most of them built at the Avro factory at Yeadon, on the outskirts of Leeds. 433 received its first aircraft – ME375 and ME457 – from the factory on 17th January and flew them operationally for the first time on the 29th in a raid on Krefeld. 424's first aircraft – ME456 and ME458 – arrived at the beginning of January and flew operationally for the first time to Ludwigshafen on 1st February.

Just six Lancasters were lost on operations in the final few months of war, a seventh crashing near Dishforth village. The aircraft had been damaged by flak and the pilot, S/Ldr Stinson, ordered his crew to bale out rather than risk landing.

Each squadron provided ten aircraft for 6 Group's final operation of the war, the daylight attack on the gun batteries on the island of Wangerooge on 25th April, all returning safely.

Both squadrons remained at Skipton-on-Swale during the summer of 1945 and were used to fly home troops from Italy. With the war in the Far East over, they were disbanded in October and the airfield closed, the land eventually being returned to agriculture.

27
SNAITH

It is possible to catch a brief glimpse of what remains of RAF Snaith as you head east from Ferrybridge along the busy M62 towards Hull. The J-type hangar is one of the few reminders that this was once a major bomber airfield.

Snaith served both 1 and 4 Groups of Bomber Command and was to be the permanent home of just two squadrons, 150 and 51, between the summer of 1941 and the spring of 1945, losing over 200 aircraft and, with them, the lives of more than 1,000 young men.

The airfield was to endure many bad times, but none was worse than that of 30th-31st March 1944, the night of Bomber Command's disastrous attack on Nuremburg. The Command's public relations department had selected that night to bring a large party of press reporters and photographers to Snaith to cover the raid from start to finish. They attended the briefing where the target was revealed for the 17 crews from 51 Squadron selected to take part, watched the Halifaxes being prepared and followed the crews out to their dispersals. Later they gathered in the station's watch office to await news of the raid and the return of 51 Squadron.

Long before the bombers began to return news was coming through of the disaster which had befallen Bomber Command that night. Eventually, the Halifaxes began to return, several showing the signs of battle. Only eleven came back. Five had been shot down and a sixth had crashed in Oxfordshire. More than a third of the squadron had gone in a single night.

In his excellent book, *The Nuremburg Raid*, Martin Middlebrook records Sgt Philip Bailey's recollections as the newspaper men watched the debriefing. 'They watched and waited so considerately whilst the lads were coming in but, as the time went on, they too became aware that there were some losses. I shall never ever forget the faces of two of them – both middle-aged – when it was quietly put to them that six crews were unaccounted for, 42 lads out of the 119 they had watched set off into the night sky. The notebooks and cameras were put away and the owners quietly left, obviously not wishing to intrude on our feelings.'

Nuremburg was the nadir of Snaith's fortunes in a bombing war in which it was to play a considerable role. The airfield site, close to the village of Pollington on the flat plain west of Goole, was among those selected for development in the late 1930s, work beginning early in 1940. Although close to Pollington, the airfield was named after the nearby small town of Snaith to avoid confusion with RAF Pocklington, then under construction 20 miles to the north. The site was bounded by the Goole-Pontefract road, the Knottingley and Goole canal and the main LNER railway line.

The airfield opened in July 1941 under the control of 1 Group, which then had its headquarters at Bawtry Hall, near Doncaster. Within a few days 150 Squadron had moved in with its Wellington IIIs from Newton in Nottinghamshire. It was to operate from Snaith until the autumn of 1941 before moving to Kirmington.

Those Wellingtons were in action almost constantly during 150's time at Snaith, attacking targets across northern Europe. Initially losses were low but, as attacks grew in intensity and the defences became ever more effective, more and more aircraft failed to make it back. On the night of 5th-6th May 1942 three of the nine aircraft sent to Stuttgart failed to return. One, JN-A, crashed in the sea off the Dutch coast, killing all six on board. Another crash-landed at Askern while the third, which had suffered flak damage, made an emergency landing at Blyton in Lincolnshire, hitting an obstruction on the runway and bursting into flames. The Australian pilot, Sgt Baxter, braved the flames to go back into the aircraft to rescue his trapped wireless operator, an act of gallantry which was to be rewarded with the George Medal.

Three more aircraft were lost in an attack on Bremen in June and another three in a raid on Frankfurt in September. 150's final loss from Snaith came on the night of 23rd-24th October when one of six Wellingtons failed to return from a mining operation off the Norwegian coast, three of the crew surviving to become PoWs.

A reorganisation of Group boundaries had seen Snaith, along with Breighton and Holme-on-Spalding Moor, transferred to 4 Group and 150's departure to the new airfield at Kirmington (now Humberside

One of the dramatic pictures taken at Snaith on the night of 30th-31st March 19-

representatives awaited the return of 51 Squadron from Nuremburg. (Via Peter Green)

Airport) marked the arrival of 51 Squadron, one of 4 Group's original squadrons, following a six-month detachment to Coastal Command. The squadron's transfer to Snaith at the end of October saw the end of its operational use of Whitleys. It was to spend two months converting to Halifaxes and flew them operationally in the New Year, suffering its first loss on the night of 9th-10th January 1943 when an aircraft failed to return from a mining operation. The first losses over Germany occurred at the end of the month when two Halifaxes were shot down in a raid on Dusseldorf.

Two Halifaxes were destroyed in an accident when incendiaries fell from one of the aircraft and ignited while pre-flight checks were being carried out. It happened during a visit to the station by a number of senior officers from Group HQ, one of whom was later to report that one of the rear gunners climbed from his turret and ran for it, not stopping, legend has it, until he reached the crew's favourite pub, the George and Dragon in nearby Pollington.

The story is told by G/Capt Tom Sawyer in his book *Only Owls and Bloody Fools Fly At Night*. He also recalls a visit to Snaith when he saw a Halifax swing wildly on take-off, going across the grass and eventually becoming airborne at a 90-degree angle to the runway. The crew – who eventually completed their tour safely – were later congratulated on being the first in 4 Group to take off sideways!

51's aircraft began using the newly-laid runways at nearby Burn, which was still under construction. One aircraft crashed at the end of January when it hit a platelayer's hut on the nearby railway line, killing one of the four men inside at the time.

That spring and summer 51 was to have a torrid time as losses went up dramatically in the all-out assault by Bomber Command on Germany's industrial heartland. Five aircraft were lost in an attack on Pilsen on 16th-17th April, 25 men being killed, seven becoming PoWs and four evading. A raid on Duisburg on 12th-13th May cost the squadron another four aircraft with a fifth force-landing at Riccall with an engine fire. Of those shot down, one was abandoned by its crew over Belgium, the aircraft falling on a bakery, killing two civilians. Another crashed in Holland where the bodies of five of the crew were buried in a ditch by German troops. Later the bodies were recovered by a local farmer and his son who reburied them on his land. Four more aircraft were lost over Dortmund later in the month with a fifth crashing at Woolfox Lodge after its hydraulics failed.

Of the three lost in a raid on Dusseldorf on 11th-12th June, one was shot down by naval gunners on a British convoy off the Norfolk coast, all seven men being picked up, no doubt to vent their anger on those responsible. 51 Squadron was one of many to question the aircraft recognition capabilities of the Royal Navy.

There was an immediate DFM for Sgt Foulsham whose aircraft was damaged by flak over Gelsenkirchen. The Halifax went into a spin and two of the crew baled out but the pilot regained control and managed to reach Sussex before crash landing.

One of the aircraft which took off from Snaith on the night of 10th August 1943 for Nuremburg was HR981 MH-D, flown by P/O MacPherson. As soon as they were airborne, the crew found the flaps would not come up and the starboard wheel was stuck half-way down. With a full fuel and bomb load the aircraft would only climb slowly while the crew managed to use the hand pumps to raise the flaps. The wheel, however, refused to budge and, after reaching 3,000 feet, they were ordered to head for the coast and dump their bombs. At that point the constant speed unit on the starboard outer engine failed. It was impossible to feather the airscrew and, as the fuel supply was cut, the engine burst into flames. By now the aircraft was over north Lincolnshire and the pilot decided to find some empty farmland to drop his bomb load, only to discover that the release mechanism would not work. He opted to belly land. At 500 feet the fire spread and the starboard inner cut but P/O MacPherson held the aircraft reasonably steady as he prepared to crash-land.

As fate would have it, the only house for miles around loomed up in front of the Halifax, the starboard wing hitting the building. The aircraft immediately burst into flames, killing the wireless operator, P/O Silvester. The building they had hit was a cottage at Cliff Farm, Snitterby, close to the bomber airfield at Hemswell. The stepson of the farmworker, Peter Clarke, was walking towards the house when he saw the Halifax crash into it. He found the door of the cottage jammed with debris but levered it open and dragged his brother and sister to safety before going back to try to rescue his mother and baby sister, this time being beaten back by the heat. Six of the Halifax's crew, in the meantime, had escaped and all were taken to the station sick quarters at Hemswell before being transferred to an RAF hospital near Lincoln.

Many of those who served at Snaith came from the far flung corners of the old Empire, including both Canada and Australia. Some came from much nearer home. F/Sgt Roland Seaman arrived with his crew from 1658 HCU at Riccall just after Christmas 1943. His home was at

Halifax II HR981 MH-D of 51 Squadron, which crashed onto a farmworker's cottage at Snit *(Grimsby Evening Telegraph)*

shire soon after taking off from Snaith for Nuremburg on 10th August 1943.

Clementhorpe Hall at Gilberdyke, near Goole, a little over a dozen miles from his first, and final, posting to a bomber squadron.

Roland Seaman, an old boy of Goole Grammar School, had been training in Beverley to be a chartered accountant before he volunteered to join the RAF. His father hoped eventually he would go into the family business.

It was a baptism of fire for F/Sgt Seaman. The day after arriving at Snaith he went as second pilot to Berlin with P/O Carder's crew. It was to be more than three weeks before he flew operationally with his own crew. Their arrival had coincided with the screening of 51 Squadron for the conversion to the new Mk III Halifax and it was in one of the new aircraft, LV778, that they went to Magdeburg on 21st January 1944, a raid which cost 51 Squadron three Halifaxes and the lives of eleven men. For a time, the operations centre at Snaith thought they had lost a fourth aircraft when MH-T, containing F/Sgt Seaman's crew, failed to return. The crew was posted as 'missing' but, almost immediately, came news that they had landed at Catfoss, almost out of fuel.

It was another three weeks before they flew operationally again, this time to Berlin on 15th February when all the 51 Squadron aircraft returned safely. Five nights later they went to Stuttgart, a raid which cost 51 one of its new Halifax IIIs. On 24th February Schweinfurt was the target, but F/Sgt Seaman and his crew had to turn for home when their Gee set developed a fault. The following night they went to Augsburg in southern Germany, a trip which lasted a few minutes under eight hours. Then 1st March saw Roland Seaman and crew over Stuttgart in MH-V, which was becoming their regular aircraft. However, for their seventh operation, a raid on Le Mans on 13th March, they took MH-Y, an ex-78 Squadron Halifax which 51 had received to replace the aircraft supplied to the new 578 Squadron before its move to Burn. The Le Mans trip was an extremely successful raid by 213 Yorkshire-based Halifaxes but, on their return, they found that as the target was in France, it counted as only a third of an operation. Two nights later they went back to Stuttgart. It was Roland Seaman's eighth operation and it was to be the last he completed. Ten Halifaxes were lost that night, including Seaman's old MH-V.

Three nights later Roland Seaman left Yorkshire for the last time as he lifted MH-Y off Snaith's main runway and joined other 4 Group Halifaxes gaining height for a raid on Frankfurt. During the raid the aircraft was hit by anti-aircraft fire and started to break up. The pilot ordered his crew to bale out. The wireless operator, Sgt Pickford, had

F/Sgt Roland Seaman, who was posted to Snaith shortly after Christmas 1943. (Mrs B. St Paul)

been struck on the head and knocked out but it is believed he was pushed from the aircraft by the bomb aimer, F/Sgt Glover, and parachuted to safety along with the navigator, F/Sgt Robson and engineer Sgt Powell. There was no escape for F/Sgt Seaman and two other members of the crew, F/Sgt Glover and the rear gunner, Sgt Baldwin as the Halifax crashed at Baumholder, but miraculously, the mid-upper gunner, Sgt Gulliver (a last-minute replacement for the crew's regular mid-upper, Sgt Walton), survived despite being trapped in his turret. The Halifax, in the meantime, had broken in half and the remains of a large section of the fuselage spun to earth. Sgt Pickford came down close to the wreckage and found Sgt Gulliver in the shattered mid-section of the aircraft shouting for morphine. He was in extreme agony with two badly broken legs and the wireless operator, unable to find anything to ease his pain, set off to find help, returning with local villagers who used a ladder to lift the gunner from the wreckage.

A telegram arrived at Clementhorpe Hall shortly after 9.30 the next morning informing the Seaman family that Roland was missing. It was ironic that, although he was only stationed nearby, he hadn't been at Snaith long enough to come home on leave.

During this period the squadron's C Flight had been detached to help form 578 Squadron, which flew its first operation from Snaith on the night of 20th-21st January 1944, all five aircraft returning safely from Berlin. In February the squadron moved to Burn, where it was to remain for the rest of the war.

Snaith was also used briefly in April by Typhoons of 266 Squadron for training for their ground attack role in the 2nd Tactical Air Force in the coming invasion. 51 Squadron itself was to play its part in the assault. The squadron lost three aircraft in each of the attacks on rail yards at Montzen and Aachen and two more in a raid on Tergnier. Three days after the invasion another aircraft was lost, crashing close to the church at Holme-on-Spalding Moor, following a raid on rail targets in France.

Not all aircraft lost were on operations. At 5.30 pm on 14th November 1944 Halifax HK844, which had already completed 49 operations, was flying over Leeds when it exploded in mid-air. Most of the wreckage came down into a field off Thorpe Lane, East Ardsley, some narrowly missing a crowded bus while the remainder fell on two nearby houses. Two of the crew are believed to have baled out but were killed by the blast along with the other five men on board.

The memorial to the 51 Squadron crew at Tingley, West Yorks. (Walter Townsend)

Miraculously, the only injury on the ground was a scratched knee suffered by three-year-old Pauline Knight, who was in one of the houses hit by the wreckage. In 1988 a memorial was erected at the site, thanks mainly to the efforts of Walter Townsend who, as a schoolboy saw the wreckage the day after the crash.

On the night of 13th-14th February 1945 most of 4 Group's Halifaxes were engaged in an attack on the Braunkohle-Benzin synthetic oil plant at Böhlen, near Leipzig. The night is best remembered for a second stage of the attack on eastern Germany which saw an all-Lancaster force raid the neighbouring city of Dresden.

The Böhlen attack was generally regarded as a failure, with thick clouds obscuring the target and icing up to 15,000 feet making conditions very bad for the 326 Yorkshire Halifaxes, which were accompanied by Lancasters drawn from two 6 Group squadrons plus eight Mosquitos from 8 Group.

Just one aircraft, a Halifax, was reported to have been lost. That aircraft, however, was to make a dramatic reappearance the following day over Yorkshire. It was one of the 51 Squadron aircraft which, probably due to heavy icing, became lost and low on fuel. The pilot realised he was not going to make it back to England and, once over Allied lines, began circling looking for somewhere to land. A British tank unit quickly became aware of the problems facing the Halifax and rigged up a make-shift flare-path from burning oil drums so that the bomber was able to land.

Back at Snaith, in the meantime, the aircraft was reported overdue. Another of the squadron's aircraft had already come to grief, crashing near the airfield while attempting to overshoot. By mid-morning the missing aircraft was deemed to have 'failed to return' and the wheels were set in motion. One of the first duties was to send out telegrams to the families of the missing crew. One of these was sent to the village of Goxhill, just across the Humber from Hull and only 30 miles from Snaith. It was there that the family of one of the gunners, F/Sgt Harry Van Den Bos, lived. He had already won a DFM on his first tour while flying with 76 Squadron at Holme-on-Spalding Moor and was a familiar sight in the village in his battered RAF cap and magnificent handlebar moustache. His family had a successful horticulturist business in Goxhill and Harry had given up a reserved occupation to become an outstanding air gunner with 76 and 51 Squadrons.

When the telegram arrived at the local post office, the postman was so concerned what the news might do to Harry's mother, he waited until he knew his father would be home before delivering it. Harry's mother, however, was adamant. She just *knew* her son was safe, and that was an end to it.

The next morning Harry's brothers were working in one of the family's glasshouses when they heard the sound of a heavy bomber nearby. They went outside and saw a Halifax flying low along the line of the River Humber on what appeared to be three engines. One of the brothers shouted for joy. It was Harry's aircraft and he jumped on his bike to get home quickly to break the news ... even though, to anyone else, it could have been just any Halifax.

A couple of hours later the postman was back at the Van Den Bos house. This time he didn't wait to bring the news that Harry was safe. At Snaith, the Halifax crew found that most of their belongings had already been distributed amongst their pals in the squadron after it was assumed, wrongly, that they had gone for the 'chop'.

51 Squadron was to lose its last aircraft on operations from Snaith on 21st March 1945 on rail yards at Rheine, MZ348 being one of two aircraft from a force of 178 Lancasters and Halifaxes which failed to return. The squadron flew its last operation from Snaith on 25th April and moved out a few days later to Leconfield. The airfield itself was used for the remainder of the year as No 17 Aircrew Holding Unit and finally closed in the spring of 1946.

28
THOLTHORPE

RAF Tholthorpe must have seemed a desolate place on the morning of 6th March 1945. The night before 25 Halifaxes of 420 (Snowy Owl) and 425 (Alouette) Squadrons RCAF had taken off on what was to be one of the last deep-penetration bombing raids from Yorkshire airfields. The target was the city of Chemnitz where 760 aircraft of Bomber Command were intended to mete out the kind of punishment suffered by neighbouring Dresden three weeks earlier. That morning nine dispersals were empty, five of them due to crashes in Yorkshire because of severe icing problems.

One of the aircraft, MZ845 from 425 Squadron, collided in mid-air with a Halifax from 426 Squadron at Linton-on-Ouse and came down at Nun Monkton Grange, only the mid-upper gunner surviving after baling out at low level. Another from 425 crashed, killing its crew, at Little Ouseburn while three more Halifaxes, all from 420, came down near the airfield, one stalling and crashing just short of the main runway, a second crashing near Tadcaster and the third near Dishforth on its return from Chemnitz. Two more from 420 and a third from 425 Squadron were lost on the raid itself.

The ninth aircraft had made a heavy landing on an American air strip in France. Among its crew was F/Sgt Raymond Scott, a young Yorkshireman who had been with the Canadians at Tholthorpe since the previous autumn.

'The icing was terrible that night,' he recalled. 'As soon as we got airborne we noticed the ice beginning to accumulate on the aircraft and we had to climb on full power for a long time to get through the clouds. The result was that it was clear we were not going to have enough fuel to get back.

'We bombed the target and then headed back to France and, once

A wheel change for a Mk III Halifax of 420 Squadron at Tholthorpe, 1944. (Yorkshire Air Museum via Peter Green)

over Allied territory, put out our Darky call for assistance and were given permission to land at Givencourt, near Rheims, which was then occupied by the Americans. When we touched down we burst a tyre and, as the Yanks didn't keep any supplies for the old Halibag, a replacement tyre had to be flown out for us. That meant us spending a day or two on the ground and the French-Canadian boys decided to make the most of it. They all disappeared and I had no idea where they had gone until, later in the day, they returned in an American jeep piled high with crates of champagne they had "liberated" in Rheims. We loaded it all onto the Halifax and when we finally arrived back at Tholthorpe the messes were awash with champagne for a day or two.'

Less than two weeks later Ray Scott and his crew failed to make it back to Tholthorpe again after a raid, this time on the Ruhrstahl steelworks at Witten. Over the target their Halifax was hit by flak and began losing fuel and power. Eventually, both port engines failed and the aircraft struggled back across the Channel before, finally, the pilot warned he was going to have to crash land. He found a likely spot and put the Halifax down in a ploughed field somewhere, he believed, in Buckinghamshire.

Within a few minutes, an RAF truck appeared and told them it was from the nearest air force establishment – Bomber Command head-quarters at High Wycombe. They were taken there and, the next morning, were called in to see Air Chief Marshal Harris, who wanted to hear all about the raid. He was particularly keen to hear about the fuel systems on the Halifax and questioned F/Sgt Scott closely for some time. 'By a stroke of luck, I happened to have the log sheet for the engines stuffed in my battledress and we were able to go through it in detail,' Scott recalled. The crew was then issued with travel warrants and, still in their flying gear, headed for London and a train to take them back to Yorkshire.

'I thought nothing more about it until a little while later I was called in by the CO at Tholthorpe. I wondered what I had done wrong but he told me he had an instruction from Bomber Command HQ to commission me in the field. I can only think I said the right things to Bomber Harris.'

Scott's was one of four Halifaxes which were lost on the Witten raid – one of them colliding with a PFF Mosquito and crashing in Belgium. Tholthorpe may have been a relative latecomer to the bombing war, but the Reaper certainly extracted his toll among the young Canadians who served there.

The airfield site close to the village of Tholthorpe, a few miles from the market town of Easingwold, had been identified as suitable for an airfield in the late 1930s and was pressed into use in the summer of 1940 as a make-shift satellite for Linton-on-Ouse. It was then little more than a large grass field and was used occasionally by the Whitleys of 77 and 102 Squadrons between August and December, which operated from Linton and Topcliffe during this period. 102 lost a Whitley soon after take-off from Tholthorpe on the night of 24th October, shot down by a Ju88C, one of the new intruder aircraft being used by the Luftwaffe. Two of the Whitley's crew were killed.

The airfield was then closed for construction work to begin and, by the time it opened again in the summer of 1943, contractors Henry Boot Ltd had laid three runways using concrete-laying machines imported from the United States and erected three hangars together with all the ancillary buildings needed by a heavy bomber station.

Tholthorpe opened as a station within 6 Group RCAF and on 13th June 434 (Bluenose) Squadron was formed there, so called because it was sponsored by the Rotary Club of Halifax, Nova Scotia, whose residents enjoyed the nickname of 'the Bluenoses'.

Formed on Halifax Vs, 434 flew them operationally for the first time

A 420 Squadron Halifax III fitted with a ventral turret for extra protection against night fighters, Tholthorpe 1944. (Yorkshire Air Museum via Peter Green)

on the night of 12th-13th August when nine aircraft took part in an attack on Milan. The squadron suffered its first casualties five nights later when three aircraft were lost on the Peenemünde raid and with them the lives of ten men, ten others surviving to become PoWs.

By this time 434 had been joined by a second squadron, 431 (Iroquois), which had been formed at Burn, near Goole, and was in the process of converting from Wellingtons to Halifaxes. By the time it became operational, 434 was suffering mounting losses in what was to prove the worst winter of the war for Bomber Command. Single Halifaxes were lost in attacks on Leverkusen, Berlin, Nuremburg and Munchengladbach, while two were lost over Munich and Bochum, and two raids on Hanover resulted in the loss of four aircraft and the lives of 29 men. 431 lost its first Halifax on an attack on 3rd-4th October when a night fighter shot the aircraft down over Belgium, three men being killed, four taken prisoner and one evading escape. 431 lost two aircraft in an attack on Hanover five nights later – another from 434 also failed to return – and among the 14 men who died was Sgt Rudd, the mid-upper gunner in one of the Halifaxes. He was just 18 years old and was one of the youngest Canadians to die on bomber operations.

It was proving a grim winter for the young men at Tholthorpe. A

271

Lancaster X KB923 of 420 Squadron at Tholthorpe in April 1945. This was one of the squadron's aircraft flown back to Canada after the war. (Yorkshire Air Museum via Peter Green)

raid on Kassel cost the squadrons five Halifaxes and the lives of 29 men. Four more were lost in an attack on Mannheim, two over Leverkusen, two over Berlin and two more in a raid on Frankfurt. The last raid mounted by 431 and 434 from Tholthorpe was on the night of 2nd- 3rd December when four aircraft, three of them from 431, failed to return, although one complete crew was picked up in the English Channel by a rescue launch after ditching.

The Mk V Halifax was being withdrawn from operations over Germany and both squadrons were due to re-equip with the much superior Mk III. On 9th December 431 moved to Croft, followed a day later by 434 Squadron.

They were replaced by 425 from Dishforth and 420 from Dalton which converted to their new Mk IIIs at Tholthorpe before becoming operational a few weeks into the new year. Conversion wasn't a painless operation, one aircraft being lost in a crash in Worcestershire, another hitting houses in Adelaide Street, Brierley Hill, Staffordshire after the crew baled out and a third crashing near Aberystwyth after the aircraft stalled at more than 20,000 feet.

Among the first operational losses was a 420 Squadron Halifax which overshot and crashed on its fourth attempt to land at Tholthorpe after a raid on Berlin on 16th February. In an attack on Stuttgart on the night of 15th-16th March, Sgt McAdam's aircraft was hit by flak and one of the crew killed. The starboard inner caught fire but McAdam decided to continue and bombed the target. The aircraft was hit by flak again and lost height, flying most of the way back at 5,000 feet before landing at Friston in Sussex. It was only then that the pilot revealed he had been wounded. He was immediately promoted and awarded a DFC. 420 lost another in a Berlin raid at the end of March while two from 425 failed to return. The Tholthorpe squadrons escaped relatively lightly at the end of the month when Bomber Command lost 96 aircraft in the disastrous attack on Nuremburg. All 14 of 420's Halifaxes returned, although one was damaged on landing, while one of the twelve sent by 425 failed to return, F/Lt Taylor and his crew being killed when their aircraft was shot down by a night fighter.

Both squadrons were in the thick of the action during the invasion period and the attack on flying bomb sites in northern France. One of these, at the end of June, led to a remarkable incident at Tholthorpe when 425 Squadron's aircraft began returning from the raid. As it was landing on three engines, the squadron's A-Able hit a second aircraft, U-Uncle, from the squadron, which was bombed up at dispersal. Both aircraft caught fire and rescuers were on the scene very quickly. They were led by the station CO, Air Commodore Ross, who was joined by F/Sgt St Germain, a bomb aimer who had just returned from the raid on Fôret d'Eawy, and a member of the ground crew, Cpl Marquet. With the assistance of LACs McKenzie and Wolfe, they managed to pull Able's pilot clear before one of the 500lb bombs on the dispersed Halifax exploded. As the wreckage blazed they heard cries for help from Able's rear turret. St Germain and Marquet used crash axes to chop a hole in the fuselage and pull the gunner, Sgt Rochon, to safety. Just as they did so, a second bomb exploded, seriously injuring the air commodore, who later had to have a hand amputated as a result of his injuries. He was to receive the George Cross for his actions and there were George Medals for Cpl Marquet and F/Sgt St Germain and BEMs for LACs McKenzie and Wolfe. F/Sgt St Germain was later awarded a DFC after being promoted and completing his tour with 425 Squadron.

The Tholthorpe squadrons suffered badly in the last winter of war. Despite the dramatic drop in Bomber Command losses, 420 and 425 lost aircraft on a regular basis, not always through enemy action. One 425 Halifax was peppered with incendiaries dropped from a Lancaster over Bochum while another aircraft from the same squadron clipped a tree at Alne, between Tholthorpe and Tollerton, after taking off for Duisburg. The aircraft spun into the ground and exploded, killing the crew. Another was written off at Carnaby when its brakes failed and it hit some trees.

Operations were also costing both squadrons dearly. 420 lost four Halifaxes in an attack on Magdeburg in a 4 and 6 Group attack on 16th-17th January. This came some ten days after 425 had lost three in an attack on Hanover.

The losses went on almost right up to the end, the last from Tholthorpe being NP946 of 420 Squadron which failed to return from a raid on the naval base and airfield on Heligoland on 18th April, one of three Halifaxes lost in the attack. Four days later 17 aircraft from 420 went to Bremen on what was to provide the squadron's last operation of the war. Over the target, however, they were ordered not to bomb by the Master Bomber and all returned safely to Tholthorpe. 425's last operation was mounted three days later when all its aircraft returned safely from Wangerooge.

Soon after the war ended both the Alouette and Snowy Owl squadrons began converting to Canadian-built Lancaster Xs in preparation for operating in the Far East. They flew their aircraft back to Nova Scotia and they were still there when Japan surrendered.

Their departure marked the closure of Tholthorpe. Today the granite memorial on the village green, unveiled by Air Vice Marshal Donald Bennett in 1986, records in both French and English the sacrifice of the men of the four Canadian squadrons who served at the nearby airfield, which is linked to the village by a lane lined with Canadian maples and English oaks. A few scattered buildings remain, including the control tower which itself has become an unofficial memorial to the young Canadians who served at Tholthorpe half a century and more ago.

29
TOPCLIFFE

Among the airfields planned for North Yorkshire during the pre-war Expansion Programme was one close to the village of Topcliffe, a few miles south-west of the pleasant market town of Thirsk. The site was only a few miles from RAF Dishforth, which had opened in the autumn of 1936. Whether that proximity worried the pre-war planners is not known, but they could hardly have envisaged the situation a few years later when Dishforth and Topcliffe were to be joined by a clutch of other airfields with virtually overlapping circuits.

At the centre of that hub of airfields was Topcliffe itself, a station which was to have as varied a wartime career as any in Yorkshire. It began life as a bomber station and later housed Canadian squadrons before becoming the centre for the training of Canadian bomber crews in 6 Group.

All that was a long way off when the station opened in September 1940. It had been built with five brick hangars and brick accommodation blocks and technical sites. The grass runways were reckoned to be adequate for the Whitleys of 77 and 102 Squadrons which were earmarked for the new station.

Both squadrons had been displaced from Driffield by the heavy air raid on that airfield in August and had, temporarily, been operating from Linton-on-Ouse. 77 was the first to arrive, flying in on 6th October under the command of W/Cmdr Jarman, and was quickly in action, losing a Whitley and the crew of Sgt Brown three days later when the aircraft crashed on return from Hanau. Among the casualties was a young Fleet Air Arm midshipman who had joined the Whitley's crew to gain combat experience. A week later S/Ldr Black was killed in a similar incident on his return from Stettin.

A month later 102 arrived. It joined 77 for what turned out to be a costly attack on Turin's Royal Arsenal on 23rd-24th November. Five of the aircraft failed to return, all because of fuel shortages. Three of them

A 77 Squadron Whitley about to land at Topcliffe, 1941. (RAF Leeming)

were from 102 Squadron, one force-landing in Kent, the second being abandoned by its crew over Sussex and the third ditching off Start Point in Devon. Of the two 77 Squadron aircraft, one hit high tension cables when trying to land in Suffolk while the second ditched off Dungeness. The pilot, P/O Bagnell, was rescued but the remainder of the crew drowned. Early in January 1941, a 102 Squadron Whitley was shot down by an intruder off Withernsea with the loss of all five on board.

Fuel shortages were a constant problem faced by the Whitley crews at Topcliffe in those days and many of the aircraft lost by the two squadrons ended their days at the bottom of the North Sea, some with their crews trapped inside. More fortunate was F/Lt Hannah and his crew who ditched off Whitby after a trip to Berlin. The crew were

276

picked up and later the bomber itself floated into Whitby harbour where it was recovered and later scrapped.

The weather was still as big an enemy to the Whitley crews as the German defenders. Never was this more clearly demonstrated than on the night of 27th-28th June 1941 when severe icing and violent storms combined with intense night fighter attacks saw 14 aircraft lost out of a force of 108 sent to Bremen. Half of them were from Topcliffe, four Whitleys of 102 Squadron and three from 77. One of the 77 Squadron aircraft was flown by 19-year-old Sgt Bernard Harpur and was hit by flak over the target. Leaking glycol, the Whitley made it back to within 100 miles of Flamborough before a Mayday was sent and Harpur made a near-perfect ditching. The crew were found four hours later by one of their own squadron's aircraft and a Hampden arrived to drop a 'Lindholme' dinghy. The pilot managed to scramble into this but it appears he was unable to inflate it correctly and it soon drifted away with Harpur clinging to it.

It was another two and a half days before the other four crewmen, two of whom were injured, were picked up by a Royal Navy ship and landed at Felixstowe. Bernard Harpur was found around the same time, but he had not survived his ordeal alone in the North Sea.

That night cost Topcliffe the lives of 21 men, among them S/Ldr McArthur who had flown on 102 Squadron's first operation of the war. Five nights later 102 Squadron lost another three aircraft in a raid on Essen while two from 77 failed to return from an attack on Dortmund.

Losses on this scale were hard to sustain, coming as they did after a series of losses for both squadrons. An attack on Schwerte earlier in the month had cost 102 two aircraft and another damaged beyond repair while one from 77 failed to return.

Four aircraft from 102 were lost, one of them crashing on its return to Topcliffe, in a raid on Hanover on 14th-15th August. An attack on Hüls early in September cost 77 two Whitleys and the lives of eleven men while a third aircraft crashed on Cromer beach after being damaged by a night fighter. These were the squadron's last losses from Topcliffe before its move to Leeming. 102, which also lost an aircraft on the Hüls raid, remained at Topcliffe until early in November before moving the few miles to the new airfield at Dalton. It bowed out with an attack on Berlin from which three Whitleys failed to return. There were no survivors.

Topcliffe was now closed to flying for an extension programme, which included the laying of three concrete runways. When it reopened

102 Squadron returned with its newly-acquired Halifaxes. It was quickly in action but on the night of 16th-17th June lost three of its new aircraft in an attack on Essen. Two fell to night fighters with the loss of all 15 men on board while the third was brought down by flak over the Ruhr, the crew parachuting to safety and spending the rest of the war as PoWs. Worse was to come a little over a week later when four aircraft, one of them from 102's Conversion Flight, were lost in an attack on Bremen. That raid cost the lives of another 23 men with just three surviving, all from the Conversion Flight aircraft.

Before 102 moved in early August to its final home of the war at Pocklington, the squadron lost another six aircraft. Two of them were lost in an attack on Hamburg. One was shot down off the German coast, the pilot managing to ditch the aircraft. Five of the crew were rescued, an act witnessed by the crew of the second Topcliffe Halifax which also ditched in shallow water, all the crew wading ashore to where they were taken prisoner.

By the summer of 1942 preparations were beginning for the formation of a new bomber group in North Yorkshire comprised entirely of RCAF squadrons. Topcliffe was to be one of those airfields and, while the formation of 6 Group was still some months away, the first Canadian squadron moved in early in August. 405 (Vancouver) Squadron was the first RCAF bomber squadron to see service in Bomber Command and brought its Halifaxes from Pocklington, exchanging airfields with 102. The squadron was working up on its new aircraft and flew operationally from Topcliffe for the first time on 9th-10th August, losing one of its aircraft and the entire crew to a night fighter as the Halifax was returning from Osnabruck. A second Canadian squadron, 419, arrived from Leeming on 18th August with its Wellingtons. It was to remain at Topcliffe until the end of September when the squadron moved to Croft. 419 took part in a number of operations during their brief stay, losing a Wellington over Saarbrucken on its first operation. Only one of the crew survived, Sgt Ledford evading capture and making it back to England. He was later to be killed flying with 434 Squadron.

On 2nd-3rd September the squadrons operated together in an attack on Karlsruhe, both losing an aircraft and all on board. The 405 Squadron casualties included the B Flight commander, F/Lt Hilton, while 419 lost its CO, W/Cmdr Walsh, who was on his 29th operation.

Another three 419 aircraft were lost on operations before it left Topcliffe, along with a Wellington which crashed during an air test

Halifax IIIs of 425 (Alouette) Squadron at Topcliffe, 1941. (Via C. Jones)

near Spalding, killing all eight on board. These included four members of the ground crew, two who had gone to monitor oil consumption and two others who had gone along for the flight.

As the sole occupants of Topcliffe for another month, among the seven aircraft 405 was to lose was its veteran *Ruhr Valley Express*, a Mk II Halifax which had taken part in the squadron's first Halifax operation, the 1,000 bomber raid on Cologne at the end of May. It was one of two which failed to return from a raid on Flensburg on 1st-2nd October, the second aircraft being flown by personnel from 425 Squadron who were gaining experience on Halifaxes.

The squadron was one of a number selected for secondment to Coastal Command and late in October was transferred to Beaulieu in Hampshire. The squadron's Halifaxes were used to ferry ground crew to their new station and, late in November, this was to lead to one of the worst non-operational accidents in Bomber Command. A Halifax carrying 15 men on a ferry flight from Topcliffe crashed close to Beaulieu as the aircraft attempted to land, killing all those on board.

As 405 moved out, a new Canadian squadron, 424 (Tiger) was formed at Topcliffe on 15th October, taking its name from the mascot of the rugby club in Hamilton, Ontario. It was equipped with Wellington IIIs and worked up at Topcliffe before the end of the year when 6

Group was formed and the Canadian flag was raised over the airfield. Its first operation was on 15th-16th January 1943 when five Wellingtons took part in an attack on Lorient. It was an attack on the same target eleven nights later which led to the squadron's first loss, three of the six men on board the Wellington surviving.

Returning from its spell with Coastal Command early in March, 405 Squadron was immediately operational again, losing four of its Halifaxes in a raid on Stuttgart on 11th-12th March. Eleven men were killed, 13 became prisoners and, remarkably, seven evaded capture. One of those, a rear gunner, later joined the Maquis and was killed fighting with them in France in December 1943. 424 was to continue operations until mid-April when it moved to Leeming before being transferred temporarily to the Middle East. The last aircraft it lost at Topcliffe was a Wellington which crashed near Maidstone when it returned from Frankfurt with engine trouble. The rear gunner, Sgt Lees, baled out just before the aircraft crashed and later made a vain attempt to rescue other members of the crew from the burning wreckage.

The formation of 6 Group had seen Topcliffe designated as a base headquarters station with Dishforth and Dalton as its satellites. The airfield, however, was now earmarked for a new role and was redesignated as No 6 (RCAF) Group Training Base and later in the year had the new airfield at Wombleton as its satellite. 1659 Heavy Conversion Unit, which was charged with training the Canadian crews from OTUs, moved in to Topcliffe from Leeming on 14th March 1943 and was to remain there until the end of the war. Over the next two years it provided a steady stream of crews for the Halifax and later Lancaster squadrons in 6 Group, losing numerous aircraft in accidents. One of these involved a crew on a diversionary raid on the Paris area in March 1944. Their aircraft was some 100 miles off track and strayed across London during a raid by the Luftwaffe and was shot down by the capital's AA defences, one of those on board being killed. A second aircraft suffered engine failure and crash-landed at Little Ouseburn.

Topcliffe is still remembered with affection by many who served there, however briefly. Eddie Eastwood was a young wireless operator with a mixed nationality crew which included three Canadians, two Americans and two Englishmen. They arrived at Topcliffe in the spring of 1944 from 24 OTU at Honeybourne to convert to Halifaxes, before they joined 431 (Iroquois) Squadron at Croft, flying Lancaster Mk Xs.

'It was, quite simply, the best station I ever served at,' recalls Mr

A 1659 HCU Halifax Mk III undergoing a major service at Topcliffe, 1944. (C. Jones)

Eastwood. 'All aircrew below the rank of flight lieutenant shared the same mess and accommodation and the food was something to behold. Even for supper we would get joints of meat, great lumps of cheese and all the trimmings. This was something I have never heard of on other bomber stations.'

The spirit at Topcliffe ws very good and Mr Eastwood, who hailed from Bedfordshire and now lives in Chester-le-Street, County Durham, still remembers the several 'good sessions' he enjoyed in nearby Thirsk with his best pal in the crew, Red Mills, the crew's rear gunner who wore the brevet of the Royal Canadian Air Force but hailed from Detroit.

'He was a great bloke and every time I think of him I still remember those days at Topcliffe when he used to show me the photo of the very good looking girl he had left behind in Detroit.' She was a girl Red was never to see again.

Eddie Eastwood was a member of F/O Jack Harris's crew and they were to progress relatively smoothly through their conversion training at Topcliffe, although they had one scare during a night-time 'circuit and bump' session.

'It was the usual practice towards the end of the course for an instructor to take two pilots on circuits and bumps to pass them ready for operational duty,' Mr Eastwood remembers. 'On this particular night we carried only a skeleton crew, the navigator, one gunner and myself together with the two pilots.

'When our turn came to fly, Jack Harris passed his test and it was then the other pilot's turn to take over. On his first landing, he panicked and the Halifax slewed across the runway, broke its back in three places and then caught fire. We all got out safely apart from the other pilot. On being told to get clear, he tried to escape without removing the hatch above his head. The instructor then did this for him only for the poor chap to land on his head on the wing. Not surprisingly, he was taken off flying duties.'

One of the oddest 'outposts' at Topcliffe was a hut constructed of empty petrol cans perched high on the cliffs north of Scarborough. It was the preserve of Eddie Henderson, a Canadian whose job it was to collect the drogues dropped by the Miles Martinet aircraft used for target towing duties.

It must have been a plum posting for Eddie Henderson. His billet was the nearby Scalby Manor Hotel and, once the firing sessions were over, his job was to collect the drogues – which the Martinet would drop in a field near Scalby Lodge – and then return them to Topcliffe. He had an unofficial assistant in 12-year-old Barry Milner, who used to cycle the three-quarters of a mile from his home in Scarborough to watch the fun and help collect the drogues. Occasionally, when Eddie was away from his petrol can perch, Barry would collect the numbered drogues and take them back to the hotel from where they were collected by transport sent from Topcliffe.

One sunny day in August 1944 Barry was on the cliffs as usual watching a Halifax firing on the drogue when, suddenly, the aircraft went into a spin and plunged nose first into the sea. The Martinet immediately dropped its drogue and flew to the nearby lifeboat station before returning to the scene of the crash. But there were no survivors from the Halifax, DG363, which came from 1664 HCU at Dishforth. Barry remembers that some time later one of its wheels was washed ashore in nearby Burniston Bay.

Back at Topcliffe the hectic pace of life went on into the early months of 1945. It was during this time that one of the worst of the crashes occurred involving aircraft from the HCU. Halifax LK878, an aircraft which had seen much service with both 426 and 424 Squadrons, lost power soon after take-off when an engine failed and crashed at Catcliffe Wood, Felixkirk near Thirsk, killing all nine men on board.

As part of the reorganisation of aircrew training, Topcliffe had been transferred to 7 (Training) Group at the end of 1944 and had become 76 Base HQ, with its satellites at Dishforth and Wombleton. This was finally disbanded in September 1945 when the RAF resumed control of the airfield.

Topcliffe was later used by the No 5 Air Navigation School and by both Transport and Coastal Commands until it was transferred to the Army in 1972 and renamed Alanbrooke Barracks.

Mona Clowes was a Yorkshire girl who served as a WAAF driver in 6 Group. She was stationed at Topcliffe but her work took her to many of the airfields in the north of the county. She now lives in Orangeville, Ontario and still looks back with affection on those days. 'I loved it,' she said. 'It was fun and an interesting outdoor life in beautiful scenery, but I got around those stations and lived the drama of it all. It was a job that had to be done.'

She recalled the airfields being laid out by an army of civilian workers very quickly, followed by young airmen from all corners of the world, strangers in a strange land.

Mrs Clowes recalled the harsh work carried out by the ground crews during the Yorkshire winters at airfields like Dalton, Skipton-on-Swale, Topcliffe and Wombleton. 'We would see them working on planes out in the open, hanging on as if by their toenails while struggling with aircraft parts in a howling wind. Even when they were in the hangars the standing joke was "Shut that bloody door", which of course was the whole front of the building.'

As the war dragged on, it became sadder and sadder for young WAAFs like Mona as aircraft failed to return and some of those which did limp back contained cold, wounded and frightened young men.

'At the height of the bomber campaign some of the aircrew messes I visited were dismal places despite the "shop" talk and occasional high jinks. Much as I admired them, I soon stopped dating aircrew for obvious reasons . . .'

She remembers how adaptable the ground crews were and what 'great mates' they made. 'They knew where to find chip shops out in the wilds in the strangest places and where there were groups of ladies providing home baking and farmers who had a few real eggs to spare.'

It was the ubiquitous 'issue cycle' which carried the young WAAFs on adventurous trips to places like Sutton Bank ("a great test for rusty brakes"), Rievaulx Abbey ("beautiful on a still summer's day") and as far afield as Harrogate, Ripon, where she remembers counting 17 pubs in just one street, and Thirsk, noted for the excellent tea shops.

Eventually Mona married an airman and they lived first in a bed-sit in Topcliffe village and then Sowerby. They would be able to walk across the fields from Topcliffe to help themselves to the odd turnip from a farmer's field for supper.

Life at Topcliffe was hectic as the heavy conversion unit there turned out crews as quickly as possible for the 6 Group squadrons.

'Many of the aircraft they had had already seen a lot of operational service and at Topcliffe they were given a lot more punishment, particularly on "circuits and bumps" as it was aptly called. There were the night cross country flights which led to several crews being killed and many others were left badly shaken. We saw one belly landing on the airfields. There was this horrible screeching of metal on tarmac and a shower of sparks. Thank God it didn't catch fire and they all got out. But not all crews were so lucky.'

She added: 'Most of the young Canadians who survived went back to their own country with warm feelings for Yorkshire, feelings which have lasted through all the years. They will never forget their time there.'

30

THE SMALLER UNITS

The airfields in Yorkshire depended very much on the various Maintenance Units across the county which provided a range of services, from the supply of bombs and ammunition to the recovery of salvageable material from crashed aircraft.

Typical of these was Kiplin Hall, near RAF Scorton in the north of the county, the home of 224 MU, whose job it was to keep the squadrons at Croft, Middleton St George, Leeming and Skipton-on-Swale supplied with bombs.

Fred Newby, now of Hexham, Northumberland served there after joining the RAF early in 1944. He recalled that Kiplin Hall itself had been owned before the war by two elderly ladies and had been requisitioned by the Army before it eventually passed to the RAF. Most of its original fittings had been stripped out (probably by the Army) and the majority of the hall was boarded up, with just a few rooms being left open for sleeping quarters and messing for the 90 or so men with the MU, which was under the command of a flight lieutenant.

Fred remembers 224 MU as a 'smashing little unit' which was left very much to its own devices. The bombs would arrive at a nearby railhead and were then stored in the woods around Kiplin Hall. Deliveries were made to the nearby airfields almost every day, using the unit's small fleet of Scammell 'mechanical horses' and three-tonners. The bombs ranged from incendiaries to 4,000lb cookies and he

Fred Newby, who served with 224 MU at Kiplin Hall, near Richmond in 1944.
(F. Newby)

recalls there was also a small supply of bombs containing poison gas. They had been there some time and were stored 'just in case'.

Ron Powell of York was an electrician at 60 Maintenance Unit at Shipton-by-Beningbrough, which was less than five miles from his home in York. After joining the RAF, he completed an electricians' course at Henlow and was asked where he would like to be posted. 'I said anywhere in Yorkshire will do and the next morning I was surprised to find I had a travel warrant and posting to Shipton-by-Beningbrough, which was as close to home as I could hope to get.'

It turned out to be so close that during the two years he was there,

Kiplin Hall pictured in 1987. It was built in the 17th century for George Calvert, founder of the State of Maryland. Today, much of the hall and the grounds have been restored. (F. Newby)

Ron "lived out" and would cycle the five miles to and from work each day. It was a practice officially frowned upon but a blind eye was applied.

The unit itself consisted of little more than a series of huts and when Mr Powell first arrived, he remembered the 'guard room' was part of an upturned fuselage of a crashed aircraft!

The job of the MU was to scour crash sites in the York area and recover everything which might be of use. As an electrician, Ron had the task of removing radios, clocks, transmitters and anything else which might be useful to the RAF. Very little was left to go to waste. Equipment which could be salvaged was taken back to Shipton, properly identified and labelled and crated up and taken to the nearby station where it was sent on to other units. Ron remembers most of the electrical equipment went to West Bromwich while all the scrap went to West Hartlepool.

So many aircraft came down in the York area that he would often cycle to crash sites, while transport would be provided for those further afield. One of the sites he had to deal with was uncomfortably close to his home in South Bank, York. He was actually on leave when a Halifax from 426 Squadron at Linton-on-Ouse exploded over the city on a grey afternoon in March 1944. Pieces from the bomber showered down over the area, with the main damage occurring three streets away where an engine from the aircraft hit Nunthorpe School and a number of houses were set on fire.

Ron's mother lived in that street and he ran to see what had happened. On his way he came across the grim sight of the body of one of the aircraft's crew in the garden of a nearby house. When he arrived there was a fire raging in one house and the sound of exploding ammunition. His mother was, thankfully, safe and her house undamaged, but there were fragments of wreckage everywhere. The landlady of the nearby Winning Post public house was the heroine of the hour and Ron was pleased to see later she had been decorated for her bravery that dreadful afternoon.

Ironically, when he reported back for duty at Shipton his first job was to go back to York to see what could be recovered from the Halifax. By that time just about every small boy in the area had a piece in his pocket as a prized souvenir.

Kiplin Hall and Shipton-by-Beningbrough were typical of several such units based in Yorkshire. Numerous other sites were used briefly by the RAF, including Plainville, which was a mile or two from Shipton. It was little more than a large grassed area which was used as a scatter site by bomber squadrons from Linton-on-Ouse early in the war when there was a real danger of airfields being bombed. Plainville itself was used on a number of occasions by the Whitleys of 58 Squadron in 1940 and 1941 before the site was finally abandoned by the RAF after surveyors decided it was unsuitable for further development.

Of all the airfield sites in Yorkshire, Acaster Malbis must be the strangest, if only for the planning that went into its construction.

It was laid out originally as a grass fighter strip, a satellite of nearby Church Fenton, but quickly proved unsuitable because of the ever-pervading mists which rolled across it from the nearby River Ouse. Rather than abandon the site, the Air Ministry appeared to compound its earlier errors by laying it out as a heavy bomber airfield, complete with concrete runways and hangars. Common sense finally prevailed and Acaster Malbis was to be used as nothing more than a relief landing ground, with parts of the site given over to bomb storage and some of the buildings being used by the No 4 Aircrew School.

It was on 6th January 1942 that Acaster Malbis' first occupants, 601 Squadron, moved in with their Airacobras, mid-engined American-built fighters which were plagued with technical problems throughout their brief operational career. The eccentricities of the aircraft were not helped by the immediate problems faced at Acaster Malbis, a waterlogged site and low-lying fog which rendered flying impossible at times. 601's stay was to be brief, the squadron moving to Digby in Lincolnshire in March 1942 where, much to their relief, they re-equipped with Spitfires. Their period at Acaster Malbis was made worse by the loss of one of their pilots, drowned when his Airacobra crashed through the ice on a flooded area alongside the Ouse.

The airfield was then passed to 21 Group Flying Training Command and became the home for W and X Flights of No 15 (Pilot) Advanced Flying Unit, which was equipped with Oxfords. It was to remain at Acaster Malbis until January 1943 and again lost a number of aircraft in the misty conditions which persisted in this part of the county. During its time at Acaster Malbis, 15 (P) AFU's Oxfords were a familiar sight across Yorkshire and one man recalls seeing them occasionally land at Tholthorpe, which was still under construction, in order that the instructor could have a smoke before continuing the lesson!

It was at this point that it was decided that Acaster Malbis would be suitable for heavy bombers. Construction teams moved in and began laying concrete runways, perimeter tracks and erecting buildings.

The airfield, however, was never destined to have its own units. Once completed, it was used solely as a relief landing ground by the Halifax heavy conversion units of 41 (later 71) Base at Marston Moor, Riccall and Rufforth. 91 Maintenance Unit used much of the site for a bomb dump serving nearby operational airfields and 4 Aircrew School was established there late in 1944. Men who passed through the school remember Acaster Malbis as a pleasant enough place (it was, after all, only a short bus journey from York). The school filled the gap between OTU and HCU and crews were able to pick up useful information on things like Gee, Monica and the latest German night fighter tactics.

The disbandment of the heavy conversion units brought flying to an end at Acaster Malbis and, following the withdrawal of 91 MU, the airfield formally closed early in 1946.

31
THE FACTORY
AIRFIELDS

Long before the RAF came to Yorkshire, the county was associated with the best in British engineering, its factories producing much of the machinery on which the Empire was built. So, when war came, it was no surprise that the Ministry for Aircraft Production should adapt those skills to supply aircraft to both the RAF and the Fleet Air Arm.

Yorkshire had three major wartime centres of aircraft building, Yeadon and Sherburn-in-Elmet, near Leeds, and Brough, just west of Hull. Today, the Brough factory still builds aircraft, notably the BAe Hawk, while Yeadon has long since become Leeds/Bradford International Airport. In addition to the factories, the airfield at Clifton, just north of York, became a major repair centre for the Halifax bombers.

At the height of the war, some 12,000 people worked for A. V. Roe on aircraft production at Yeadon, over half of them women. The factory covered more than 37 acres and two housing estates had to be built nearby to help accommodate the thousands of workers brought in from all parts of the country. Its contribution to the war effort was prodigious, producing over 700 Lancaster bombers and 4,000 Ansons.

It had all been so different a few years earlier when a site on Yeadon Moor was identified as a possible site for a civilian aerodrome by Sir Alan Cobham as part of his municipal airports campaign. When Yeadon opened for flying, the Yorkshire Light Aeroplane Club – it was the oldest in the county, having been formed in 1909 – moved in from Sherburn-in-Elmet. In 1936 one of the new RAF Auxiliary squadrons, 609 (West Riding), was formed there as a light bomber unit, transferring two years later to Fighter Command.

A Yeadon-built Avro Anson Mk I, fitted with a Bristol turret. (Peter Green)

During 1939 it became clear that Britain's aircraft industry was going to have to be put on a war footing and the general manager of A. V. Roe, Roy Dobson, visited Leeds to look for a suitable site for a 'shadow' factory. He quickly identified Yeadon as ideal and by December 1939 work was under way on constructing the first phase of the aircraft factory.

In the meantime, 609 Squadron moved to Catterick soon after the outbreak of war and, although the airfield was still nominally under the control of Fighter Command, it was used as a 'scatter' site by 51 and 58 Squadrons of Bomber Command, then at Linton-on-Ouse. This was to be only a brief semi-operational interlude in the wartime life of the airfield at Yeadon. Later in the year it was used by 4 Group of Bomber Command to house its communication flight and as the base for the central maintenance organisation. Both of these were later to move to York. Then it was used briefly by the Tiger Moths of 20 Elementary Flying Training School and of the Leeds University Air Squadron.

By August 1940 work started on components for Avro Ansons, the aircraft which was later to be produced in great numbers at the factory. Yeadon's first Ministry of Air Production contract was awarded for

291

One of the many. A Yeadon-built Lancaster, LM418, PG-S of 619 Squadron at Coningsby in Lincolnshire. It was wrecked in a crash-landing at Woodbridge after being badly damaged during the Nuremburg raid of 30th-31st March 1944. (C. Jones)

construction of the Albermarle but this was quickly shelved in favour of the Hawker Tornado, a single-engined aircraft powered by a Rolls-Royce Vulture engine. Five aircraft were produced but the project was then abandoned. The Vulture engine proved unreliable – it powered the ill-fated Manchester bomber – but the airframe was later used in the development of the Tornado's successor, the Hawker Typhoon. The Yeadon factory was finally finished early in 1941. It provided excellent working conditions for its employees. The canteen could seat up to 7,000 workers, it had numerous first class air raid shelters, was comprehensively heated and even included air conditioning.

By the time production reached its peak at Yeadon in 1944, 53% of its 12,000 employees were women. Apart from the 300 brick bungalows built by the Ministry of Aircraft Production for married employees in Yeadon itself and nearby Guiseley, there was a hostel for 700 'singles' at Horsforth while many other workers were billeted out. A fleet of 150 buses was used to ferry workers out from other areas of Leeds and Bradford.

Full Anson production was under way by May 1941 and the first

Yeadon-produced aircraft, W2612, was air tested on 21st June. That particular aircraft was one of a number crated and then shipped out from the Clyde bound for Australia where it was due to be used by the RAAF. However, the ship carrying the aircraft was torpedoed on 10th September and today the remains of Yeadon's first Anson lie on the bottom of the sea somewhere off West Africa. Of the first 50 Ansons produced at the factory, nine eventually found their way to Australia, eight to Canada and four more to South Africa. Of those 50, only one was to survive the war and that was wrecked in a crash in France in 1946.

All Yeadon-produced aircraft were flight tested from the nearby airfield and, apart from those crated and sent abroad, were collected by pilots from 7 Ferry Pilots Pool, which was based at Sherburn-in-Elmet for delivery to RAF units around the country.

By the summer of 1941 Yeadon had been chosen as one of the 'Lancaster group' of factories and was awarded a contract for the building of 350 aircraft, most of them Mk IIIs, fitted with American-built Merlin engines. The runway at Yeadon had to be extended to handle the air-testing of the new bombers and more workers taken on to handle the additional work – there was to be no reduction in Anson production.

Lancaster production at Yeadon reached its peak in the early summer of 1944. Most were delivered to squadrons in Lincolnshire and East Anglia although early in 1945 a batch of 19 were sent to 424 and 433 Squadrons at Skipton-on-Swale, which had been flying Canadian-built Mk X Lancasters. All were used on operations in the final months of the war and one, ME456, QB-K of 424 Squadron, was lost in an attack on Dortmund on 21st February 1945.

Towards the end of the war Yeadon produced a few of the Lancaster's successor, the Lincoln, and some 150 of the transport variant, the Avro York. But, in August 1946, staff at the factory heard that production was to cease completely at Yeadon and the last aircraft – fittingly, an Anson – was completed on 16th August that year.

There was some limited use of the airfield by the RAF after the war but Yeadon's future was in civilian aviation and the first scheduled services were operating by the mid-1950s. In January 1959 the airfield was taken over by the Leeds and Bradford Airport Committee and work began on a major expansion programme intended to turn the wartime airfield into the major international airport it is today.

*A Lysander of the 4 Group Communications Flight, which operated from RAF York.
(Sir Guy Lawrence)*

If Yeadon became the wartime home of Avro in Yorkshire, then the
pre-war airfield just north of York was the home of Handley Page. It
was there, at RAF York, that 48 Maintenance Unit was set up to repair
and rebuild many hundreds of the Halifax bombers which were to
serve on Yorkshire airfields during the Second World War. Aircraft
damaged in battle, in heavy landings or just worn out by constant use
went through 48 MU and appeared at the other end, hopefully as good
as new.

The airfield had opened in 1936 as York's municipal aerodrome and
was run by Yorkshire Aviation Services on behalf of the city council. It
was built just north of the pre-war city boundary on land between
Clifton and Rawcliffe, bounded on one side by the A19 and the other
by the B1363. It was a typical pre-war airfield, with lots of enthusiastic
week-end fliers and a varied social calendar. All this came to an abrupt
halt at the end of August 1939 when the airfield was requisitioned by
the RAF and civilian flying ended.

Initially, RAF York – known locally as 'Clifton' – was used as a scatter
site by 51 and 58 Squadrons at Linton-on-Ouse but in December 1939 it

The famous gates at Brough, pictured in 1939. (Brough Heritage Centre)

was taken over by Army Co-operation Command and was used by 4 Army Co-operation Squadron, which was equipped with Lysanders. Armstrong Whitworth set up some repair and maintenance facilities at the airfield for the Whitleys then in use on nearby airfields and this was to set the pattern for the airfield for the remainder of the war.

In 1941 48 MU opened and with its establishment the airfield underwent extensive redevelopment, which included the laying of three concrete runways and the construction of a large number of hangars. By the time the work was finished the airfield had no fewer than 14 – twelve Blisters, one T1 and the pre-war hangar which remained from its flying club days.

At the end of April, York was subjected to one of what became known as the Baedeker raids by the Luftwaffe, so called because the targets were largely cathedral cities chosen from a pre-war Baedeker guide to Britain. The bombs which hit the airfield were well concentrated and damaged the officers' mess, the guard room, the station headquarters and several of the hangars.

Severe though the damage was, it was quickly made good and work carried on at Clifton. The airfield itself was still being used by Army Co-operation Command and 169 Squadron, which operated Mustangs, were visitors in November and December 1942 before moving to Duxford. Other visitors around this time included 809 Squadron Fleet Air Arm with its Seafires. Early in 1943, 231 Squadron replaced 4 Army Co-operation Squadron, remaining at the airfield until the summer. It was followed by a series of Air Observation units equipped with Austers.

By the end of the war Yorkshire was full of unwanted Halifaxes. Some were being converted for transport work but the majority were

A Brough-built Blackburn B2, pictured in 1937. It served with 4 EFTS at Brough before moving to Cosforth in 1941. (Yorkshire Air Museum via Peter Green)

marked down for scrap and the airfield just north of York was chosen as the centre for much of this work. Several hundred aircraft were eventually broken up, most of which were flown in by their crews from airfields around the county. One of these crashed on a row of nearby houses and killed a number of civilians.

Once the Halifaxes had been disposed of, 48 MU was disbanded and the airfield returned to civilian use. There was some post war flying but early in 1950 the land was acquired by York City Council and redeveloped for housing and retail development.

Brough's links with Britain's aviation history date back to 1915 when the site was first identified by Mark Swann, one of Robert Blackburn's most trusted employees, as suitable for testing the land and seaplanes then being built by the company at its factory in the former Olympia skating rink in Roundhay Road, Leeds. Up to that point, the company had been using part of the adjacent Roundhay Park for testing its aircraft but that was now clearly unsuitable.

By the following year a small hangar and slipway had been constructed and trials began on the prototype of a new seaplane. The small airfield was then commandeered by the Government as the No 2 (Northern) Marine Acceptance Depot became an erection, storage and test centre for many of the aircraft then going into service with the Royal Naval Air Service.

The end of the Great War brought only a brief respite in flying at Brough. Blackburn's saw an opportunity to use the airfield for a passenger and freight service to Holland and formed the North Sea Aerial Navigation Company to operate this. It proved to be short-lived, but Brough had now become established as vital to the future of the Blackburn company.

The factory in Leeds was well-equipped but, with no adjacent airfield, its future was limited and by 1925 the company was already beginning to switch production to Brough, where a flying school had now been established. By 1932 all production had moved to Brough and it was there that the company's new trainer aircraft, the B2, first flew that year.

Pre-war aircraft development at Brough saw the emergence of a number of aircraft which were to play supporting roles in the conflict to come. Notable among these was the Skua, the fighter/dive-bomber which went into service with the Fleet Air Arm in 1937. On 26th September 1939 a Skua from HMS *Ark Royal* earned its place in history by being the first British fighter to bring down a German aircraft in the Second World War. Skuas were to be the mainstay of the FAA in the early days of the war and, despite their limited range and fighting capabilities, acquitted themselves well until more advanced machines became available.

Another major project at Brough in the months leading up to the outbreak of war was the development and construction of the Botha. Designed as a medium twin-engined reconnaissance and torpedo aircraft, the first of 242 Bothas ordered from Blackburn's rolled off the production line shortly before the outbreak of war. Production reached a peak during 1940 when 30 aircraft a month were being built, and when work ceased in 1943, 380 Bothas had been delivered to the RAF. Its limited range, however, quickly precluded it from front-line service and the Brough-built Bothas were used as communication aircraft and, most successfully, as operational trainers for bomber crews.

When Botha production ended at Brough, the company began work on its most successful wartime aircraft, the Barracuda, designed originally by the Fairey company and built by a consortium which included Boulton Paul and Blackburn's. It was built for the FAA as a light attack bomber and torpedo aircraft and, after an uncertain start, went on to prove its worth in numerous theatres of operation,

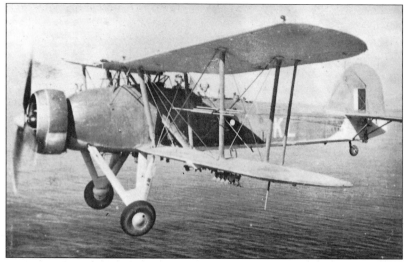

A Sherburn-built Swordfish of 834 Squadron. (Peter Green)

including successful attacks on the *Tirpitz* in Alten Fjord in April 1944 and on Japanese oil installations in the Far East. Work began at Brough in February 1941, with the first completed Barracuda flying out on 23rd October 1942. When production ended in June 1945 some 700 Barracudas had been built at Brough, production reaching a peak in June 1944 when 45 aircraft were built.

While all this was going on in the Brough factory, the RAF ensured that maximum use was made of the adjacent airfield. This was officially taken over by Flying Training Command which established No 4 Elementary Flying Training School equipped with a mixture of Tiger Moths and Brough-built B2s. They had to share the airfield facilities with the Blackburn-produced aircraft and this, inevitably, caused problems for both parties. The solution was to reopen the old night landing ground at Bellasize, just south of Gilberdyke, as a relief landing ground and this was in use until July 1945 when 4 EFTS left Brough.

During the war the Royal Navy made extensive use of American-built aircraft which were provided as part of the Lend-Lease agreement. But they needed extensive modifications to enable them to carry British equipment and this work was entrusted to Blackburn's.

However, as production of the Barracuda got under way at Brough it became necessary to switch the work elsewhere and it was eventually placed with Boon & Porter, which produced the modification kits to

Blackburn specifications. Some high priority modification work was still retained by Blackburn's and this was carried out at Brough, in addition to its other factories at Sherburn-in-Elmet, Leeds and Dumbarton.

By 1943 it became clear that it was uneconomical for US Navy-specification aircraft to be brought by sea to England and then converted. The answer was to set up a British modification centre in the US and this was established at Roosevelt Field. The assistant chief engineer at Brough, Mr J. Hall, was loaned to the Admiralty and served as chief engineer at Roosevelt Field until 1945. It was a scheme which worked very well and, by the end of the war, Blackburn's reported that some 400 modifications were incorporated in 4,000 aircraft processed through the scheme, 600 of them by Blackburn's themselves.

Blackburn's was not alone in feeling the pinch when the war ended and was to merge with General Aircraft Ltd. The merger brought with it General Aircraft's work on the GAL 60, a large transport aircraft which was eventually built at Brough as the Blackburn Beverley. This was widely used by the RAF until eventually replaced by the American-built Hercules. The first Beverley flew from the airfield at Brough but later much of the flight testing was done from the nearby wartime airfield at Holme-on-Spalding Moor, which had been acquired by the company for its test programme.

It was the start of a post-war renaissance at Brough, where the next aircraft off the production was the NA39, later named the Buccaneer. Today the Brough factory is part of British Aerospace and has played a major part in the construction of such outstanding aircraft as the Harrier, BAe146 and the Hawk.

Blackburn's second centre of production in Yorkshire was the airfield at Sherburn-in-Elmet, near Leeds. Sherburn had been used in the First World War as an RFC Acceptance Park from where Blackburn aircraft manufactured in Leeds first took to the air. It closed in 1919 but seven years later was being used again for civilian flying when the Yorkshire Light Aeroplane Club moved there, remaining until 1931 when it moved to Yeadon. Some flying did continue until 1939 when the airfield was requisitioned and opened as a Fighter Command airfield. It had limited facilities but, nevertheless, was used briefly by Hurricanes of 73 and 46 Squadrons stationed at nearby Church Fenton in the summer of 1940 and early spring of 1941.

In the meantime, Blackburn's had set up a repair depot at Sherburn and when the company was awarded the contract to build the

Swordfish torpedo aircraft for the Fleet Air Arm, the company chose Sherburn as the site for the work. By early 1940 they had begun work on a factory adjacent to the airfield. Remarkably, the first aircraft had been produced by the end of the year and between 1941 and 1944 the Sherburn factory turned out around 1,700 Swordfish together with a huge quantity of spares. The Swordfish was the last biplane to see action with the Royal Navy and despite its apparent obsolescence, proved to be one of the most effective carrier-borne aircraft of the war. Later the repair depot was responsible for handling modifications to many of the American-built aircraft going into service with the FAA. The airfield also became the base for 5006 Airfield Construction Squadron, which was responsible for repairing damage on airfields throughout Yorkshire.

In the late summer of 1942 the Airborne Forces Experimental Establishment whose job it was to try out new ideas, filter the good from the bad and help prepare Britain's airborne forces for the forthcoming invasion of Europe, arrived at Sherburn. It had its own staff and aircraft and many of the airframe and engine fitters were WAAFs. Among them was a young Sheffield girl, Renee Percy, who found herself posted there in the summer of 1944 after a spell at the Empire Air Armament School at Manby in Lincolnshire.

'We shared the airfield with the Blackburn factory nearby, which used it for testing the Swordfish biplanes they were building,' remembered Renee, now Mrs Renee Newsam of Sheffield.

'Much of our work was experimental. I recall Halifaxes being fitted out to air-drop jeeps from low level for paratroops to use. Other aircraft were fitted out with communications equipment to link up with soldiers on the ground. Some of the aircraft there were so strange we didn't know exactly what they were. We also saw a number of gliders being tried out.'

As an engine fitter Renee was obliged to fly in some of the aircraft following major work. One particular aircraft she worked on was an Armstrong Whitley Albemarle, one of the twin-engined aircraft being used at Sherburn as part of some glider trials.

'I went on leave before the job was done and when I came back, I was hardly off the station (which was right alongside the airfield) when a chap I knew there saw me and shouted: "I thought you were dead!" It seems while I was away the work on the Albemarle was finished and another WAAF had gone in it for the engine test and it had crashed and all aboard had been killed.'

Accommodation at Sherburn was typical spartan wartime RAF – cold and draughty Nissen huts. No concessions were made for the WAAFs. 'We were treated just like the men and expected to endure just the same hardships,' said Mrs Newsam. One consolation was that Sherburn was handy for Renee's home in Sheffield, where her family kept a town centre shop which had miraculously survived the Luftwaffe's blitz.

As Christmas 1944 approached, living conditions were becoming uncomfortable for the station staff before orders came through for the entire unit to move to Brockenhurst in the New Forest. It turned out to be an eventful journey for the staff, who were all carried in one train which had to shelter in a tunnel during a raid on a nearby town, an unpleasant experience for everyone on board.

Sherburn was also the home of 7 Ferry Pilots Pool, whose job it was to fly new aircraft from Sherburn and Yeadon to units around the country. Most of the ferry pilots were women and they flew their own Anson 'air taxis', delivering batches of pilots to various locations where they would collect aircraft for delivery.

Sherburn quickly reverted to civilian flying after the war and the factory which once produced the Swordfish was turned over to producing scales for grocery shops.

32

THE

CIVILIANS

The contribution made to the war effort by the ordinary men and women of Yorkshire was enormous. The county's mines produced the fuel and its foundries the steel for the industries which kept the armed forces supplied with the weapons they so desperately needed. Its factories built aircraft, guns and vehicles. And its farms produced the food to feed the workers and supported the hundreds of thousands of young servicemen and women who served at the county's airfields and military camps.

The cost of all this for Yorkshire was considerable. Over 2,000 civilians were killed in air raids while many more were killed in the crashes involving British aircraft. In Hull alone over 150,000 were rendered homeless by air raids and large tracts of Britain's biggest county were lost to the demand for yet more airfields.

It was on 20th June 1940 that the threat of aerial warfare became reality to the people of Yorkshire. Early that morning a German aircraft dropped a single bomb and a few incendiaries close to the Chapman Street railway bridge in Hull. Little damage was caused and no one was injured. But it was a taste of what was to come.

Hull became one of the most badly damaged of all British cities in a series of air raids which left 1,200 people dead, more than 3,000 injured and 152,000 homeless, and which damaged or destroyed 86,715 houses. Many of the city's major factories were hit and it was only after the war that the scale of concern over morale among the civilian population at the height of the raids became public knowledge. A series of heavy attacks in the late spring of 1941 burnt the heart out of the city and led

This was where many Yorkshiremen learned to fly – Swallow IIs of 4 EFTS at Brough in August 1938. (Yorkshire Air Museum via Peter Green)

to the unofficial evacuation of many residential areas.

The big raids began in March 1941. Thirty-eight people died on the night of 13th March, 91 five nights later and 52 late on the night of 31st March, among them the staff of the ARP control HQ at the corner of Ferensway and Spring Bank, which was destroyed. Two weeks later 57 were killed, 50 of them in a shelter in Ellis Terrace off Holderness Road which took a direct hit.

The attacks reached a peak in early May. On the night of 7th May, 203 people died and another 165 were seriously injured as much of the city centre and the Riverside Quay area was devastated. The following night the Luftwaffe returned and this time the weight of the attack fell on the docks, Hedon Road and the north and east of the city. Two hundred and seventeen civilians died and 160 were badly injured and major fires were started in the big timber yards on the docks. German pilots later reported that the glow of the fires could be seen from the Danish coast. So many of the victims of these two raids could not be identified that a communal funeral was held for 200 victims. It proved such a traumatic event that the city authorities decided not to repeat it should Hull suffer on this scale again.

A series of small-scale raids cost the lives of another 75 civilians in the weeks to come before the Luftwaffe returned in force on the night of 18th July. Reckitt's factory was badly damaged along with Spillers' mill and the casualties for the night were 140 killed and 108 seriously

A Lysander Mk II of 613 (City of Manchester) Squadron, pictured at RAF Firbeck in the harsh winter of 1941–41. (613 Squadron Assoc., via Noel Wade.)

injured. This turned out to be the last large-scale raid on Hull but the city's agony was still not over. Forty-four died on the night of 3rd September and another 26 in July the following year.

The Luftwaffe was to have a nasty surprise for Hull in the closing weeks of the war. Intruder aircraft which had followed Yorkshire-based bombers back to their bases on the night of 4th March 1945 sprayed the city with cannon fire while a single raider killed 12 and injured another 22 a few nights later on the very last attack of the war.

Sheffield had suffered badly in the winter blitz of 1940. Some 760 people died in a series of heavy raids in December which caused enormous damage in the city centre, destroying many well-known buildings. In the worst incident, 77 people sheltering in the unstrengthened cellar of the city's Marples Hotel died when the building collapsed onto them. Eighteen were killed when a public shelter in Porter Street took a direct hit and five patients died when one of the city's hospitals was damaged.

But, as in most of Britain's bombed cities, it was the packed working class communities which suffered most. Whole streets of terraced houses were reduced to piles of rubble by the Luftwaffe and many owed their lives to the communal shelters and the ubiquitous 'Andersons'.

Evacuees f̶   ̶ull enjoying a game on a farm at Barrow-on-Humber in 1939.

Leeds and Bradford were spared destruction on this scale but the city of York suffered badly in what became known as the Baedeker raids of April 1942, so called because it was rumoured that the targets – which included York, Canterbury, Exeter and Norwich – were selected from the Baedeker Guide to Britain in retaliation for the damage caused by the RAF to the ancient cities of Lübeck and Rostock. The raid was carried out by some 20 aircraft and among the many buildings hit was the city's railway station.

The towns of Yorkshire also suffered more than most from the dangers of having the RAF as their neighbours and many more civilians were killed and injured by crashing aircraft. Typical of them was Goole, the inland port which shared with York and Lincoln the sometimes dubious honour of being surrounded by milling aircraft. Gordon Campsell was then growing up in the town and, as with most schoolboys at the time, he found the war extremely exciting with the ever-present possibility of picking up pieces of shrapnel from the anti-aircraft defences around the town's docks or finding souvenirs from crash sites.

But the real horror of war was brought home to him one day when, during his early-morning paper round, he heard two Halifaxes had

Aftermath of the Baedeker Raid in York as clearing up work begins in one of the city's residential areas hit in the attack. (Yorkshire Evening Press)

collided over the town during the night and had crashed. One had come down nearby, hitting the Peacock Hotel in North Street, badly damaging the pub and nearby houses. The other had crashed on open land just across the Ouse. It was only when he arrived at Goole Modern School that he found that the crashing bomber which flattened the Peacock had killed one of his classmates, 12-year-old Jim Stanley, as well as an elderly lady who lived next door. Also wrecked was the Tower Theatre, Wardle's garage and Robinson's furniture shop, together with its scout headquarters, which were on the second floor. The crash started a serious fire but Gordon, who now lives in York, remembers that the Tower was open for business again within a relatively short period.

Earlier in the war, Mr Campsell remembers a Wellington bomber hitting the primary school which stands at the corner of Boothferry Road and Dunhill Road, taking the roof off the main building before crashing into a small annexe. It occurred early in the morning when the school was empty so there were no civilian casualties.

Young evacuees from Hull arriving at New Holland station in North Lincolnshire in 1939. (Grimsby Evening Telegraph)

On another occasion he was woken at 2 am by the noise of an approaching aircraft. It seemed to just clear the house roof before he heard a thump and the next morning saw for himself the wreckage of a Halifax which had crashed on Westfield Banks, near the town's fever hospital. Those at the scene told him no one had escaped from the Halifax. He was to witness another crash himself. 'It was 6.45 in the evening and I was on my way to my piano lesson when I heard the sound of an aircraft and looked up and saw a Mosquito, probably from Church Fenton where they were based at the time. Suddenly, the aircraft exploded right before my eyes and I watched it spiral down before it crashed in West Park in Goole.' In those days most of the park had been turned over to growing vegetables as part of the Dig For Victory campaign but a small square had been left in the centre for the youngsters in the area to kick a ball about. The Mosquito plunged into this very spot, fortunately deserted at the time.

Towards the end of the war he saw yet another crash, this time involving a Spitfire, the wreckage of which was only recovered from

A familiar sight for all those who lived near Yorkshire airfields – F/Lt Hunter's Halifax JD475-Z heads a queue of 78 Squadron Halifaxes about to take off for Berlin from Breighton, 31st August 1944. This particular aircraft and its crew failed to return from a raid on Mannheim six nights later. (Sir Guy Lawrence)

marshes near Crowle in the mid 1990s, just across the county border in Lincolnshire.

'We were in the school yard when we saw four Spitfires flying in line astern. It looked like they were playing follow-the-leader, wherever the first one went, the others followed. Then we clearly heard the crack of machine gun fire and the leading aircraft caught fire and fell away from the formation. We saw the pilot bale out and his parachute opened while his aircraft disappeared in the direction of Crowle. We watched the pilot come down and he landed right in the middle of the river and quickly disappeared. They didn't find his body for three weeks and we heard he was an American.

'There was a lot of speculation about why the aircraft was lost and we heard they were practising gunnery. We most definitely heard the sound of machine gun fire and we were certain someone fired by mistake. I often wonder when they recovered that Spitfire at Crowle if they found any bullet holes in it.'

Arthur Skate's father was one of the police officers stationed in Selby during the war and had to attend the scene of many of the numerous crashes around the town, later describing the scenes in great detail to his son. One involved a Halifax coming down on fields at the back of Abbot's Road. The crew walked away unscathed, only to be killed in action a few weeks later. Another came down at Thief Lane, Barlow on its approach to Burn, the aircraft clipping trees in a nearby wood and then ground looping when its undercarriage ran into a ditch as it crash-landed. PC Skate helped pull two survivors from the wreckage but the remainder, including the rear gunner who was trapped in his turret, died.

Arthur was then a 15-year-old schoolboy and was, like most boys in Selby at the time, 'plane mad'. Whenever he had any free time he would cycle out to Burn and stand by the railway crossing, where they were unlikely to be moved, and watch the Halifaxes taking off and landing.

Selby itself suffered one of the worst wartime crashes in Yorkshire when a Halifax from the heavy conversion unit at nearby Riccall collided with the spire of St James's church in May 1944 and crashed into nearby houses, killing all those on board along with eight civilians (see the chapter on Riccall).

Eric Welbourn grew up on Moor Farm at Balne, less than a mile from the main runway at Snaith, an airfield he still refers to as 'Pollington'. One of several crashes he remembers involved a Wellington, probably from 150 Squadron, which he spotted on its approach as he was leaving church. Suddenly, a red flare went up, warning the pilot not to land. As the Wimpey tried to overshoot it lost power and the pilot elected to crash-land in fields near the family's farm. 'He seemed to have made a perfect landing until the aircraft hit a ditch between two fields. A wing struck a tree and the aircraft spun round before coming to rest. The pilot suffered a broken arm but the rest of the crew were OK, they had taken up crash positions in the rear of the aircraft.'

On another occasion he remembers hearing a Halifax come down one foggy morning across the road from the farm. A local railway signalman was on his way to work by cycle at the time and he came across the Halifax's crew sitting on a wooden fence at the side of the road. They had no idea exactly where they were but they did know they had left an unexploded bomb on their aircraft and they wanted to stay as far away from it as possible. The signalman went to his nearby box where he raised the alarm while the seven airmen, still in their flying gear, were invited in to Highfield Farm, much to the delight of 12-year-old Eric Welbourn.

There was another occasion when a number of bombs exploded in the bomb dump at Snaith and nearby houses were only saved by the deflection of the blast by a railway embankment.

He would often watch airmen from Snaith (often with a WAAF on the cross bar) cycle past on their way to the nearby Four Horse Shoes public house where they would be able to dine on eggs and bacon and drink until all hours. Other favourites were the George and Dragon at Pollington and the Horse and Jockey, where a tradition was established by members of 51 Squadron to leave their ties behind the bar and collect them again after their next operation. Many ties were never to be collected.

They were not the only reminders of service life to go uncollected. A poignant reminder of the losses from Yorkshire airfields came to light at the end of the war when staff at Boots in Selby were given the job of throwing away all the unclaimed photographs which had been brought in for processing by aircrew from the nearby airfields. Many showed happy groups of men gathered around Halifaxes, men who had failed to return from operations within days of the films being handed in for developing.

The small town of Pocklington, which stands near to the old Roman road which links York with Hull, was closer than most communities to the airfield which bore its name. This cheek-by-jowl existence inevitably led to a great bond of friendship between the town and the RAF and, in particular, the two squadrons mainly associated with the airfield, 405 and 102. Today the parish churchyards in both Pocklington and neighbouring Barmby Moor, contain the graves of many airmen from both squadrons killed while flying from the airfield. Twenty-one of those men, and station commanders, are also commemorated in the names of streets in Pocklington itself.

One of the many inconveniences people in Yorkshire had to endure was the blocking off of roads around many of the county's airfields. Some obstructions were only temporary but still caused a few hackles to rise. Peter Roberts remembers his first operation as a flight engineer in a Lancaster of 49 Squadron at Fulbeck in Lincolnshire in January 1945. Once back over England the weary crew was ordered to divert to Pocklington and the Lancaster, U-Uncle, overshot the runway, smashed through the boundary hedge and came to rest on the main Hull-York road which ran alongside the airfield. The crew, shaken by their experience, were taken for a meal and a rest before returning to look at the remains of their Lancaster as dawn broke. Just at that point a civilian bus appeared and was stopped by service police.

'The driver jumped from his cab and began to remonstrate loudly with the first RAF bod he could find. "Tha can't leave that bloody thing

A wartime picture of Betty's Cafe in York. (Taylor's of Harrogate)

there, tha knows. A've got ta get these people to work!" making out as if the Lancaster had been placed there on purpose!'

The young men and women who served on the bomber, fighter and training airfields became very much part of the way of life in Yorkshire between 1940 and 1945. They filled the trains, the buses and, of course, the pubs and bars. The most famous of these was Betty's Bar in York where the Oakroom in the basement became the haunt of service personnel stationed throughout the county. The bar – known to countless bomber crews as 'The Dive' or the 'Briefing Room' – owed its popularity to the fact that it was one of the few places in York to have a liquor licence.

Betty's was then, as it is now, York's best-known place of refreshment. There was a shop on the ground floor with tea rooms on the first and second floors. The oak-panelled basement housed the bar. Behind the bar hung a very large mirror and at some point early in the war air crew began scratching their names on it. Exactly how the practice started no one is sure. One story tells of airmen using the barmaid's engagement ring to scratch their names – another tells of a specially designed pen which was used. Whatever the origins were, the practice quickly caught on and was positively encouraged by the owner and founder of Betty's, Frederick Belmont. By the time the war ended there were some 568 names on the mirror. Most were left by bomber crews from Yorkshire's airfields while other contributors included American airmen, soldiers, sailors and a few members of the Women's Auxiliary Air Force. The bar has long since disappeared but the room, now part of Betty's Cafe, retains its oak panelling and a section of the mirror still hangs in it as a memorial to its wartime customers.

Today, Yorkshire is studded with memorials to the young men who flew from the county during the war, including the astronomical clock and book of remembrance in York Minster which commemorates some 18,000 airmen of many nationalities who died flying from Yorkshire. Several smaller memorials were erected by members of the public, among them one at Tingley on the outskirts of Leeds to a crew from Snaith killed in a crash there in 1944. At the unveiling of that memorial, Walter Townend, who was largely responsible for its erection, dedicated a poem to all those who flew from Yorkshire in the Second World War, which concludes:

Over the span of years, time takes its toll.
Pitted runways slowly disintegrate, no longer in their prime.
Familiar buildings long gone, whilst others have a different role.
The ghosts of yesteryear still appear from time to time.

No longer the fumes and roar of engines fill the air.
Huge iron birds poised, waiting the call to gather.
Their innards gorged with death-dealing fare.
More than once was heard a voice to murmur: 'Our Father…'

Fingers of light probed the skies already glowing.
Our safety is assured because we are immortal.
Over the target, though, true Hades altered their knowing,
The final count would be far less than the total.

They who were youthful and now able to return,
Recall sometimes with anger, oft times with remorse.
Their friends' lives extinguished for a lesson to learn.
To overcome evil, was it worth it? Of course!

BIBLIOGRAPHY

Aircraft Down 1: Air Crashes Around Wetherby 1939-1945, Brian Lunn &
    Lee Arbon (Hardwick Publications)
A History of 77 Squadron, Harry Shinkfield (pb. Shinkfield)
A North-East Coast Town, T. Geraghty (Kingston Upon Hull
    Corporation)
A Short History of RAF Leeming (RAF Leeming)
Action Stations 4, Barry Halpenny (Patrick Stephens)
Aerodromes in North Yorkshire and Wartime Memories, David Brown (pb.
    David Brown).
Air Battle of the Ruhr, Alan Cooper (Airlife).
Aircrew, Bruce Lewis (Orion).
Avro Lancaster, Harry Holmes (Airlife).
Based at Burn, Hugh Cawdron (578 Association).
Bombers Over Berlin, Alan Cooper (Kimber).
Bomber Squadrons of the RAF, Philip J. Moyes (Macdonald and James).
Brave and True: The History of 466 Squadron, Alby Stevenson and Stan
    Parker (Stevenson & Parker).
British Military Airfields 1939-45, David J. Smith (Patrick Stephens).
Cheshire VC, Russell Braddon (Odhams).
Coningham, Vincent Orange (Methuen).
Duel of Eagles, Peter Townsend (Cassell).
Failed to Return, Bill Norman (Leo Cooper).
For Valour: The Air VCs, Chaz Bowyer (William Kimber).
Flying Through Fire, Geoffrey William (Allan Sutton).
From Hull, Hell and Halifax, Chris Blanchett (Midland Counties).
If You Can't Take a Joke, Ron Read (Box Publicidad).
Mother Worked at Avro, Gerald Myers (Graphics).
Nicolson VC, Peter Mason (Geerings).
One Wing High, Harry Lomas (Airlife).
Only Owls and Bloody Fools Fly at Night, Group Captain Tom Sawyer
    (Kimber).
RAF Bomber Airfields of World War Two, Jonathan Falconer (Ian Allen).
RAF Bomber Command Losses in the Second World War, 1939-44, Volumes
    1-5, Bill Chorley (Midland Counties).
Selected for Aircrew, James Hampton.

The Battle of Britain: The Jubilee History, Richard Hough and Denis Richards (Hodder & Stoughton).

The Bomber Battle for Berlin, John Searby (Airlife).

The Bomber Command War Diaries, Martin Middlebrook and Chris Everitt (Penguin).

The Hampden File, Harry Moyle (Air Britain).

The Wellington Bomber, Chaz Bowyer (Kimber).

The Handley Page Halifax, K.A. Merrick (Aston).

The Berlin Raids, Martin Middlebrook (Viking).

The Nuremburg Raids, Martin Middlebrook (Allen Lane).

The Battle of Hamburg, Martin Middlebrook (Allen Lane).

The Thousand Plan, Ralph Barker (Chatto and Windus).

White Rose Base, Brian Rapier (Air Museum York).

York Memories of the Second World War, York Oral History Project.

ACKNOWLEDGEMENTS

The author wishes to thank everyone who has helped in the preparation of this book. The response to appeals for information, generously carried by most of the county's newspapers, was astonishing. Many of those who replied served on the multitude of airfields to be found in wartime Yorkshire, others were the civilians who became used to having the RAF (or RCAF in the case of North Yorkshire) as their neighbours. Many provided memories of those days while others were able to provide photographs to help illustrate this chapter in Yorkshire's illustrious history. Great help has been given, too, by the various squadron associations with their roots in the White Rose county. It is gratifying to note that while those that were left continue to grow old, the strength of their comradeship shows no sign of diminishing. Finally, special thanks are due to a Lincolnshire man, Peter Green, whose generosity, enthusiasm, knowledge and, of course, his immense photographic collection, know no bounds. Without him this – and many other – aviation books would be the poorer.

INDEX

316

SQUADRONS